REORDERING THE NATURAL

Humans and Animals in the City

Reordering the Natural World is a fascinating account of the many and varied ways in which animals and humans interact in the urban context. In looking at these interactions, Annabelle Sabloff argues that the everyday practices of contemporary capitalist society contribute to our alienation from the rest of nature. At the same time, however, she reveals the often disguised affinities and sense of connection that urban Canadians nonetheless manifest in their relations with animals and the natural world.

Sabloff reflects on how the discipline of anthropology has contributed to the prevailing Western perception of a divide between nature and culture. She suggests that the present ecological crisis has resulted largely from the ways in which Western societies have construed nature as a cultural system. Since new ideas about nature may be critical in changing humanity's destructive interactions with the biosphere, *Reordering the Natural World* is invaluable in exploring how urban Canadians develop and sustain their current relationship with the macrocosm, and in considering whether these relationships might be altered by reconceptualizing anthropology itself as an integral part of natural history.

With this unique text, Sabloff not only provides provocative insight into the study of relations between humans and the natural world, she lays a cornerstone for building a new structure for the study of anthropology itself.

ABELLE SABLOFF is a doctoral candidate in the Department of Social ropology at York University.

Reordering the Natural World

Humans and Animals in the City

ANNABELLE SABLOFF

UNIVERSITY OF TORONTO PRESS
Toronto Buffalo London

© University of Toronto Press Incorporated 2001
  Toronto Buffalo London
  Printed in Canada

  ISBN 0-8020-4832-3 (cloth)
  ISBN 0-8020-8361-7 (paper)

Printed on acid-free paper

Canadian Cataloguing in Publication Data

Sabloff, Annabelle, 1944–
  Reordering the natural world : humans and animals in the city

  Includes bibliographical references and index.
  ISBN 0-8020-4832-3 (bound)   ISBN 0-8020-8361-7 (pbk.)

  1. Human–animal relationships.   2. Urban ecology.   I. Title.

  QL85.S22 2000   304.2'7   C00-931815-1

University of Toronto Press acknowledges the financial assistance to
its publishing program of the Canada Council for the Arts and the
Ontario Arts Council.

This book has been published with the help of a grant from the Humanities
and Social Sciences Federation of Canada, using funds provided by the
Social Sciences and Humanities Research Council of Canada.

University of Toronto Press acknowledges the financial support for its
publishing activities of the Government of Canada through the Book
Publishing Industry Development Program (BPIDP).

This book is for Anik Bay, my daughter,
who makes everything worthwhile.

Contents

Preface

In an age in which the perennial question of where human beings fit into the natural order has taken on more practical meaning and urgency than ever before, it is somewhat surprising how little we actually know about human relationships with the rest of nature. We seem to have enquired into these relationships least of all in contemporary urban Western culture, relying on, and frequently lamenting, an often-stated declaration that people in cities are distanced and disconnected from nature. What is missing from such discussions is a close-up scrutiny of how human beings actually interact with other living beings in the city. How do contemporary urban people in the West imagine, encounter, and experience the natural world? How does the urban context influence these imaginings, encounters, and experiences? How, if at all, do these perceptions and practices change?

This is the subject of this book. As one central theme, it addresses how humans and animals relate to one another in the urban context, and considers what this relation tells us about our current perceptions of ourselves and other beings in the order of nature. Among other things, the book traces evidence of a strong sense of connection with nature manifested by people in cities – connection actively sought, established, and defended.

This book has had a long developmental history. Its origins lie in ethnographic fieldwork I conducted in Toronto for my master's thesis in anthropology. The bulk of the research was done between 1986 and 1988, with some data collection continuing to 1991. Revisions to the manuscript for publication were frequently interrupted by other projects, but the time lapse did enable me to make many informal observations in succeeding years, mainly to corroborate or to revise, where necessary, original interpretations.

I carried out participant-observation in diverse settings: humane societies, veterinary clinics, dog and cat breeders' shows, pet stores, family homes, grass-roots animal-rights organization meetings, an animal-rights movement protest march. Interviews in the ethnographically classical minimally structured mode, most lasting between two and four hours, were held with individuals, families, and groups of unrelated persons – a group of employees from the Ontario Humane Society, a writers' group, and a readers' discussion group. I interviewed persons who kept pets and persons who did not, families with pets, mixed groups of pet-owners, non-owners, and people who did not like animals, pet-store clerks, a number of animal-rights activists, an animal-control officer, the manager of a pet shelter, a veterinarian, and several veterinarians' assistants. In all, forty-six people were interviewed in depth, with the great majority of those interviews being audiotaped, and the rest recorded by hand. All direct quotes from respondents in this study are verbatim.

The late 1980s and early 1990s proved to be a notably rich era for animal-rights activities in Toronto as well as for mass-media stories on animal welfare and animal rights. Therefore, direct data-gathering methods were supplemented by media news items. Radio, television, pamphlets, and newspaper articles became a bountiful source of primary data – treated, that is, as culture-bearing news, not as cultural analysis.

With a theme as large as the one tackled here, my research was necessarily limited to a small part of the immense range of human–animal relations in our society. There are obviously important areas not covered here that, if better known, undoubtedly would colour the interpretations and opinions I have ventured. I restricted my enquiries to three domains of cultural life: the domestic, workshop or 'factory,' and civic domains. But probably the most important limitation on research of this kind, research that seeks to understand interspecies behaviour, is the incapability of a researcher specialized in one discipline to engage effectively in another specialized field of study. My own lack of knowledge and training in observing animal behaviour in depth obviously limited my capacity to present an adequate accounting of the animals observed or discussed. To conduct this kind of in-clusive ethno-ethology properly awaits a level of interdisciplinary collaboration we do not yet have. Thus, hemmed in as it is by its somewhat restricted scope, this essay is meant to be suggestive, not definitive, as must be the case with all such studies. I hope the findings and interpretations presented here will nonetheless pique the interest of scholars, researchers, and an interested public enough to motivate further discussion and enquiry.

This book is not strictly an anthropological monograph. The many questions that arose in the course of research and analysis led me to address some of the larger issues these local findings pointed to: questions of how we establish the concepts and beliefs we hold, how we live with contradiction, how we change our minds and our behaviours, or how we resist change; and what all this might tell us about how we respond to environmental crisis. It was perhaps inevitable that anthropological assumptions would become part of this related body of questions. In any case, another central theme in this book is the role of anthropology in shaping our ideas about the place of human beings in the order of things. Probably much more often unintentionally than intentionally, anthropology has influenced much of our thinking in this area, yet its practitioners have seldom reflected critically on their own most basic assumptions about human–animal relationships. I offer here a modest critique of my discipline and suggestions for a renewed practice that could do justice to the interspecies relationships that human beings everywhere seem to find so (positively or negatively) compelling.

A few words about word usage are in order. Many of the words important to this study are old ones; they thus enfold a lot of history and a lot of compressed meaning, not all of it congruent. Such terms are difficult to define precisely and to everyone's satisfaction, but in certain places in the text I have attempted to provide some definitional foothold. For 'nature,' as an example, for the most part I used the definition implied or stated by virtually all of my respondents, that is, 'all the living world exclusive of human beings.' At the points where I used another definition, this has been made explicit in the text. For 'culture,' I provided a definition, however loose, that would emphasize the ceaseless dynamism of process. In another key instance, the term 'the West' (or 'Western civilization') has become too controversial to allow me to unpack it briefly in the text. The history encapsulated in this term, fraught as it is with some now-discredited ideologies and now-repellent practices, should not be forgotten. But this study is a local one, and this locality is deeply informed by a longstanding tradition we still call 'Western.' Other terms, such as 'Anglo-European,'

'Euro-American,' 'North American,' 'Canadian,' or 'North' (versus 'South') simply do not capture the breadth, the depth, and the nuances of the tradition that shapes and constrains human–animal relations in Toronto today. Until we can find a term for this cultural process that is more resonant with a changing world order, I have opted to keep the old terminology. Indeed, the very loadedness of 'Western' is, I believe, well suited to a basic premise of my overall position, which is, put in its most general terms, that to know where we are going, we need to know where we come from.

Acknowledgments

I owe a great debt to many individuals. Anik Bay's passionate concern for animals opened my eyes to a relationship seldom articulated and rarely taken seriously. Neil Evernden's work in environmental critique, his generosity with his ideas and time, and his patience turned my world around. York University professors Penny Van Esterik, my original thesis adviser, Margaret Rodman, and John Livingston, all of whom along with Neil Evernden were my thesis committee members, encouraged the publication of my work and continued their support through the years. Professor Michael Bodemann of the University of Toronto introduced me to the engaging rigours of urban fieldwork. York professors Peter Harries-Jones and Judith Nagata provided valuable theoretical contributions. Virgil Duff, executive editor of the University of Toronto Press, provided unflagging support that carried me through lots of rough spots. Anne MacLennan, Rosemary Aubert, and the anonymous readers of the manuscript gave brilliant suggestions for making it much better. John St James's guidance made the text much clearer. Anik Bay has always been the toughest and most honest of critics. All these people helped make the work a reality.

Long-term support of all kinds was forthcoming from Nomi Berger, Gail Burns, Maureen Jennings, Carl Kent, Jane Murray, Sandra Sabloff, Wayne Skinner, Cheryl Sourkes, Susan Sweeney, Evelyn Wolff, Brenda Yagod, and Elliott Yagod. Many thanks are due to June Ardiel, Alec Capon, Ken Borden, Robert Sprachman, Donna Griffith, and the Cadillac-Fairview Corporation for the generous loan of photographs of public art in Toronto.

My work owes its greatest debt to the many people who shared their opinions and anecdotes with me and gamely went to work putting into words hitherto unvoiced thoughts and feelings about nature, animals, and the relationships between humans and animals. The debt extends to the many animals who, in their own way, acted as superlative informants, had I but the powers to understand them better. The riches all my informants gave so freely in reflection, story, instruction, passion, and just doing what comes naturally can never be captured adequately in a book. However, I hope that I have been able to convey at least a fraction of the great-heartedness with which all shared their activities and their tales.

REORDERING THE NATURAL WORLD

'The Pasture' (1985, bronze) by Joe Fafard (b. 1942), Toronto-Dominion Centre Courtyard, Toronto (photo Daniel Weiner; courtesy Cadillac-Fairview Corporation)

The Pasture in the Metropolis

We wake, if we ever wake at all, to mystery ...
Annie Dillard (1974)

You will find it in the depths of the financial district of Toronto, at the bottom of a narrow steel canyon of high-rise buildings: a cow pasture. A small herd of cattle lies stolid and imperturbable in a rectangle of grass amid incessant weekday buzz, electric metropolitan night, and weekend silence that falls suddenly, uncannily, in such places. Incongruous in that alien space, yet weightily and reassuringly present, the cattle rest unmoving, as if cast in bronze. As, indeed, they are.

Slightly larger than life-size, fully formed, muscle and bone clearly visible beneath bronze skin, the seven cows in Canadian artist Joe Fafard's *Pasture* take up all the space in their small allotment of grass that their living being would take up in life, and a bit more. As imposing as they are in size and sheer improbability, their demeanour is nonetheless not heroic. They are ordinary, just plain cows, dipped it seems rather than cast in bronze.

Startled at finding these creatures in the centre of the metropolis, you are compelled by the sense of living nature these manufactured things evoke. Even if your experience of living cattle is minimal, you are jolted by a visceral 'recognition.' You may feel wonder, pleasure, a most unexpected and confusing sensation of 'rightness': cattle in the heart of the city! Or you might sense a joyful disorder; or experience, perhaps, an unhappy discord. You will not be alone if you even feel affronted by the creatures' confinement to the too-small space set aside for their urban pasturage.

Why are these cows at once so enthralling and so disquieting? What is it about them, as built as the skyscrapers surrounding them, that so disturbs the urban order? What do they tell us about our relations with the natural world?

This study is, in large part, an attempt to answer these questions.

Nature and the City

It was divine nature which gave us the country, and man's skill that built the cities.
Marcus Terentius Varro (in Rybczynski 1996)

Cities are artifacts.
Witold Rybczynski (1996)

We begin with a paradox: 'Nature is where I go to when I want to get away from the city.' I heard many variations on this statement in the course of my fieldwork. Urban life is inimical to nature, people would say sadly, or angrily, or with resignation. Yet nature, almost universally defined by my respondents as nonhuman living beings, is in fact everywhere woven into the fabric of the city. Cities teem with animal and vegetable presence. Rivers, creeks, and major bird migratory flyways trace their paths below ground and overhead. Wildflowers flourish between long-disused railroad ties. Family and feral dogs and cats roam every neighbourhood. Squirrels colonize trees. Many species are attracted to the city precisely because of the cityscape itself. Raccoons, rats, and other scavengers seek out household garbage cans, fast-food waste bins, and city dumps. Bats, sparrows, finches, and hawks like attics, wall cavities, hanging flowerpots, and high-rise ledges. Warm concrete and asphalt provide comfort to reptiles. Termites, a tropical order, have plenty of wooden porches and foundation posts in which to fatten without ever having to venture outside. Butterflies, earthworms, insects of all shapes and sizes, birds that know a good meal when they spy it, all are attracted by the hidden world of gardens tucked in behind countless houses or in out-of-the-way community plots. On a peninsular landfill in Toronto known as the Leslie Street Spit, telltale tracks suggest that the city has created welcoming niches for people-shy weasels, muskrat, snowshoe hares, foxes, and coyotes.[1] Is there truly an absence of nature in the city? Or is this an urban myth? And if it is, why is this so?

HUMANS AND ANIMALS IN THE CITY

It is a revelation to itemize some of the ways in which people interact with nature as most people define it, and particularly with animals, in cities. Not only does urban wildlife in innumerable forms maintain their species in every nook and cranny of the concrete jungle, but North Americans actively seek out animals. They flock to conservation areas, zoos, marine parks, circuses, rodeos, and bird sanctuaries, all found within city limits. 'African safari' parks lurk at the very edges of municipal boundaries. Toronto is built atop a system of natural ravines, a favourite walkers' and cyclists' haunt, that shelters vegetation, streams, rocks, and animals somewhat from urban development. And one of the most popular draws to downtown Toronto for a number of years was a duck that had chosen an ornamental pond between two massive high-rise complexes to breed successfully and launch her ducklings. Her human fans were legion, loyal, and protective, if baffled by the duck's choice of nesting place.

Pets are abundant in Western life, and the interest in keeping, breeding, selling, and schooling companion animals continues to grow. Through humane societies and animal-welfare activism, North American and European city dwellers even attend to the social and political concerns of animals, and do so with sustained enthusiasm and commitment. As a society we delight in nature programs on television, video, and film, and stories in print. Nature art, perennially in and out of mainstream fashion, never seems to fade away entirely. The omnipresence of animal toys and games and the beast-ridden names of sports teams and automobiles also attest to this fascination. Many years ago Edmund Leach pointed out the abundance of animal terms of abuse in the English language – 'pig,' 'cow,' 'bitch,' 'mule,' 'fox,' and so on. And as so many other scholars and clinicians continue to remind us, animal images and symbols are not only a part of our languages and urban popular cultures; they also play a significant role in our dreams and phobias, our religions and folklore – whether or not we perceive them to be part of our daily lives.[2]

Within the precincts of the city itself, even a partial inventory illustrates to what an astonishing degree our Western economy depends on, and a typical urban setting engages in, practices related to animals and the natural world. Such an inventory would encompass animal food eaten by humans and other animals; skin, wool, fur, feathers, bone, fat, and organs processed for other commodities; cosmetics, pharmaceuticals, and household products tested on animals for human consumption; medical and surgical procedures perfected on animals, and specimens used in student training; research and pet livestock bred; grooming operations and veterinary clinics; extermination and control facilities; and countless other industries, professions, and trades engaged in some way in breeding, maintaining, studying, selling, protecting, controlling, or transforming animals.

Artist Joe Fafard's metropolitan *Pasture* reminds us too that the city flourishes because somewhere 'in the country' (as if backstage), seldom seen and rarely comprehended but critical to the city's continuing existence, can be found our primary use of animals: their endless reproduction and slaughter for our food. The city, self-absorbed and completely self-referential, easily forgets its dependence on the rest of the natural world for its subsistence, comforts, and vanities.

Along with our survival needs and other economic interests we hold in animals, and apart from their symbolic meanings, a number of the interactions in which urban Westerners engage with other animals are significantly *social* in nature, in the earliest English sense of that word as 'companionate,' implying fellowship, relationship, or intersubjectivity. Geographer Yi-Fu Tuan has documented how humans throughout recorded history have taken pleasure in associating with other life forms: from groves, gardens, and waterfalls, through companion animals, to animals as curiosities and as entertainment. Many of my informants would have responded wholeheartedly to the Swiftian irony in biologist James Serpell's assertion that '[t]he keeping of animals as companions is clearly not essential to human survival. We can live without it – just as we can live without singing, dancing, music, art, laughter, and friendship.'[3]

The City versus Nature

Despite copious evidence of plants and animals and of animal-related activities in the city, however, most informants insist that 'nature is where the city is not,' and are persistently reluctant to register urban interactions with nonhuman life. When respondents do register them, they frequently do so offhandedly, idly, playfully, or peripherally, suggesting that the subject is unworthy of serious reflection or commentary. People, it seems, are disinclined to recognize *any* urban being, human or nonhuman, as natural.

The human–nature link is minimized both in serious reflection and in discourse. Most people in urban society are not usually aware of animals as a central or serious personal or societal concern. 'If you did away with all the animals in the city, you would be missing something,' said one of my informants, 'but you'd be hard-pressed to say what it is.' Our everyday metropolitan thinking about nature is inchoate and our reflections are undeveloped. We no longer borrow metaphors from human–animal relations with the ease with which we increasingly take them from, for example, human–computer interactions. With the exception of the terms of abuse and names of sports teams and automobiles noted earlier (a suspicious enough assortment in itself), Western society's common metaphors, as ecological historian Carolyn Merchant has noted, no longer derive from the natural world.[4]

Today, it is almost impossible to imagine a world without something separate from ourselves we call 'nature.' Yet, there must have been such a time – without separation – for our ancestors. Indeed, such thoughts are not so alien to us that we cannot imagine early humanity as a truly *native* species, living life's rhythms mostly in concert with, at times in conflict with, but always *in*, a habitat: part of the given. And if we can grant that possibility, we might wonder whether all of humanity, including people coming of age in the twenty-first century, might have taken some crucial aspects of character and inclination from such an early imprinting, immersed in habitat. Yet today in the West, apart from that odd, mostly unaccounted period of ecological affinity in late childhood and early adolescence that writer Edith Cobb explores so effectively,[5] individuals no longer seem able to tap effortlessly into this state of belonging for any length of time.

Biophilia and the Totemic Imagination

Nonetheless, human beings yearn to be part of the whole. People never cease to seek to connect with other life. The stream of *biophilic* practice[6] – literally, the love of life forms, the neologism Edward O. Wilson coined to capture humanity's intense interest in and search for connection and relation with other organisms – is an integral part of

Western society. Many urban North American practices make this yearning manifest – the care of plants, gardens, and backyard bird feeders, the weekend flight to the country, burgeoning pilgrimages to glimpse a whale. At the same time, this biophilia is muted in our society and is largely unnamed as a motivating force. We have also lost what we could call our shared *totemic imagination*, that is, our ability collectively to name and experience the world as natural-beings-in-habitat, as animals, sharing the world in relationship with other beings. But the muting of biophilic tendencies and the loss of totemic imagination are more than losses: they are, I believe, *active forfeitures* that we all inevitably, although inadvertently, pay out in the service of a sense of coherence and continuity. They are part of a contract we have accepted as the price of cultural order. And as a result of our impaired totemic sensibility we are unknowingly but deeply *perplexed* in the presence of the real and not scientized natural world. Not only can we not decide whether we are observers or participants in this world (or perhaps its creators), but even as observers our depleted collective imagination cannot contain and refuses to entertain the irreducible complexities of nature. In this study we will follow the implementation of the cultural contract we in the West have made with the rest of nature, and the consequences of our impoverished imagination for our fellow creatures and ourselves.

Nature, it would appear, gets a name, a shape, and a weight as we feel ourselves separating from it. Having lost touch with our own creaturely nature we feel removed from the whole, until finally, in its latest incarnation, nature becomes 'environment': a stage-set, a backdrop to human life. But now that this backdrop is damaged, and wilful, and reactive in ways a backdrop usually is not, we have had to begin to question this metaphor for nature and our relationship to it. We have found to our bewilderment that our loss of the use of metaphors from the natural world has resulted in a dulled, ill-equipped imagination, with significant consequences for our ability as a society to deal with our current environmental problems.

ANTHROPOLOGY AND ENVIRONMENTAL CRISIS

In trying to solve our latest environmental crisis, the threat of collapse of some of the planet's major ecosystems through human activity, we in the West seem unable to arrive at a world-view, not to mention a practice, that can encompass both human desire and the earth's needs.

What lies in the way of coming to benign solutions for a matter so critical for all of us, for all of life?

Over the last few decades of the twentieth century, a growing cluster of homegrown critiques placed Western culture itself at the root of the problem. This body of critique maintains that the problems do not lie centrally in the fact that Western capitalist hardware – its technology, commerce, industry, and urban templates – has overrun the globe. Although this may indeed account for many ills, the critique goes deeper, basing itself on a realization that we no longer are, if we ever were, confronted with a mere 'fix-it' situation. The environmental crisis lies, rather, in the very sources of *how we think*, in the basic and often submerged premises we hold about the world. Our ecological impasse has a lot to do with the way in which Western society has defined nature and prescribed or influenced human relations with the rest of the biosphere. We are suffering as a direct result of the way in which we in the West have constructed nature as a *cultural system.*[7]

This indigenous critique is situated at another level than the usual material and instrumental analyses of environmental issues favoured by many mainstream researchers and policy makers. Borrowing much from the insights of anthropology (although as a discipline, anthropology itself has arrived only very lately at addressing these issues), this critique is moving into intangible regions, probing elusive yet tenacious aspects of culture that motivate and colour all levels of consciousness and action and yet often remain out of awareness. The newer critique is venturing into untracked places where crucial boundaries of shared reality are drawn: buried regions where, from culture to culture, certain shapes of possibility are felt as real, others as imaginative if fantastic, and still others as sheer non-sense. In these explorations of the deeper aspects of culture we have entered unmapped terrain where *basic categories of experience* are moulded – categories of perception, thought, feeling, and everyday practice: the terrain of geographies of the mind.

No longer content to be on the sidelines, anthropology itself is now adding its voice to this indigenous critique. Indeed, as we will see, while anthropology has successfully played a central role in keeping nature and culture separate up until now, no discipline is better situated to explore the key categories and boundaries of culture that matter here, or more equipped to enter the unknown conceptual and emotional territory we have tended to keep virgin in the West: the no-man's land between culture and nature, habitation and habitat, humans and other living beings. In this exploration, we will enquire into the utility of emphasizing anthropology as a form of natural history.

I suggest that, having suppressed our totemic imagination, we in the urban West have lost critical elements of language and imagination with which to make sense of the rest of the natural world, and of ourselves in it. We manifest a *poverty of discourse* related to nature, to other animals, to human–animal relations; nor are we able to speak coherently about human beings as natural beings, as animals, or, most significantly, as animal *subjects*. I will argue that this muting, this cultural dispossession, is significantly implicated in our failure to act in concert to forestall environmental collapse. It is our cultural contract, in my view, that threatens our capacity to think with appropriate complexity about our endangered environment, and that contract accounts in large part for difficulties in finding our way to environmental solutions. For Western culture, and for the discipline of anthropology, retrieving our muted totemic imagination and exploring the unknown territory it occupies will be, I believe, a central task for this century.

Cultural historian Raymond Williams warned some time ago: 'We need different ideas because we need different relationships.'[8] New ideas about nature will be critical in changing humanity's destructive interactions with the biosphere. Influential essays on how to approach the crisis, among them a number of United Nations reports, are unequivocal about the need for a global change in human relations with the environment.[9] But how a society relates to the natural world is inextricably grounded in how its members conceive of nature. How, then, can we expect conceivers of planetary solutions such as the Brundtland Commission of the 1980s or the Rio reformers of the 1990s, not to mention ordinary society, to improve relations with the rest of the natural world if there is a poverty of categories of shared discourse in which to cast and scrutinize such human–animal and human–nature relationship? *Can people think clearly about nature and human–nature relations if we cannot talk clearly about them?* Indeed, how can those we must entrust with conceiving solutions understand the natural world if they do not know how human beings *habitually* shape ideas and behaviours with respect to that world, or how, in real life, we manage to change such ideas and behaviours? In examining urban perceptions of nature and other animals, I am interested not in grand theory but in the local practices of people in the everyday conduct of their lives. Grand theory to date has been singularly unsuccessful in addressing the environmental crisis. What do ordinary people, that is, people living their everyday lives outside their 'expert' roles, whatever these may be, think and feel and do about nature? Enquiry into these realms forms the core of this book.

The Phenomenal City

Does the city itself have something to do with this absence of thought and language concerning the natural world? The city is the quintessential symbol of human ingenuity and handiwork, the triumph of the artificial, of the intentionally humanly created. It is the master arena for the creation and re-creation of contemporary Euro-American and increasingly, Third World, cultural life. It is the primary medium out of which has developed much that is characteristic of Western habitus. Urban habitation, the pace and sensations of city life, and cultural products influenced by the city have become our most familiar environment, the context in which most Westerners, indeed most people in the world today, live out their lives, conceive their relations with others, and negotiate their place in the natural order of things.

Furthermore, as is the case with cultural contexts generally, the city is neither inert nor a mere backdrop but exerts a critical if hard-to-define pressure on human consciousness. It is as if the city, being understood as the quintessential 'humanly built environment,' can be experienced in no other way. I suggest in fact that the city – as a cultural arena bounded and defined by its built environment – is apprehended by both its residents and visitors precisely as *an arena for not-experiencing the living world*. Perhaps it is the case that in the city what is built by human hands fits and is registered but remains unmarked, while what is not built and thus does not fit is marked as anomalous – 'matter out of place,' in Mary Douglas's famous epithet. A common response to matter out of place is to ignore it, even to not-perceive it. As a result, and all dispassionate evidence to the contrary, the city continues to be experienced by its natives as a place where 'nature is not.'

I will explore how important to maintaining a sense of order is the human capacity to not-see, to not-register, and even actively to mute some aspects of the given world. Our Western idea of nature with its associated practices – that is, nature as a cultural system – depends for whatever coherence and order it can claim to have not only on what we agree to perceive, but also on what we jointly agree to elide from our perceptions.

It is here, I think, that we can begin to comprehend the vexatiousness of artist Fafard's *Pasture*. The cattle, artifacts themselves, are so resonant with life that we cannot, as long as we are in their presence, ignore them or their evocation of nature. Like a mote in the eye, they are insistently, frustratingly, matter out of place.

In the West, as elsewhere, the relations of ordinary people with the natural world are reflected in their interactions with other animals. This book, based on ethnographic research I conducted in Toronto at different times during the past decade, presents my observations and reflections on how people in the city interact with other animals and the natural world. How do we in the West, primarily urban dwellers, encounter the natural world? How do we perceive, think about, and regulate our interactions with animals and other life forms? How do we go about ordering our relations with the rest of the natural world? In the pages to come, I will describe how Western practices between humans and other animals are constructed and reproduced. Enquiring into ways in which different cultural domains or contexts call up different patterns to order and guide human–animal relations, I will explore the critical role that metaphor plays in shaping these patterns. I will also consider ways in which people try to change the order of things, that is, to reorder the natural world.

From the vast choice of cultural contexts available, I have selected three domains of Canadian cultural life in which to examine human–animal relations. I suggest that a different relation between humans and animals obtains in each domain, each patterned by a separate metaphor that constrains our cognitive ordering processes, influences our emotions, and guides our behaviour in different ways. I will argue that the relations we observe or hear about so often – companion animals treated like coddled children, livestock farming operations structured like assembly lines, animal rights promoted as a struggle for the rights of citizenship – are not accidental, not mere anthropomorphisms nor mechanomorphisms, although they may be that as well. Rather, and perhaps more interestingly, they are contextually influenced behaviours based on the few metaphors we have available to live by. I will examine how and why this comes to be so, and what this means for our ability – both as a culture and, for anthropology, as a discipline intimately involved with humans in habitat – to reorder our relations, as we clearly must, with other animals and with the rest of the living world.

To return once more to Fafard's installation, *The Pasture*, I would guess that one reason this work so persistently discomposes its viewers stems from its ability to call up such deep contradictions. We experience in these cattle a sense not of nature represented in art but of something more unsettling: a sense of actual nature petrified, captive, quiescent; nature enculturated, encased in bronze, a metal never encountered in the natural world, a humanly invented alloy. Here is nature suitable for a modern Western metropolis. At the same time, there is something else here. In these stolid cattle, we are in the presence of nature 'at large': indifferent to the skyscrapers, the ceaseless weekday noise, and the throngs of hurrying people – the very built environment that constitutes our urban world. Too massive and realistic to be ignored, appropriating a green patch that human beings (at least in summer) are prohibited by a chain barrier from sharing, the cattle seem to transcend the built environment. They are nature as unencumbered as humanity is encumbered by the city. In this setting it is the cattle that set conditions and obstacles for the human beings around them, while in turn being impervious to human interference. Here is nature, oddly, set free.

The Pasture brings home the deep ambivalence that city dwellers seem to feel toward the natural order. Trickster figures, shape-shifting with the regard of every passerby, these cows suggest to us, perhaps without our quite being aware of it, dissonances between city and country, past and present, self and other, domestication and enculturation, living things and made things. They call up fundamental questions concerning the order of things. As the bovine bronzes lie there surrounded by glass and steel, rooted to their patch of city grass, something feels out of order, out of place. Is it the grass-appropriating cattle, or the sky-obliterating buildings? Or is it something else? Something, not consciously felt to be missing, but at last, unexpectedly, *in* order, *in* place: a long misplaced piece of an infuriating puzzle found at last? Perhaps the sculptor[10] has restored something that has been too long lost to the heart and soul of the city: a faint recollection, a longing, a hidden knowledge. Imagine Fafard's cattle as *missing metaphors* retrieved from the ether of urban cultural memory and garbed in bronze – as a baby's first pair of shoes may be: preserved to act as a weighting of memory, an anchoring of the once-known, and a means, over time, of plumbing past understandings.

As we try to deal with the planetary crisis on the international stage, we need at the same time to try to find our own missing metaphors. We will have to accept and openly affiliate with nonhuman life that we now admit only under false pretenses into our urban lives. We will need to imagine cool streams flowing beneath city pavements, patiently watch weeds breaking through concrete, permit ourselves the stillness to sense the darting movements shooting from tall building cornices just beyond our peripheral vision, and hear the rush of wings over the noise of traffic – to register the *structures of feeling*, in Williams's evocative phrase, through which individuals and communities live their history as they participate in making it. Fafard's obstinately present cows remind us of the need to recognize and acknowledge our totemic relationship, animal subject to animal subject – even in the city – with the rest of life. For until the human imagination is truly seized with the notion of itself as an animal in relationship with other animals, until we retrieve – or invent – that crucial missing metaphor, there will be no revolution in our discourse, in our culture, or in our environment – no long revolution at all.[11]

PART ONE

Constructing the Natural Order

Nature is an hypothesis every society needs.
Neil Evernden (1988)

Chapter One

Nature as a Cultural System

Humans and nature construct one another.
Alexander Wilson (1992)

A NEED FOR ORDER

In one of their genesis stories the Iatmul people of New Guinea, so Gregory Bateson tells us, relate how order comes to be in the world. In a conundrum familiar in the West, the Iatmul need to know how water was separated from dry land. They say that in the beginning the crocodile Kavwokmali paddled in the water with its front and hind legs, thus keeping the mud from the bottom stirred up and suspended in the water. The culture hero Kevembuangga killed Kavwokmali with his spear, and as a result the mud settled and dry land appeared. In the West's struggle to understand the same problem, the Judaeo-Christian tradition says that Yahweh commanded that the waters be separated from the dry land, and so it happened.

Bateson goes on to note that what we have in these stories are two diametrically opposed theories of order. Among the Iatmul, order will emerge of itself if disorder or randomness is prevented. In Western theory, an outside agent is necessary to impose order on inherent chaos. Despite these important differences, in both accounts order and differentiation are paramount concerns.[1] These and other genesis tales the world over serve to underscore the deep and pervasive need in cultural life to order and to explain order. A yearning for order in our lives seems to be a basic human motivation. We long to be able to tell stories about ourselves that are coherent, that fit with the realities we perceive.

This desire, this leaning toward order, may well be an urge we share with all the rest of life.[2]

Perhaps the human search for order contains within its core a desire for limits, for checks, for clues with which to circumscribe the meaningful and to make sense of the overwhelming data of living. In as plastic a medium as humanity is said to be, the search for collective certainties must be, at one level, a search for forms people can shape their lives to. This would be so not only for individual people but also for scholarly disciplines. Anthropology's search for theories to explain the diversity of patterns manifest in human cultures is at least partly motivated by this yearning for limits. As philosopher Richard Rorty puts it: '[D]esire for a theory of knowledge is a desire for constraint – a desire to find "foundations" to which one might cling, frameworks beyond which one must not stray, objects which impose themselves, representations which cannot be gainsaid.'[3] For inherent in the ordering process is an anxiety that stems from the daily experience of contingency, probability, choice, error, and the inevitability of flux and change. People yearn for order precisely because it is not a given but presents itself, and then only intermittently, as possibility. Embedded in the ordering urge is the need to stabilize one's living environment in the face of change: we seek at least enough certainty to be able to tolerate the fortuities of history, and enough order to brave the risks of intentional *reordering*.

As Mary Douglas illuminated for us in *Purity and Danger*, where order is sought, disorder must lurk: they are part of the same process.[4] Not only may people have an apprehension of a vast unknown or a sense of chaos outside the known world that they have difficulty naming or even conceiving; there is also, often enough, what appears to be an active desire within social and cultural life – certainly in highly heterogeneous societies, but evident as well in the ethnographies of more homogeneous ones – for derangement, confusion, disarray; an urge, as French sociologist Alain Touraine says one of his student informants of 1968 put it, to 'bust up the works.' Leaving aside other motivations, we can make cultural sense of this in at least two ways. First, there is the testing of traditional cultural boundaries. How firm are they? How much can we rely on them, even in times of change? At which points do they maintain their 'immovable objectivity'? Where do they crumble in the face of such irresistible forces as refutation, resistance, subversion, parody, irony, and – deadliest of all – plain indifference? Perhaps we are reassured by the durability of our cultural ramparts in the face of such offensives. Second, the assault on the given order of things may have a lot to do with people's diminishing satisfaction with the ability of the givens, the traditions, to 'explain' enough of what matters. Chafing under the conservatism and inertia of the achieved order of another time and other interpretations, we try to change the inherited order to fit our own particular historical moment better. Whatever other important things it may accomplish for people – and we cannot discount the sheer 'for the hell of it' carnival gratification such instances call up – the turn to disorder is also, and importantly, indicative of a search for a more complex order, for theories that save more of the appearances than the extant tradition can do. It is a para-doxical desire: through instigating disorder (or we might see it as *creating history*), the hope expressed is, I believe, to discover the deeper regularities of the universe.[5]

ORDER AND CULTURE

Victorian naturalist Frank Buckland found upon taking the train in England that he had to pay for a monkey, which was counted as a 'dog,' but not for a tortoise, which was deemed an 'insect.' To the auto-cratic administrators in that heyday of the British railroad, the category 'insect' encompassed reptiles.[6] As this incident illustrates, ordering also has to do with where people agree (or submit) to place the de-marcation lines in the phenomenal continuum. As anthropologists never tire of asking, where are the perceptual, conceptual, and social boundaries drawn from society to society? Boundaries, as we are aware, are only infrequently coextensive from culture to culture even in societies that name similar concepts. Our most common, taken-for-granted words, such as 'nature,' 'culture,' 'human,' 'animal,' 'history,' 'ecology' – some of the terms I explore in this book – are all concepts ordered not only by their definitions, but also, and critically, by where each society, or at times subgroup, places the boundaries between them. And then, as these concepts are demarcated, contained, and insisted upon in each society, they become political actors in their place and time, exerting discernible effects on people. Had Frank Buckland stood his ground and denied that the mammal in his company was a dog or the reptile an insect, he might have remained on the platform eternally, stranded with his monkey and his tortoise but with no ticket, all for an excess of indissoluble boundary lines.

Stripped to one of its most basic tasks, anthropology consists of the effort to observe and make sense of how human beings under different conditions collectively create and look after stable boundaries and frameworks that order and contain change. Anthropology is a disciplined effort to understand the mechanisms that permit that stability, that containment, those boundaries to be maintained and adapted, or renegotiated, in the face of history, and across successive generations. This is of course what culture – anthropology's coin of the realm (and a word the discipline has come to dread defining) – is all about. The term 'culture,' as appropriated and developed in anthropology and recently diffused in its disciplinary sense to other discourses, is basically a way to talk about how people go about ordering their cosmos and their everyday lives. A restless process, culture is a verb in noun disguise.

Another means by which some anthropologists explore culture and order is a concept I will play upon throughout this essay in both theme and variation forms: *habitus*, in Pierre Bourdieu's usage of the term. In his effort to express the tendencies of people in any society to behave sufficiently recognizably to one another to be able to interact, communicate, and carry on their cultural life, Bourdieu, in his theory of practice,[7] develops the idea of habitus thus: as unconscious predispositions toward perception, thought, action, and emotion inculcated or enculturated into the body schema of each individual, inscribing each of us with the time, place, and objective conditions of our birth. People born or brought up in the same community in the same generation or era, sharing, in varying degrees, habitat, tradition, and history, would also share propensities to perceive and interact with their world in particular ways. Yet these culturally and historically shaped patterns are not behaviours so tightly patterned as to be regimented, insists Bourdieu, but are, rather, *inclinations*, permitting individuality to shine through. Habitus is thus, in Bourdieu's words, a 'subjective but not individual system of internalized structures, schemes of perception, conception, and action common to all members of the same group or class and constituting the precondition for all objectification and apperception ...'[8] It need hardly be said by now that membership in different categories of race and gender no doubt affect habitus as much as, if not more so, than does class. In any event, as a way of proposing how human society gets arranged so that people can understand one another and coordinate their activities and projects sufficiently to get along, the concept of habitus proves extremely useful to the argument I will develop.

Yet another preoccupation of anthropologists engaged in investigating cultural ordering processes has to do with the non-random patterning of social life. In the task of interpreting others' understandings of the cosmos anthropologists are confronted, sooner or later, with the very rock-bottom of cultural life: they find themselves immersed in realms of *metaphor*. Indeed, the analysis of metaphor is considered by some ethnologists to be at the very heart of anthropological enquiry.[9] For, if one is so inclined, all of culture can be understood as metaphor, as an *as-ifness*, as a way that people in different societies, including our own, come to agree to name, describe, narrate, and in this way make sense of the ultimately unnameable experiences of life. '*Knowing* is nothing but working with the favourite metaphors,' Friedrich Nietzsche said, 'an imitating which is no longer felt to be an imitation.'[10]

Metaphor, that unstoppable faculty of the human mind to make associations, most often between an experienced and named domain of life and an apprehended but unnamed domain, is a fundamental mechanism for the patterning of cognitive and behavioural practice and emotional life. Far from being a mere decorative verbal trope, metaphor has long been recognized as a basic and pervasive mode of human cognition, and may be basic to animal cognition and behaviour as well.[11] In their important and aptly named book *Metaphors We Live By* linguist George Lakoff and philosopher Mark Johnson declare that our whole conceptual system, in terms of which we think, feel, and act, is fundamentally metaphoric in nature.[12] To them metaphors we live by are ones that, originally creative, are now so widely, routinely, and unreflectively shared in the culture and have become so deeply embedded in everyday life that people have come to think and speak of one thing as if it were *literally* the other, and act accordingly. In the West, for example, animals bred for scientific manipulation are often spoken about and treated literally as if they were non-sentient disposable laboratory materials or mini-factories (see below, chapter 4). Once metaphors become deeply and subconsciously rooted, they no longer appear to the users to be imaginative bridges from the known to the unknown. Operating at the level of 'common-sense knowledge' or 'practical consciousness'[13] in the *doxic*, uncritical manner of cultural models, and often unverbalized, they appear to be natural and inevitable, reflecting the way things 'are' – and, by implication, defining the way things 'are not.'[14] To think of an animal as kin, for instance, elicits, in the human at least, much the same feelings and associated behaviours toward the animal as exist between a human parent and its young (see below, chapter 3). And, since defining one domain in terms of another suggests a set of guides for actual behaviour, metaphoric mapping from one domain to another also furnishes a practical framework for organizing activity. Fostering certain associations while muting or denying others, metaphors we live by provide us with a fairly delimited set of possible relations and operations, borrowed from the familiar sphere, to engage in. For example, defining animals as citizens provides animal-rights activists with a clear and detailed program of action for advocating the rights of animals under law (see chapter 5).

A bit like trying to catch the tail of Coyote, the Trickster, the Shape-Shifter, a primary activity of the anthropologist consists of translating into one's own (always metaphoric) understandings the webs of metaphor others live by, to the degree that this is possible: tracking sources, resonances, dissonances, and cross-connections, and fashioning from all these some sort of cultural ethos or consistency that at least approaches the flavour and degree of consistency experienced when immersed in the lives of others in the field.[15] Since metaphor, like habitus and like cognition in general, is embedded in particular habitats and specific cultural and historical eras, the anthropologist's interpretive conundrum results largely from the fact that, inescapably emic, metaphor works only if understanding and experiencing one kind of thing in terms of another occurs and is interpreted from the native's point of view. Thus, metaphors we live by act as cultural models, for, historically shaped entities themselves, they in turn shape collective thought, action, and sentiment, what can and cannot be conceived, done, felt. It would seem that it is largely through the shared natural poetry of our lives that we come to order and predict the world.

At bottom, then, most social and cultural anthropologists, when observing and interpreting culture as systems of relation and meaning, as 'ways of knowing,' are most deeply interested in the basic premises, rules, boundaries, inclinations, and metaphors by which peoples actively order their thought, their behaviours, their societies, and their worlds, and in how they contain and explain disorder and chaos. In keeping with this orientation, I use the concept of culture throughout this discussion in this active sense, in terms of 'ordering process.' Employing Raymond Williams's invaluable historical dictionary, *Keywords*, and seeking to emphasize both the dynamic and the attentive, intentional features of its practice, I define culture as ways in which people 'tend to' the ordering of their worlds under different conditions.[16] The argument throughout this book, then, stripped to its essence, is all about order: how, through the process we call culture, the category we call nature, and the spontaneous poetry of everyday life we call metaphor, the West creates it, preserves it, disrupts it, reworks it, and, unendingly, resists its dissolution.

NATURE AS A CULTURAL SYSTEM

Just as culture is understood to be constructed by human beings as a way to interpret the experienced world in a stable, ordered, and collective way, so too is nature a constructed concept. This is, of course, not to say that there is no nature 'out there,' just that what is 'out there' is so variably understood by different groups at different times and places. In any case, amidst the abundant evidence afforded by ethnographers of humankind's propensity to fashion diverse categories out of the continuum of life, one clear universal is the enduring human preoccupation with nature and other animals. Encompassing in the term what each group considers to be the living aspects of its environment, or all those phenomena not created by human beings, whether implicitly understood or explicitly named, nature appears to be a universal medium that commands a response. The delineation of an accepted and acceptable relation of humankind to nature constitutes one of the most significant ways peoples everywhere tend to the ordering of their world. In one form or another nature is recognizable as a fundamental 'cultural system' in all societies. Indeed, all peoples may be said to acquire a *nature-habitus* in the course of enculturation, a term, borrowing from Bourdieu, I will use to emphasize the largely unconsciously held yet shared proclivities of individuals to perceive, conceive, and act within or upon the physical world in characteristic ways conditioned by their particular tradition and history. As Williams observes, 'the idea of nature contains an extraordinary amount of human history.'[17] Nature, the hypothesis every society needs and every culture constructs, is itself an active process that, as will become evident in chapters to follow, demands constant tending by the people who live by it.

Although, strictly speaking, as environmental philosopher Neil Evernden remarks, there can be nothing that is not nature – formally, as a concept, it has no opposite in Western culture[18] – in practice it is not a well-defined idea. Until recently, people rarely displayed the need to define the term with any precision. My informants all readily accepted my unadorned questions about nature, apparently 'knowing' what the word meant. True, on reflection some had difficulty deciding whether certain things were 'inside' or 'outside' of nature, but they had no doubt there was something called nature, and that it related somehow to living things. Also, interestingly, they construed some things, even living ones, as 'not nature,' or 'not in nature,' or 'not natural.' Thus, in practice if not formally, contemporary Westerners conceive of nature not as everything but as a meaningful if loosely arranged cluster of things and events, as a dynamic yet ordered whole. In the West as elsewhere, then, nature, while not totally free of inconsistency and dispute, is construed in an ordered way, as a cultural system.[19] It is a particular cultural system not only because its natives conceive it to be so, but, more important, because through our nature-habitus we actively live our lives as though it were so.

Ethnographers have shown us that as a species, we humans are not in agreement about where we truly belong in the natural order. People in different societies express this conundrum in different ways, trying to find their place among other species or to make a place for at least some plants and animals within the sphere of human society.[20] Perceiving our choice in Western culture to be to align ourselves with either the beasts or the angels, our ordinal ambivalence echoes throughout Western history. '[A]s a member of two orders of being at once,' notes historian Arthur Lovejoy, '[man] wavers between both, and is not quite at home in either.'[21] Nor has anthropology, as a Western cultural enterprise, succeeded in escaping the problem, as we will discover.

Received wisdom in contemporary Western culture tells us that in our hyper-urbanized, post-industrialized society machines have become our predominant metaphors.[22] Yet James Fernandez, among others, claims that animals are humanity's primordial metaphors.[23] And how shall we explain the distinctly non-utilitarian jolt, the sudden lift of the heart, the bolt of I–Thou recognition, on coming upon Toronto's metropolitan cattle in their urban pasture? Does nature, perhaps underlying, or co-stratified with our machine metaphors, still drive our primordial metaphors? Despite the view of many intellectuals since the industrial revolution that the ethos of Western culture consists almost exclusively of an uncritical worship of the machine, it seems to me that the very naming of nature and the lengthy history of the idea of nature itself[24] connote the West's deep and enduring concern about how human beings fit into the natural order of things. Indeed, all of occidental science is based on faith in an order in nature and in the ability of humanity to understand something of that order.[25] In whatever way we understand it and live it, nature is the way the

West orders and articulates its particular view of the universe from where we are situated in time and place. Whether we are aware of it or not, nature is one of our principal ways of knowing: of ordering our percepts, concepts, and emotional responses, our social and political interactions, our productive practices, and our metaphysics. Nature is a hard pea embedded under many layers of cultural ticking: even at its most somnolent and mechanistic, the West has always been alive to nature's ability to keep us awake in the night with vague stirrings, to toss us and turn us, leaving us cross and restless and wordless, and wistful in the morning.

While we may agree that in Western as in all societies nature is a primary ordering concept, what may not be so clear is that it is an unsettled and dynamic one, continually being re-enacted and renegotiated – whether consciously or not – in the course of cultural life. For, as my informants demonstrated, once prodded into articulating what they think 'it' is, people begin to perceive even enculturated nature (nature as commonsensical and therefore self-evident) as remarkably complicated. As a vague reference the word nature feels known; but when people are asked to bring the concept to the foreground of their attention for description, elucidation, and examination, this effort brings to awareness nuances, discrepancies, and outright disagreements in views among people, providing a glimpse of culture involed in the very *act* of inventing nature.

The Nature-Culture Divide

The most notorious feature of Western nature-habitus, as it appears to a number of critics in the current era of collective awakening to environmental crisis, is the dualism that pervades our modern view of humanity-and-nature.[26] While in a formal sense nature as a concept may have no opposite, the nature-habitus we live and practise in the West appears to be solidly based on the assumption that nature does indeed have an opposite, and that is culture in its broadest sense: all that human beings have made and all that we are. Claude Lévi-Strauss, in characterizing the passage from nature to culture as the central problem in anthropology, best articulates the evolutionarily tinged, progressivist leaning that presumes a decisive split between these worlds: nature and culture, animals and humans, are separate orders of being.[27] This presumption is foundational to much of everyday and scientific discourse to this day. As environmental historian Clarence

Glacken notes, even when people pay lip-service to a conception of humanity as part of nature, the ensuing argument, whatever its substance, almost invariably is built on the nature-culture divide: nature quite rapidly metamorphoses into all that is nonhuman. This divide is so deeply ingrained in our nature-habitus that we seldom notice the discrepancy between assertion and argument.[28]

In this sense, nature refers to a relation. Nature is the other against which humanity is defined. Each is here defined by the *absence* of the other. (It is this pervasive zero-sum underpinning of our modern nature-habitus, I think, that the refractory presence of Fafard's seven cows deep in the heart of Toronto disturbs so much.) If any co-presence is suggested, it is a highly distanced one, taking the form of man observing nature. As historian of science Donna Haraway points out, 'Man is not *in* nature partly because he is not seen, is not the spectacle.'[29] Indeed, as she suggests elsewhere, professional reputations are at stake if the nature-culture boundary is crossed. So critical is this relation of absence considered to be that scientific conventions would view interactions between human observer and animal observed in the field, or their representations in print, as potentially polluted and scientifically suspect, perhaps even discreditable. Yet ambivalences between 'scientific objectivity' and 'anthropomorphic empathy' are not always easy to deny. They are apparently particularly difficult to dissemble in primate field research. Let us take, for instance, the studies of George Schaller, Jane Goodall, and Dian Fossey. Where these consummate primatologists could not refrain from empathic emotions and 'anthropomorphic leaps' – where, in other words, they crossed the line – each of them felt compelled to publish separate accounts of their work for scientific and lay audiences. Thus, we have 'objective,' distanced, ethological accounts of animal behaviour in doctoral dissertations and scientific journals, and more intimate, 'subjective,' boundary-confounding, interactive accounts for a more general public in journals like *National Geographic* or in popular books. In such ways do Western scientists try to maintain or, as Haraway puts it, 'apologize for violating' what should be a more 'neutral' relation between animal and human.[30]

This metaphor that many people, and significantly most scientists, live by – the 'given' that we in the West are living out a *fundamental rupture* between nature and culture – takes two principal forms. In the first, in contrast to many (perhaps most) other cultures worldwide, the West, through its advanced scientific knowledge, has 'demonstrated' repeatedly that the gap between human and animal, culture and nature, is unbridgeable: there is a dimensional disjunction between the two orders of being. Usually judged to be lodged in, or manifested by, an intellectual, linguistic, or spiritual capacity, there is an extra 'something' that humanity is possessed of that other beings simply do not have, and this absence diminishes the latter. With the evolutionary leap to mankind this unique capacity, whatever it is judged to be, and the cultural evolution it fosters have left the rest of nature in the dust. Of course, the unique capacity keeps changing with each new piece of information that provides evidence for other animals' capacities for tool use, intentionality, inventiveness, communication, consciousness, emotion, culture, and so on, but the boundaries between human and animal, like the portable partitions in today's offices, have become a fixture of our modern nature-habitus.[31]

In the second form of the 'fundamental rupture' metaphor, it is the West that has lost something irrevocably: the sense of belonging to and in a natural habitat. Unlike many other, technologically simpler societies that have a survival stake in the moment-to-moment interaction with the natural world, so this version goes, the West of globalized capitalism, urban sprawl, and cyberspace has completely lost touch with its original roots in the natural world. The world of the technologically unsophisticated native on the margins of Metropolis, it is assumed, is a world blessed in the connection it has retained with nature and animals, and the West suffers by contrast;[32] not least in its inability to come to terms with impending environmental catastrophe, for which it is primarily responsible.

Anthropology's own ethnographies have shown decisively that the dichotomy between nature and human beings is not a universal human response to the physical world.[33] To cite but one of many instances, the Koyukon Indians in the boreal forest of subarctic Alaska have been the subject of anthropologist Richard Nelson's research and a part of his life for many years. Nelson considers it likely that from earliest times most of humanity has understood the natural world according to principles similar to those of the Koyukon and other native North American peoples. In the necessary interactions with nonhuman life that include killing for food and at times being killed in turn, the Koyukon accept moral responsibility for the animals in their habitat. Nelson observes: 'For Koyukon people, nature is the greatest power, and humans must humble themselves to it. The key to this humility is respect – through the innumerable of gestures of politeness and through adherence to rules or taboos. A strict code of morality extends beyond the enclave of human society to include the entire community of life.'[34] This way of knowing includes a recognition of the animals' reciprocal moral codes. A Koyukon man said of the Canada goose, 'Even if it had the power to knock you over ... I don't think it would do it.'[35] Restraint is perceived as part of all of living nature. And human beings not only must practise self-control but are also tempered by the rest of nature. The world that humans watch and interact with returns the gaze, keeping humankind within the bounds of moral restraint: 'There's always something in the air that watches us,' a village elder said to Nelson.[36] On another occasion he was told: 'The country knows. If you do wrong things to it, the whole country knows. It feels what's happening to it. I guess everything is connected together somehow, under the ground.'[37]

Among the Koyukon, humans and animals are bound together in ways that challenge a Westerner's comprehension. All animals contain both material and spiritual dimensions. All creatures, says Nelson, 'no matter how small and inconspicuous, carry the luminescence of power.'[38] When a hunter has 'luck' in hunting, it might be said that 'something' took care of him, this 'something' being the animal's spiritual power. A Koyukon elder told him once that every hair on a brown bear's hide has a life of its own, 'so it can't keep still; it can't keep its temper. It takes a few years for all that life to be gone from a brown bear's hide. That's the kind of power it has.'[39] Nelson's own nature-habitus frustrated his desire to understand the spiritual relationship between humans and animals in that society in any depth, as he himself freely admits. He could grasp, however, that an all-embracing affinity and connectedness with nonhuman life pervaded the thought, behaviour, and belief of these people. Among hunting-gathering peoples, he says, the intricate weaving together of nature and culture is like the exchange between living cells and their surroundings. 'Animals are our food,' they say. 'They are our thoughts.'[40]

In contrast, Lévi-Strauss's famous phrase 'animals are good to think' always had an 'understood' clause that, when fully expressed, would be '*the disjunctions between humans and* animals are good to think.' The muting of any totemic imagination or sense of human being as creaturely being, as sharing the same phenomenal world with others – a characteristic feature of Western nature-habitus – stems directly from the nature-culture divide. This muting tendency is especially prevalent in contemporary scientific disciplines, where differences between humans and other animals are highlighted while continuities are downplayed or discounted altogether. But, as writer Jeffrey Masson remarks, '[t]o refuse to see commonality ... is to deliberately widen the gap.'[41]

In this connection, it is interesting that one of the most notable of recent efforts to bridge the nature-culture gap in biology, sociobiology, has been the object of often virulent critiques from many quarters of Western intellectual life. Sociobiology, the 'Great Synthesis,' as Edward O. Wilson called it,[42] is an expressly stated attempt to link human behaviour with the rest of nature. Basing their work on evolutionary theory, its proponents have tried to show that all animal behaviour, including that of humans, is a result of the pressures of natural selection on specific genes or gene combinations to maximize individual fitness and the reproduction of fertile offspring. As a result, behaviours are 'built in' and are not susceptible to environmental change. Collective behaviour is the product not of emergent properties of social life but of the aggregation of the individual behaviours of all the group's members.[43]

The devastating critiques of sociobiology are well known: its confusion of a generally acknowledged evolutionary drive for an organism to manifest 'relative advantage' over others with its insistence on the organism's drive to 'maximize fitness'; its reliance on a narrowly deterministic concept of 'genes,' and its flagrant disregard of basic genetic evidence that environment and genetic make-up interact in complex ways to manifest a particular phenotype; its conflation of individual with group behaviour; and so forth. Sociobiologists seem woefully unaware of history, cultural diversity, and contextual flexibility, not to mention imitation, borrowing, and invention in the shaping and changing of behaviours in human life. A frequently underscored flaw of sociobiology is its wholesale and unexamined use of Western market and competitive capitalist metaphors that are specific, as Marshall Sahlins points out, to a particular epoch of Euro-American history and culture – in other words, its unacknowledged subscription to a nature that is 'culturally figured'; not to mention the related tendency to characterize behavioural 'norms' in grossly ethnocentric terms that are Western, middle-class, white, and largely male. These are most often the rational and ideological sins of a 'pop' or 'vulgar' sociobiology, but the more rigorous scientific sociobiology shares in some of these as well. For many of sociobiology's critics, apart from the lack of evidence for many of its assertions, the most egregious of its flaws is its apparent lack of awareness of, or concern about, the fascistic dangers inherent in a poorly examined conception of our social and cultural dispositions as not only natural but inevitable.[44]

There are two things I find particularly interesting in this extended onslaught: first, the efforts of most critics to single out what sociobiology says about humans without considering whether it might not also be reductive, perhaps even wildly wrong, about other animals as well; and second, the fervour of the critical response. To my mind the primary error of sociobiology lies less in its diminishment of humans than in its a priori oversimplification of all *other* beings, for this, in large part, becomes the model applied to humans. Quite without evidence, sociobiologists appear to believe that all nonhuman animal behaviours are inherently simple: virtually completely genetically determined, without agency or flexibility, without interior complexity or emergent social organization. In turn, the significant error of many of sociobiology's *critics* is that, although outraged by the reductive characterization of humans, many of them rush to accept this same simplified notion of other animals. The critics rarely bother to ask whether, being quite wrong-headed in their estimation about human beings, sociobiologists might be equally wrong-headed about other beings. The sociobiology debate seems to have widened the gap between nature and culture even further.

The ruckus has also had an unfortunate effect on some people interested in studying human–animal continuities, influencing them to turn away from any such inquiry altogether, either because they are incensed by sociobiology's simplistic reasoning itself or for fear of being tarred with the brush of a discredited science. For any approach that poses similar questions, even from very different premises, is frequently uncritically categorized in the sociobiology slot.

The second interesting point is the furor this hypothesis (hardly a 'theory' or a 'new synthesis,' as had been hoped) provoked. Of course, it is no wonder that the critique flew fast and furious to counter the narrowly deterministic, simplistic mechanisms proposed for human social life (a model that has proved, disquietingly, widely appealing to lay audiences and a number of introductory biology textbook authors[45]). And yet, I cannot help but wonder whether the intellectual uproar also had something to do with countering the temerity of some scientists, however misguidedly, to attempt to bridge the gap between nature and culture. Perhaps the poor reasoning of sociobiology and its extreme stances in pop sociobiology were more or less unconsciously welcomed by many scientists and others because they unwittingly reinforced the nature-culture divide with which we are so comfortable, and which we are loath to give up, having nothing, at present, to take its place. And of course, the nature-culture divide is useful in so many ways.

We constantly need to remind ourselves to ask who gains from 'a particular construction of the way things are.'[46] For one thing, the habit of representing nature as a separate order of being, as all the material world except us, permits us to forget that it is we human beings who have constructed our perceptions of nature, our polarizations, and our practices. If we believe we have nothing to do with nature, we can do nothing about it. 'Why criticize a sunrise or a frog?' asks Evernden.[47] Or our genes, if they have such an iron hold on our behaviour and our social structures?

In contrast to the fit between the conditions of life and the consciousness of human–animal *connectedness* among the Koyukon of subarctic Alaska, it is the nature-culture *divide* that has proved so immensely useful in modern Western society. For Evernden, the maintenance of nature and culture as separate orders of being is necessary to keep the idea of humanism alive. Humanism is defined against the material, natural world. 'Unless we have this absolute separation,' he comments, 'we cannot claim the unique qualities that justify our domination of the earth.'[48] In this view, nature becomes merely the raw material for exploitation by human culture and especially by globalized capitalism. For Haraway, the complex interrelations among colonialism, gender, class, racism, and research inherent in the nature-culture divide as we live it ensure the status quo of our present institutions of power and control.[49]

A discipline born in and of the West, anthropology has always, nevertheless, been as much a critic of its culture as an expression of it. But in the case of the nature-culture debate, mainstream anthropology has largely assumed, without much critical assessment, its own culture's general ideas of nature with all their attendant ambiguities and contrarieties. In turn, the discipline has contributed significantly to these culturally specific ways of knowing the natural world – also, I believe, largely without being aware of its impact on the general culture. In this, anthropology, looked at as a *practice*, as a Western cultural system, tells us perhaps more about its own nature-habitus than about that of the people so wonderfully described in its monographs.

Chapter Two

Anthropology and the Natural World

The spirits leave the island when the anthropologists arrive.
Haitian proverb (in Hans Peter Duerr 1985)

Despite the durability of the nature-culture divide in everyday and scholarly life, anthropological interest in human interactions with the rest of nature has always been lively. This is not surprising since, to most if not all the native peoples anthropologists have studied, the natural world was perceived, as among the Koyukon of subarctic Alaska, to be integral to their own and could not be separated out from their cultural life as an autonomous entity. Ethnographies therefore abound with exquisite descriptions of the relations of humans to other life forms. Ecological and economic anthropology in particular have focused on human–habitat relations (although primarily from a utilitarian perspective). Indeed, the entire discipline's record in documenting human relations with the rest of nature is exemplary. Of all Western disciplines, anthropology has been the most consistent and exhaustive in its recording of human–animal relations, from up close, in depth, and across many cultures.[1] Problems arise, not in the reports themselves, but rather in their interpretation.

ANTHROPOLOGY'S NATURE-HABITUS

Since human beings rely so absolutely on animals and the rest of the biosphere for their very survival, and since most if not all the peoples studied by anthropologists are keenly aware of this fact, some description of human–animal interactions will naturally be basic to all but the

most specialized of ethnographic studies. Yet the human–animal relationships investigated worldwide are not characterized simply and
unequivocally by utilitarian concerns. The anthropological record
demonstrates, rather, an extraordinary diversity of interaction patterns
and relationships, often within one culture. At the same time, it reveals
how Western anthropologists tend to interpret these varied phenomena. It is primarily in these interpretations that the discipline's particular perspectives on the natural world, particularly its deep dedication
to the nature-culture divide, show themselves most clearly. I will concentrate on four aspects of anthropological analysis of human–animal
relations characteristic of much of the ethnological record, and a fifth
that is embedded in the structure of anthropology as a discipline.

Interspecies Sociality

One of the most remarkable findings from the ethnographic record is
the wealth of evidence for the sheer sociality of much human–animal
interaction in general, the abundant evidence of biophilia: from the
close, affectionate relations some peoples have with their dog teams
or their herds of cattle or pigs to the popularity of animal taming and
pet keeping under highly diverse and sometimes surprising circumstances. Such interspecies sociality has been found even where hardship and privation are not infrequent conditions of life.[2]

However, the overwhelming majority of ethnographies that describe
human–animal relations proceed to analyse them from a particular
and rather peculiar perspective. In most such studies, among them
many that have become classic texts, the ethnographer tends to divert
his or her focus away from an analysis of the human–animal relations
observed toward what is taken to be their 'truer' significance in casting
light on various other – by implication more important or more fundamental but always human-centred – aspects of the culture under study.
Instances these concerns may be modes of human subsistence, of classification, mentation, myth-making, ritual, and so on. The underlying
assumption, sometimes implicit and sometimes, as in Lévi-Strauss,
explicit, appears to be that the human–animal relation is at bottom not
really of interest or value – indeed, cannot reasonably be countenanced
– *as a relation in itself*. It is only of special interest because it is presumed
to act as a symbol of something else that *is* of value, invariably supposed to be some intra-human concern. As Lévi-Strauss states: 'The
animal world and that of plant life are not utilized merely because they

are there, but because they suggest a mode of thought.'[3] The focus has rarely been on observing and recording human–animal interactions with a view to examining the significance of interspecies relations as social relations in and of themselves.[4]

In his book *Beast and Man*[5] Roy Willis provides an instructive and quite representative example of this attitude. He compares the configurations of human–animal relations and their symbolism in three cultures: the Nuer of the Sudan from Evans-Pritchard's accounts, the Lele of the Congo as documented by Douglas, and his own work among the Fipa of Tanzania. Willis's primary interest lies in exposing the structural synonymy between conceptions of wild and domesticated, animal and human, female and male and their symbolic meanings for the human communities involved. In the process he manages to provide a breathtaking wealth of observations on interactions between humans and animals that, to my mind, cry out to be explored 'nakedly' – that is, just as they were enacted, albeit in the presence of the ethnographer. For, after all the symbolic, cognitive, and materialist analytic avenues have been trodden and all the deep anthropological interpretations have been exhausted, the greatest mystery remains unexplained: what is the visceral meaning for these human beings, and for the animal beings involved, of daily coexistence and the social give-and-take between the species?

In the course of his discussion of Evans-Pritchard's classic account of the Nuer, Willis passes on to us many instances of the physical intimacy with which the lives of these people were intertwined with their cattle. Cattle were socially identified with the descent group and lineage of their owners, and since Nuer males and females took a name from one of their oxen, Willis observes, 'a Nuer genealogy often sounds like an inventory of a kraal.' The Nuer tended to define all social processes and relationships in terms of cattle, and sometimes called their oxen 'friend.' In addition, their association with their cattle provided them with a poetic and 'metaphoric language capable of embracing the whole Nuer universe.'[6] The Nuer were too identified with their cattle to think of them abstractly and with detachment, as scientists might, although they did demonstrate the detached curiosity of the latter with wild animals. Here is an example of Evans-Pritchard's account of Nuer attachment to their cattle:

The men wake about dawn at camp in the midst of their cattle and sit contentedly watching them till milking is finished. They then either take them to pasture and spend the day watching them graze, driving them to water, composing songs about them, and bringing them back to camp, or they remain in the kraal to drink their milk, make tethering-cords and ornaments for them, water and in other ways care for their calves, clean their kraal, and dry their dung for fuel. Nuer wash their hands and faces in the urine of cattle, especially when cows urinate during milking, drink their milk and blood, and sleep on their hides by the side of their smouldering dung. They cover their bodies, dress their hair, and clean their teeth with the ashes of cattle dung, and eat their food with spoons made from their horns. When the cattle return in the evening they tether each beast to its peg with cords made from the skins of their dead companions and sit in the wind-screens to contemplate them and to watch them being milked.[7]

It is evident that acute and sympathetic observation does not fail ethnographers in their descriptions of human–animal interactions, particularly in non-Western societies. Yet, at the same time, there appears to be a singular failure to perceive as profound and mysterious the interspecies acts observed and recorded so faithfully. Ethnographers appear to readily accept without further curiosity that 'primitive' peoples would have such intimate and apparently satisfying relationships as a matter of course, as part of some animistic worldview. It would seem that, at least until quite recently, Western ethnographers have had difficulty in conceiving that some true significance, for Westerners as well as for other peoples, might attach to the prosaic social aspects of the human–animal relation itself. Embedded in this failure of imagination seems to be a reluctance to entertain the possibility of the other in this particular dyad as an Other, as a subject.

Interspecies Subjectivity

Anthropology has always been concerned with the exotic Other, in the sense of 'unknown subject.' Since the late 1960s anthropologists have been witness to and willing participants in a more self-conscious ethnographic practice and concern with their relation to the other.[8] But until a few scholars began to publish work on actual human–animal relations – for example, Myrdene Anderson on the Saami of Finland and Norway and their dogs and reindeer, Elizabeth Atwood Lawrence on the relation between humans and horses in the American West, and Barbara Noske on the domesticated animal as other in Western societies, and until Tim Ingold published the proceedings of the 'What Is an Animal?' conference in 1988[9] – the other was by and large limited to other humans, and did not include other species.

Yet, as the passage from Evans-Pritchard demonstrates (along with many other descriptions of human–animal relations in the anthropological literature), it is not difficult to gain the impression that for many of the peoples studied, the animals in question *are* subjects: recognizable individual beings of another species with whom people have significant, often emotional, social relationships. Here is what Fernandez has to say of the village people in Asturias, Spain, and their relation to their cattle:

> Cows and calves have an enormous weight in village life. They are a constant topic of conversation. When one is shown the family pictures, photos of cows and calves are as likely to tumble out amidst the shuffle. And a family given a picture taken five years earlier of the father and baby posing before a cow team pulling a hay cart spent most of an excited half hour remembering those cows with nostalgia. I don't know all there is to walking cows from the stable through the streets and up to the pastures. But there is a satisfaction in it for men and women that makes them highly resistant to government efforts to consolidate their scattered meadows ... For if they were consolidated one would no longer walk one's cows about one's wide world.[10]

Similarly, Clifford Geertz describes how Balinese men related to their gamecocks:

> [They] spend an enormous amount of time with their favorites, grooming them, feeding them, discussing them, trying them out against one another, or just gazing at them with a mixture of rapt admiration and dreamy self-absorption. Whenever you see a group of Balinese men squatting idly in the council shed or along the road in their hips down shoulders forward knees up fashion, half or more of them will have a rooster in his hands, holding it between his thighs, bouncing it gently up and down to strengthen its legs, ruffling its feathers with abstract sensuality, pushing it out against a neighbor's rooster to rouse its spirit, withdrawing it toward his loins to calm it again.[11]

Geertz notes that the men spent 'what seems not only to an outsider, but also to themselves, an inordinate amount of time with them,' seeing to the minutest details of their feeding, grooming, ceremonial preparation, exercise, and general care.[12]

But again, something happens in these and similar ethnographies as the analysis proceeds. The subjectivity (the *thereness*) of the animal for the native person often fades into colourful background data on the page, while the anthropologist finds the real significance of the animal to lie in some exclusively human preoccupation. Geertz himself goes on to say: '[L]ike most of the rest of us, the Balinese are a great deal more interested in understanding men than they are in understanding cocks.'[13] The nonhuman being is simply not perceived as an appropriate anthropological subject.

In calling attention to this pervasive tendency in anthropology, Lawrence writes: 'Much of the anthropological work previously done in the sphere of man's association with animals has virtually discounted the contribution of the animal as a living creature with certain distinct characteristics of its own that influence its role in the relationship.' Citing as an example a classic work on the horse in Plains Indian culture in which the horse was cast as a 'tool,' she states that a major consequence of this tendency is a 'negligible account either of the influence of the animal's requirements as a large herbivore or of the psychological and spiritual effects of human interactions with an animal of its particular nature.' She points out that observing and describing the animal as a subject does not preclude but rather enriches any additional perspectives an anthropologist might wish to explore. And therefore, uniquely for an anthropologist, she has set as a goal for herself to 'expand the traditional ethnographic perspective by including, as far as possible, the input of the animals themselves in these associations.'[14]

In sum, there are many ethnographic instances in which the native group being studied insists on including animals and other biota as significant others with a subjectivity of their own, while the anthropologist reports this as a mere curiosity, or as a surface expression of a deeper symbolism referring solely to the intra-human social order. Attributing subjectivity or personhood to an animal is nothing more than the native's 'unconscious anthropomorphism.'[15] As a result, and with few exceptions, anthropologists have given short shrift to the notion that the animal in question is truly, to the native, a subject. Even in the face of informants' statements to the contrary, scholars often ignore the possibility that it may be the social relationship itself – a relationship between subjects of different species – that is held to be

significant, even central, by members of the host society. This consistent oversight strengthens Marshall Sahlins's claim that the founders
of modern ethnography 'never really overcame the assumptions of
practical reason deeply embedded in their conceptual frameworks,
and as such, the English and American styles of anthropology that followed them never really got to the heart of the cultures with which
they were concerned.'[16]

Human–Animal Relations in the Urban West

While we may take issue with how ethnographers have interpreted
their information on human–natural relations among non-Western
societies, we cannot quibble with the wealth of description they have
provided. The situation is quite different in Western societies, especially in urban settings, where we are faced with a scarcity of discourse
or reflection from either the social or biological sciences on the subject.[17] Why have the human and life sciences so seldom focused on
non-utilitarian human–animal relations in contemporary Western society as a domain worth investigating?[18] In the introduction I suggested
that in the West, urban settings, experienced as places for encountering
and interacting with the built environment, envelop their human
inhabitants in an impression that these are locations where nature does
not, or *should not*, exist. This might account in part for the scholarly
silence. There is no doubt, as well, that such studies would bring to
light awkward and unsought insights into Western culture itself, forcing an undesirable examination of the complicated and uneasy relations between humans and animals in this context. Perhaps such study
would be as disconcerting as the spectacle of Fafard's obdurate Toronto cattle lying unyielding in their metropolitan pasturage, fixed to
the earth, embodying the solid essence of stock, while market abstractions blink and byte rapidly and ceaselessly high up in the steel aeries
of the urban canyon.

Non-verbal Communication

A fourth area that has had immense impact on the nature-habitus
of anthropology has been the glorification of spoken language over
all other forms of communication. This feature of information-sharing,
using words and syntax, is only one aspect of an extraordinary range of
communication that human beings, as well as other animals, possess.[19]

Yet, especially with the proliferation of structuralist theory and its privileging of human language both in itself and as powerful metaphor, any
hope of support for examining non-linguistic communication between
humans and other species was essentially blocked. An example here is
the disproportionate focus on teaching other primates a human-type
language rather than trying to understand the communication patterns
of apes and other animals, as well as those between other animals and
human beings. Further, in the effort to teach primates, little attention
was paid to what *was* known about the usual content of many primate
communication patterns: that they clearly conveyed information of an
emotional nature. Even with this knowledge, most of the primate language researchers did not pay special attention to this aspect of ape
communication, and thus the language teaching, for the most part, did
not emphasize words to express emotion.[20]

Yet, even the privileged position of spoken language, this bastion of
human uniqueness that not even primates could master, was severely
shaken with the discovery that the African grey parrot could not only
imitate human sounds, it could combine the words into meaningful
phrases that indicated the transfer of original concepts through
speech.[21]

This, then, appears to constitute some of the central legacy of the
nature-culture divide that makes up anthropology's nature-habitus:
the muting of the social aspects of human–animal relations in different
societies; the elision of the intersubjectivity of many of these interactions; almost complete silence about human–animal relations in the
West other than use-relations, particularly in industrialized urban settings; and the slighting or outright neglect of non-verbal communication. Equally important, if not more so, I believe, is a fifth feature that
merits mention: the *absence of dialogue* concerning the human being
as animal subject, manifested largely in anthropology's fragmented
nature and in the concomitant failure of its totemic imagination.

Anthropology's Fragmentation

At the turn of the twentieth century, against Franz Boas's vigorous
efforts to build a science of humanity encompassing organic, linguistic,
cultural, and historical facets in equal measure, the still-young discipline of anthropology opted to separate into the various branches we
take for granted today: physical anthropology, linguistics, ethnology,
and archaeology. Swept away in this fragmentation was the opportu-

nity to engage in the study of humankind as *cultural creature*, that is, as both organic and cultural being.[22] From that time the organic aspects of the study of humankind lay solely in the province of physical anthropology, and ethnological theory developed unburdened by the idea that human subjects were also animal beings. When anthropology gave up that sense and understanding of human being as both subject *and* animal being, other animal beings lost the possibility of subjectivity. Sociality, equality, and intersubjectivity in human–animal relations became unthinkable. Is it any wonder that, as they say in Haiti, the spirits leave the island when the anthropologists arrive?

The curtain of silence between physical and cultural anthropology remains essentially drawn. Physical and cultural anthropology still rarely converse; when they do, it is not usually a conversation initiated by anthropologists studying human beings. The discourse is rather among some primatologists who struggle with the methods of a positivistic biological science while accumulating, via those same methods, evidence of animal interiority, subjectivity, and culture as I have defined it – as a dynamic, interactive tending to the ordering of one's world. By and large, however, Western physical anthropologists' primary interests lie in investigating a particular human being only as representative of a species, as object, in primatology as in the rest of physical anthropology. Haraway cites, in comparison, the studies of some Japanese primatologists, who consider it scientifically necessary to recognize, observe, and describe the life of each and every member of a troupe, sometimes upwards of two hundred primates. Here, the animals are clearly approached as subjects.[23]

While there is some development in primatology in bridging a nature-culture gap, we observe no parallel changes in the study of human nature. In the West, physical anthropology still remains primarily a study of objects, while cultural anthropology, particularly since the 1960s, tries to conduct a study of subjects. Since that era of 'reinventing anthropology,' concepts of the other in the post-colonial period have been more complexly conceived. However, this turn toward self- and other-reflexivity has been limited to intra-human affairs. Anthropology did not cross the Great Divide into human–animal relations in the same political, self-reflexive way it did when faced with the residues of human colonialism. With natural colonialism still hegemonic, the old primitivist-progressivist notions of 'Other' and 'Self' remained (and remain) embedded in human–animal relations; in this terrain, Western metaphors retain the We/They of colonial discourse.[24]

The failure of physical and cultural anthropology to establish a scholarly dialogue has resulted in the reification of the split between human being as natural object and human being as cultural subject, and anthropology tends doxically to maintain this 'division of labour,' as Haraway puts it.[25] Thus, the boundary between nature and culture, and especially between human and animal, remains virtually impenetrable, despite the increasing rhetoric about bridging the nature-culture gap. The sociobiological debate merely drove a deeper wedge into the divide. In cultural anthropology at least, the discussion pertaining to the human being as culture-making animal subject has been silenced.

This same split between creatureliness and subjectivity results in the muting of interspecies relations that, as we saw, is a feature of so many ethnographic texts. It is difficult for Westerners to think of humans as subjects and as animals simultaneously, and equally hard to think of animals simultaneously as creatures and as subjects. If animals are not subjects, how can we interpret relations between humans and other species as intersubjective, or social, and why bother to consider forms of communication other than verbal intercourse? Only human beings can be subjects, exotic or otherwise, and only intra-human relations can be considered as real relations; all other relations are to be characterized in metonymic, not metaphoric, terms. The closer we are to the discipline's 'home' – the contemporary urban West – the less likely are human–animal interactions to be considered of ethnographic interest. If there is to be any discussion of animals and of human–animal relations, it is most comfortably left at the 'primitive' end of the human 'primitive-civilized' polarity.[26]

The result of this unexamined attitude is the maintenance and reinforcement of the boundary between nature and culture. This, I would say, is one of the more important tasks, among the many necessary to sustain the great Western cultural enterprise, that has fallen specifically to the discipline of anthropology to carry out. As Evernden notes, 'The conceptual purity of the domain of Nature is a condition for the security of the realm of humanity.'[27] Anthropology, unreflectively for the most part, has acted as one of the primary guardians of the purity of that border. This is not a mere figure of speech. In terms of research on wildlife, as we saw in chapter 1, human–animal interactions are actually treated as data *contaminants*. Thus, anthropology's duty to Western hegemony – forged as the science itself was, after all, in the smelters of that same late-nineteenth-century Euro-American culture – is fulfilled by policing this precious border, this first, now last, and most important, colonial outpost of imperialist pretensions. Such a heavy charge laid upon the field makes it equally difficult for practitioners to posit as researchable terrains the animal subjectivity of human being and the interiority and subjectivity of animal being, not to mention meta-anatomical continuities among the species or the depth and intricacies of human–animal relations. The Great Divide between nature and culture, whether thinly or thickly drawn, is still perceived as a real, if two-dimensional, line: it is a limen, a threshold, one to step over rather than through. This divide is not yet seriously entertained in the discipline as a vast unmapped territory, a literal no-man's land. It would doubtless come as an appalling thought to anthropologists to view themselves as cherubim with flaming swords keeping the threshold between nature and culture inviolate. But contemporary practice must lead us to the conclusion that the field as a whole still holds firmly to the view that there *is* a threshold, and once one has stepped over the limen of the Garden – of nature – there is no going back, not even a viable standing still, only a going forward in the passage from nature to culture. And Western anthropology, positioned east of Eden with swords ablaze (although perhaps wavering somewhat at last), continues to fend off thoughts of return.

A fascinating glimpse into the impact of these tendencies in the discipline can be found in the debates on totemism that took up so much scholarly energy in the first two decades of the twentieth century.

TOTEMISM

Defined broadly as 'an aspect of the way in which man conceives of the relationship between the social and the natural world,'[28] totemism, a key theme in anthropology for the century from McLennan to Lévi-Strauss, told us, in practice, much more about how Western anthropologists conceive of the relationship between the social and natural world than about the conceptions of some generic 'man.' Thus, anthropology itself provides an excellent example of the attenuation of the totemic imagination in Western culture.

As an anthropological concept totemism was held to consist of a cluster of three necessary traits: the existence of groups in a society named after some animal or plant; the idea that the human group is descended from and related to this animal or plant; and the treatment of the totem as sacred. Such clusters, with many variations, were found to be widespread on every peopled continent. Studied by turns as a form of magic, mistaken genetics, primitive religion, means of social organization, thanksgiving for adequate subsistence, mechanism for domesticating nature, exemplar of the deep structures of concrete human thought, and metaphoric predicate for the inchoate human subject,[29] all of these hypotheses appeared to have some merit in some circumstances and not in others, or to explain persuasively some aspect of all totemic activity while failing to capture the whole.[30]

Despite decades of focused scholarship, a vast collection of examples from many disparate parts of the world, and much debate in learned societies and in print, Western thought could not agree on the 'purpose' of totemism. Eventually it was noted that the forms totemism took in America, Africa, and Australia were too different to be studied together. By 1920 Arnold Van Gennep listed no less than forty-one theories put forward over the preceding few decades, and concluded that the one certainty to be gleaned from them all was a negative one: that totemism did not symbolize the clan or any other concrete or even idealized social entity.[31] Finally (and to their credit), burdened with too much theory and too little empirical information, the first generation of anthropologists retired their pursuit of the unsolved riddle and turned with more hope to fieldwork.[32]

By its own admission, anthropology could not grasp and never did resolve the totemism debate; it soundly defeated the most knowledgeable of scholars. Even the most recent attempt, by Lévi-Strauss, to show that totemism was merely a way to organize human thought, left much to be desired. Why did this happen?

The one commonality that pertains throughout the vast collection of instances of totemism – *the transparent and marked sense of affiliation and continuity between humans and other animals* – was precisely that which was *not* considered to be of major interest in these debates. As with the ethnographies discussed above, such an expression of closeness between human and animal could not, it seems, count as significant. As a way of ordering human–animal relations, that cluster of traits we call totemism appeared to originate from an alien metaphor to live by, and proved to be untranslatable; metaphoric systems the Occident lived by could not accommodate it. Missing the requisite memory or imagination, the Western mind could only understand a relation with the natural world in metonymic terms, as 'good for something.' It could thus only grasp totemism as an institution, a humanly created enterprise to fulfil or at least explain specific intra-human needs. It could not be understood and studied as what it purported to be in every single case: a *relation* – an only partially mediated state of being and connection between species. Further still from mainstream anthropological thought would be the possibility that totemism, in all its variations, might be a primary means of expressing, perhaps even celebrating, the animal subjectivity of human being in the midst of other subjects inhabiting the natural world.

Yet the ethnographies themselves are not always obscure, the native speakers not particularly incomprehensible. As Lévi-Strauss reports in *The Savage Mind*, the Carrier Indians told a Western ethnographer:

> We know what the animals do, what are the needs of the beaver, the bear, the salmon, and other creatures, because long ago men married them and acquired this knowledge from their animal wives. Today the priests say we lie, but we know better. The white man has been only a short time in this country and knows very little about the animals; we have lived here thousands of years and were taught long ago by the animals themselves. The white man writes everything down in a book so that it will not be forgotten; but our ancestors married the animals, learned all their ways, and passed on the knowledge from one generation to another.[33]

Although totemism proved confounding and ultimately recalcitrant to Western anthropological categories of thought, at the very least we cannot doubt that the abundance of material on totemism attests to the widespread expression by this means of a profound sense of affinity, intersubjectivity, intimacy, communication, and responsibility that human beings, living under vastly differing conditions, have felt to exist between themselves and other creatures in the natural world. Yet, because of our collective loss of a totemic imagination, this remains for Western culture, I submit, the deepest, the least fathomable, mystery of the other.

These are not merely intramural issues. Not only has anthropology uncritically taken on much of the West's nature-habitus, it has been immensely, although largely indirectly, influential in shaping that nature-habitus. How does the discipline influence Western society's perceptions of nature, culture, human–animal relations, and environmental concerns? What are we *constrained* from seeing and experiencing as a result?

THE INFLUENCE OF ANTHROPOLOGY ON
WESTERN CULTURE

Ever since its inception as a distinct scholarly endeavour, anthropology
has had repercussions beyond its own academic borders, influencing
(at times intentionally, at times not) other scholarly disciplines and
capturing the imagination of the general public as well. An enthusiastic educated laity avidly consumed, and even helped produce, through
research subsidies, many of the early projects in Anglo-European
anthropology.[34]

Anthropology's direct influence on strategy and policy making in
national and regional political contexts should not be forgotten. Beginning with its close connection with Euro-American imperialist expan-
sionism in the later nineteenth century, the discipline provided both
research-and-information officers and critics of colonial policy and
practice, sometimes in the same person. During the Second World War
anthropologists were recruited for war intelligence activities, and
thereafter provided their governments with insights into international
relations and relations with indigenous peoples. And since the results
impressed the powerful, that is, the decision makers (whether policy
ultimately reflected this or not), anthropology's ideas were ever more
legitimized and often enough diffused to policy makers and the general public. French anthropology has been even more closely affiliated
with philosophy, politics, and activism than other traditions.[35]

Paradoxically, anthropology is most particularly influential as a
principal arbiter of the nature-culture debate. This is, after all, its scientific territory. Indeed, it may be argued that anthropology's is *the* legiti-
mizing discourse related to conceptualizing nature and culture in the
West. Intentionally or – more often – not, directly or indirectly, anthropology has reflected and also irrevocably affected the shaping of public
opinion, perception, and practice regarding humans and other animals, culture and nature, and environmental concerns.

Ethnographers have brought to the attention of the West a wealth of
information concerning the world-views of peoples that are very different from those of Western societies. But through their ethnographic
interpretations many Western anthropologists have also given to the
world a sense that all peoples everywhere were and are primarily
interested in and preoccupied with intra-human affairs. To consider
that human beings might have strong, not to mention acknowledged
and even formalized, bonds with other animals and with the physical

environment, and that these might be of primary importance in their world-views was, with few exceptions, as we saw, either interpreted symbolically or glossed over in other ways, or indeed ignored completely. As a result, the boundary between nature and culture, so uncompromisingly drawn in Western society, was often inadvertently emphasized in the interpretation of other cultures as well. Without a totemic imagination to bring to the field, the interpretation of others' ways of knowing must necessarily miss – or, as in Nelson's situation with the Koyukon, simply be unable to grasp – any such connection, at least in an immediately meaningful, phenomenal way.

Even when theories evolve, their later incarnations are not always disseminated to colleagues, and seldom to other disciplines or to the wider world. Lévi-Strauss provides us with an instructive example. The fundamental opposition between nature and culture was a key principle of Lévi-Strauss's structural premises. But he modified this opinion somewhat when, in 1969, in a preface to the revised English edition of *The Elementary Structures of Kinship*, he admitted that after twenty years he thought the boundary was not as straightforward as he had once thought. This preface, indeed, could be read as partly refuting important aspects of his theory, posited as the latter is on the opposition between nature and culture and the attempt to reconcile the two through myth and ritual. Had Lévi-Strauss begun with his later hypothesis, one that stresses continuity rather than disjunction and opposition, his conclusions might well have been quite different, with perhaps radical import for anthropology as a whole. But he buried his altered views in his preface to the revised English edition and reissued this edition with, as he admits himself, virtually no substantive changes to the text itself. This decision has inescapably affected and will continue to affect generations of anthropologists who came after him and others who have been greatly influenced by Lévi-Strauss's structuralist concepts. Indeed, his 1969 statement is a remarkable one, and deserves at least a partial airing here:

> As far as the contrast between nature and culture is oncerned, the present state of knowledge and that of my own thought ... would seem in several respects to present a paradox ... By this hypothesis [that the division between nature and culture may be a purely human invention], the contrast of nature and culture would be neither a primeval fact, nor a concrete aspect of universal order. Rather it should be seen as an artificial creation of culture, a protective rampart thrown up around it because it

only felt able to assert its existence and uniqueness by destroying all the links that lead back to its original association with the other manifestations of life. Consequently, to understand culture in its essence, we would have to trace it back to its source and run counter to its forward trend, to retie all the broken threads by seeking out their loose ends in other animal and even vegetable families. Ultimately we shall perhaps discover that the inter-relationship between nature and culture does not favour culture to the extent of being hierarchically superimposed on nature and irreducible to it.[36]

It is interesting that while Lévi-Strauss changed his mind about the disjunctions between nature and culture, he nonetheless helped to maintain the unbreached boundary *in his practice*. For he had always been one of the most eloquent voices in the discipline naming this boundary and thereby strengthening its liminal potency. But when the moment came, he refused, to all intents and purposes, to *unname* it.

And so it is that anthropology has effectively – because silently, unmarkedly, inadvertently, unconsciously – colluded to secure the borders between culture and nature not only for itself and its sister disciplines, but for society at large.[37]

What are we constrained from seeing, experiencing, and imagining in the wake of contemporary anthropological practice? Above all, I think, we are constrained from noting continuities, continuities of the sort Darwin saw.[38] We miss the sense of human continuity with the rest of nature, not so much in the genetic, hereditary, evolutionary, or structural sense, as in the sense of lived experience – of affiliation, rivalry, affection, hostility, fear, greed, judgment, friendship, deceit; of communication, the care and nurturing of tradition, *funkionslust* (that is, taking joy in the exercise of one's given abilities),[39] and so on through the living gamut of practice and emotion. Further, by privileging the visual, observational, representational, and linguistic aspects of cultural life over other senses, anthropology has managed to minimize the multiple sensuousness of human nature: our hearing, smell, taste, touch, pheromonal senses – senses we share with other animals in obtaining important data about the environment. By muting these in ethnography[40] as well as mis-recognizing them in their everyday lives as do other Westerners, anthropologists suppress their own and others' animal-memory, their experience of the vital animal nature in human life.

In assuming the role of guard rather than geographer of the Great Divide, anthropology has helped maintain a language and practice of polarization. As a result, anthropologists no longer have at their disposal webs of metaphor through which to imagine and express a richer apprehension: the possibility of an all-pervasive continuity between nature and culture.

How deep truly is this disjunction between nature and culture in Western ways of knowing? Is the 'fundamental rupture' scientists and others are convinced exists in the Western world-view as stable a construction as it is made out to be? Is it possible that this Great Divide is, in practice, more myth than a metaphor we live by?

'The Iron Horse' (1994–6, Stratem FRP, steel) by Robert Sprachman (b. 1959),
Yonge Street south of Davisville Avenue, Toronto (photo Donna Griffith;
courtesy Donna Griffith, Robert Sprachman).

'Domestic Animals' (1928, stone), artist unknown, Toronto Humane Society, River Street, Toronto (photo Alex Capon; courtesy Alex Capon, June Ardiel)

'St Francis and the Wolf' (1956, Indiana limestone) by Thomas Bowie (b. 1905), The Guild Inn, Toronto (photo Alex Capon; courtesy Alex Capon, June Ardiel)

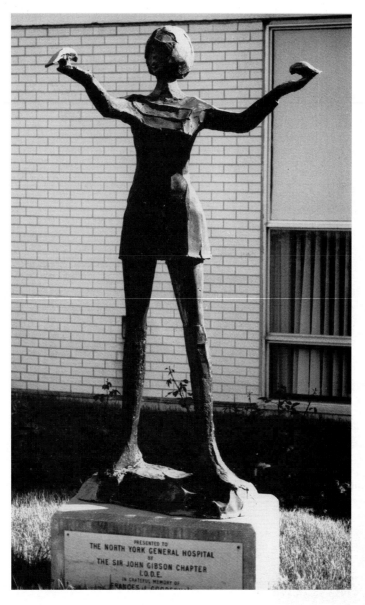

'Girl with Birds' (1974, bronze) by Barry Shaw-Rimington (b. 1923), North York General Hospital, Toronto (photo Alex Capon; courtesy Alex Capon, June Ardiel)

'Flight Stop' (1979, fibreglass) by Michael Snow (b. 1929), Eaton Centre, Toronto (photo Alex Capon; courtesy Alex Capon, June Ardiel)

'Shibagau Shard' (1989, granite rock) by Bill Vazan (b. 1933), Yorkville Avenue and Yonge Street, Toronto (on loan to McMichael Gallery of Canadian Art, Kleinburg, Ontario, since 1996) (photo Alex Capon; courtesy Alex Capon, June Ardiel)

'Cross Section' (detail, 1984, terracotta) by William McElcheran (1927–99), Toronto Transit Commission subway entrance, Atrium on Bay, Dundas and Bay Streets (photo Annabelle Sabloff)

'Remembered Sustenance' (1992, bronze) by Cynthia Short (b. 1949), Metro
Hall, Wellington Street West, Toronto (photo Alex Capon; courtesy Alex
Capon, June Ardiel)

PART TWO

Human–Animal Relations in the City

We do not even know why we respond a certain way to other organisms, and need them in diverse ways, so deeply.

Edward O. Wilson (1984)

Chapter Three

Reproducing the Natural Order: The Domestic Domain

The purpose of obedience training is to teach the dog to be a better member of the human family.

Ralston-Purina pamphlet

Love brings opposites together into a single unit, while it holds together those things which are moving apart.

David M. Schneider (1980)

KINSHIP AND THE DOMESTIC DOMAIN

In a busy shopping mall, a crowd gathered around the entrance to a pet store. The attraction was a small beige puppy in the arms of a store clerk. People craned their necks to see, asked questions, jostled each other good-naturedly while trying to get close enough to touch the animal. The clerk told us that the dog would not get much bigger as an adult. With its high, domed forehead, long cocker spaniel–like ears, large liquid brown eyes, and an expression much like a contented infant resting in its mother's arms, I couldn't resist the aesthetic and emotional pull of the little creature. It was evident that many others could not either: a living magnet, the pup managed to attract and pull crowds of people, otherwise intent on their various privately motivated tasks, toward its appealing vital being.

Human–Animal Bonds

As we saw, it was zoologist Edward O. Wilson who first gave the term biophilia to this urge to explore and affiliate with other life forms. Remarking that we still do not know why we respond so deeply to other organisms, he speculates that the human mind harbours a 'natural' – by that he means innate – desire to love other living things, a desire shaped and supported by evolutionary forces. Whether 'innate' or the cultural product of many centuries of intimate human–animal interaction in the course of daily living, evidence for some kind of biophilic propensity in Western culture seems difficult to refute.[1] My own ethnographic fieldwork on human–animal relations abounded with overwhelming evidence of the attraction, sense of affiliation, and empathic bonds many people feel for other species, even in a highly urbanized environment. 'I just move inside when I see an animal sometimes,' a woman told me. 'People say, "tugging at your heartstrings," you know, when you see somebody you love? It happens with animals as well.'

Of all human–animal relations, the keeping of companion animals, or pets, is one of the most intriguing. Historian Keith Thomas considers pets to be domesticated animals that fulfil three conditions: they live with humans in their homes, they are named, and they are not eaten.[2] By definition, then, they do not serve (not primarily at least) an economic function. There is no obvious need for their presence in any society, and they require ongoing effort and expense to maintain and keep thriving. Yet this relation has been recorded in many societies across time and space.

Some historians place a friendly human–wolf association as far back as 60,000 to 125,000 years. A late Palaeolithic burial site in northern Israel, about 12,000 years old, seems to speak to us across the ages. In it were found an elderly human of unknown sex and a five-month-old domestic dog buried together, the dead person's left hand carefully arranged to rest on the puppy's shoulder. The ancient Greeks were known to have lavished affection on animals, especially horses, dogs, and birds. In Roman life, poetry and prose, pictorial art, and funerary objects bore witness to a deep fondness for pets and other animals. The ancient Hebrews were instructed by their religious laws to attend to the animals under their care with the consideration they would extend to kin and servants. This included providing a day of rest for animals as well as the other members of the household, and giving assistance to any suffering being, human or animal, even on the otherwise inviolable Sabbath. Among early Christians, even though animals were outside the realm of Christian theology, monks and nuns kept pet animals despite their superiors' strict rules against it, and Christian hagiography portrayed many of its saints in intimate communication and tender interaction with animals and the rest of the natural world. It was said, for example, that St Godric of Finchale would go out barefoot in winter to save shivering animals and release birds from snares. Indeed, in the Western world today, even non-Christians have come to consider St Francis of Assisi, at least informally, the patron saint of ecology and the environment.[3]

The human–animal pet relation has also been amply documented in societies where economic uncertainty and even hardship may have been encountered with some frequency.[4] Early accounts of Indians in North America by explorers, missionaries, and other travellers to colonial territories tell how the tribes they met kept tame raccoons, moose, bison, wolves, bears, and many other species, and how they lavished affection and care on their dogs. According to biologist James Serpell, one traveller reported: '[T]he red races are fond of pets and treat them kindly; and in purchasing them there is always the unwillingness of the women and children to overcome, rather than any dispute about price.'[5] Serpell further relates how the Spanish explorer Hernandez, visiting Mexico in the sixteenth century, described the natives' pet relation with the raccoon: 'Domesticated and fed in the house, it is constantly pestering people it knows and will follow them with great affection. It lies next to them and rolls around happily in the soil, amusing itself and gamboling in a thousand different ways.'[6] One nineteenth-century British naturalist recorded twenty-two species of quadrupeds living tame among the villages of the Amazon basin. A Swedish explorer in Australia noted in 1884 that the aborigines reared their pet dingoes 'with greater care than they bestow on their own children. The dingo is an important member of the family; it sleeps in the huts and gets plenty to eat, not only of meat but also of fruit. Its master never strikes, but merely threatens it. He caresses it like a child, eats the fleas off it, and then kisses it on the snout.'[7]

Roy Rappaport, studying the importance of pigs to economic and ritual life among the Maring of New Guinea in the 1960s, described how young pigs were treated as pets. At first carried in arms, then led on a leash, and at last trained to follow on their own, baby pigs accompanied their mistresses everywhere until four or five months of age or longer. They were petted, talked to, fed with tender care, and slept in the women's houses. Rappaport writes, '[I]t is hardly facetious to say that the pig through its early socialization becomes a member of a Maring family.'[8]

Pet keeping appears to be among the most unambiguously social (as well as culturally shaped) behaviour patterns that human beings display with respect to animals and the natural world. In a culture as deeply steeped in an ideology proclaiming the materialist basis of every cultural pattern as is Western civilization, the ubiquity of pets is a significant anomaly, and no satisfactory theory has yet been put forward to account for this persistent interspecies relation.

A veterinary assistant told me that she had brought home a kitten for her cat-hating husband. 'After two weeks,' she said, 'without a cat he would be lost. He's grown to love them. And that happens all the time. You grow to love and see why they're so important to people as a companion, as a friend.' Although an infrequent visitor to pet stores myself, once inside on a mission of 'participant observation,' I found the animals to be deeply engrossing, whether they were active mammals with twitching snouts and tails, torpid lizards frozen into graceful positions, or absolutely motionless tarantulas with thick hairy legs. I frequently had difficulty turning my attention away from the animals toward the people watching them, the intended focus of my observation.

People who interact at all voluntarily with pets are simply not impartial to them. In quite an unselfconscious way they behave with extravagant affection toward these animals. They stroke, pat, hug, tickle, scratch, kiss, and cuddle them with abandon. Clerks in pet stores, male and female, cradle their charges against their breasts, stroking and gentling them when removing them from their cages for cleaning or to show to store visitors. The patrons themselves, and pet owners in their own homes, seem to get the greatest pleasure out of exclaiming tenderly over the animals, making clicking, whistling, chirruping, and snuffling noises to get their attention. They fondle them endlessly and feed them tirelessly. From infants to the aged, regardless of gender, people appear to be irresistibly drawn into intimate contact with these creatures, and are delighted at any sign that their attention is reciprocated. 'You do get attached,' reflected one woman about her tank full of large goldfish. 'You don't think you're attached to fish, until they start reacting, doing things that they always do. Or doing things when I approach – they probably see me and think, "food!"' she chuckled. Another woman, describing her young daughter's response to a family pet, was explicit about the relationship: 'She would hold that cat, and hug it, and it came to her, and they bonded.'

Sometimes people are not fully aware of the bonds that have grown between themselves and an animal until the animal dies or is lost. In a group discussion one person confided that, to her great surprise, she wept when one of her cats died. 'I wouldn't have predicted I'd do that,' she said. Another participant told about a letter in the newspaper: 'It said something about the writer being so upset when his dog died – or his cat, whatever – and he felt foolish, because he was so attached to it.' And a third, who did not keep pets, said, 'I'm actually a bit afraid to get attached to an animal because I don't want to lose it, and don't want the pain of losing it.' On my second visit to interview a respondent, I found out that one of this woman's two cats had been diagnosed with advanced lung cancer and put to death during the previous week. My respondent was quite devastated, breaking into tears from time to time throughout the interview. Her remaining cat seemed very much at a loss as well, keeping close to her all evening and shedding great clumps of orange hair.

One man described what happened when his neighbours took care of his family's dog while they were on vacation. He related that the neighbour family 'fell in love with the dog. Before, the wife was afraid of him and the husband didn't like him, but when we came back, they had all adopted this dog. They would take the dog for drives in the car, sometimes without telling us.' He went on to describe his neighbours' new interactions with their dog. From the upstairs window of his own home he would look out over their adjoining back yards and see the housewife, at home alone during the day, bringing her tea to the fence between the properties. Sitting by the fence, she would sip her tea and talk to the dog. 'So anyway,' my informant continued, 'when Casey died, she went into a serious depression, and I'm talking a *serious* depression. She carried around a towel and cried all the time.'

We can thus find plentiful evidence that individuals feel a profound attraction toward other species, not infrequently counter to their own initial intuitions. This should not really be too surprising, for if we have lived in a 'natural' or more rural environment not only for the entire period of human evolutionary development but throughout virtually the entire development of Western as well as other civilizations, there is a logic to the idea that this attraction to other species is deeply rooted, whether biologically or culturally, or both. Even if the logic of biophilia is taken too far and too simplistically, by some sociobiologists, for example, I for one cannot disagree with Edward Wilson when he says: 'We are in the fullest sense a biological species and will find little ultimate meaning apart from the remainder of life'.[9]

Kinship as a Metaphor We Live By

People do not experience the bonds between themselves and the animals they call their pets as vague and diffuse. These bonds are structured and experienced in particular ways. In its more general form, the human–animal bond in Western urban life is modelled on relations between human beings. The analogy between pet and human person is often quite transparent. A poster featuring a portrait of a dog's head, widely distributed in the Toronto public transit system, proclaimed: 'Rabies – it's no way for a friend to die!' A veterinarian's office provided copies of a pamphlet entitled: 'Yoga for Cats.' And a woman on a British television documentary exclaimed: 'They're not animals – they're fur people!' a designation echoed by writer May Sarton in her book, *The Fur Person*.[10]

People love to converse with animals. My informants all admitted to talking routinely to their pets, and many insisted that they got a response. Said one person: 'When we come home Max [the family's cat] is quite vocal. He greets us at the door with lots of talk, so he is sort of telling us what his day has been like.' In pet stores animals are addressed as other commodities never are. They are treated to an unending human cacophony, noises of appreciation and approval emitted by children and adults alike: 'Aw! You're just a honey, aren't you?' or 'Will you come home with me?' and, everywhere, 'You're so cute!' Talking birds are very popular with patrons, who patiently repeat phrases over and over as they gingerly stroke the bird's feathers and try to avoid the sharp beak at the same time. I found myself entranced to hear the clear, clipped, genderless, and utterly unexpected 'hello' that Cassius, a favoured pet-store parrot, greeted me with, to the pride and delight of his caretaker. I longed for the bird to perform again and again so that I could capture an odd and unnamed emotion, one I could not pin down, a fleeting unitary sense of alienness and familiarity that Cassius's greeting evoked in me.

While people frequently describe the relation to a pet in terms of companionship, friendship, or respectful colleagueship, by far the most common metaphor, the one most plainly yet unreflectively expressed and enacted – in Bourdieu's vocabulary, the one most redolent of doxa, of unwavering acceptance – is that of kinship. Every interview I conducted with people who kept pets yielded a reference, implied or explicit, to the pet as a family member. One respondent, reminiscing about the hunting dogs her father kept when she was a child in England, recalled: 'They would sleep on our beds or on the couch, or whatever you're not supposed to let dogs do, but they did it; they were just like one of the family. But once a week, they would go out hunting for game.' In another instance, when I asked an informant whether he considered the household cat to be in any way part of his family, he replied with resigned emphasis: '*Max* thinks he's part of the family!' The mother in another family interview reported with a bemused laugh why she thought their golden retriever Zack was part of their family: 'I mean, I come home and he's the only one that comes to greet me at the door! What can I tell you?' (In the *Odyssey* Homer related that when Ulysses returned home to Ithaca after twenty years' absence, it was his old dog Argus who was the first to recognize and greet him.)[11] Her husband added: 'Well, I think a dog fits into the family. Like, I see these ads that show dogs that look like their masters and masters that look like their dogs.' And then, just like the family that anthropologist James Fernandez went back to visit in the Spanish village of Asturias, where pictures of children and cattle prompted animated discussion among the villagers about the cattle, this urban Canadian family would not rest until I had thoroughly inspected the pages and pages of photographs from their family albums portraying, at all stages of puppyhood, all their dogs, the latest of which was present at the interview.

One woman participating in a group discussion said: 'I never thought about it much before today, but I can't help likening some of our attitudes to animals to attitudes toward children. Children are nice to be around because you can be playful and you don't have to be adult, and maybe there's some similarity to animals.' Others in the group agreed. Another said: 'Animals are like little children a bit. They're simple. They don't have politics driving them. Their needs are fairly basic and fairly communicated.' A third participant speculated: 'I think they are like children in that there is a part of their nature that is still ... that we don't use all the time, not anymore.'

Thus, it seems clear that urban Canadians openly, easily, and frequently liken pets to family members.[12] This is not limited to a mere figure of speech, however; people also routinely, and in minute details, treat their pets like family members. Indeed, *a primary organizing metaphor for human–animal relations in the Western urban domain, one we live by, is the metaphor of kinship.*

Why kinship? we might ask. Why not a metaphor of another sort, based on some other set of relations? Other metaphors and models are certainly possible, as anthropologists, travellers, and other itinerants have documented. For example, according to a nineteenth-century visitor to Brazil, the relationship of the Caraja people of that region of the world to their tame cormorants was not one of kinship, but rather one of host to guest. Traveller Peter Fleming tried, in vain, to show these people that they could train their cormorants to bring them fish if they fastened rings round their necks. 'In conception, rather than in execution,' he wrote, 'this project amused them very much; it is clear that they thought of the birds always as guests, never as servants.'[13] The Fipa of Tanzania, by contrast, seemed to have an unsentimental, utilitarian attitude to all animals, according to Roy Willis, who had done fieldwork among them. Cattle and other livestock were just different forms of wealth to them, with no other symbolic value. Good-humoured tolerance could be detected from 'pet names' desultorily given to animals, for example, 'Old Scratcher' applied to a chicken, 'Old Fusspot' or 'old Shitter-at-God' for a goat. Dogs and cattle were given no pet names. The generic 'animal' might be used as a mild insult aimed at other human beings. The Fipa were tolerant of rats, mice, and other forms of what we would call 'vermin' and usually consider to be loathsome. They also seemed to be quite neutral toward wild animals. They had, remarks Willis, a 'businesslike appreciation of the profits and dangers to be found in the bush.'[14]

To find out why kinship is such a compelling metaphor to live by in the urban Canadian, and indeed North American, field, we need to turn to the domestic domain for a brief critical examination of the cultural and historical meaning of this sphere of life in the contemporary Western world.

The Domestic Domain

In her theory of cognitive practice, psychologist Jean Lave highlights the importance of context in influencing meaning. Not only the specific setting but also the arena or cultural orbit, which is the context of the setting itself, are crucial.[15] For example, cognitive activity taking place in a home is also occurring 'in the domestic domain,' with all that implies culturally, and cognitive activity in the setting of a pharmaceutical laboratory is simultaneously taking place 'in the market place.' In addition, Lave emphasizes the *relation* between person and context.

As she observes in her practice approach to cognition, a theory of practice enables one to think less simplistically and more dialectically, both in terms of the person-acting-in-the-setting and in terms of the interrelations of persons, actions, and settings. The terms alone are not enough, she insists, it is their relations that count. As well, in this view cognition is conceived as situationally specific activities of persons-in-settings, implying that all activity is inextricably grounded in, while at the same time it acts as a grounding for, specific cultural and historical, as well as spatial, 'moments.' 'A theory of cognitive practice,' says Lave, '... take[s] learning, thinking and knowledge to be historically/culturally specific, socially constituted, and politically tempered, and argues that they structure the social world writ large as well as being structured by it.'[16] In this view there is no 'neutral' context. Thus, in the 'real world,' cognition, activity, and context are all interwoven, and the context is best viewed as a conjuncture of particular cultural, historical, and spatial conditions, inevitably steeped in ideology.

Now, granted that the context has a significant effect on the cognitive and behavioural patterns that relationships take, what is there about the domestic domain in Western culture that evokes kinship as a primary metaphor to live by for human–animal relations?

It may seem obvious that the pre-eminent human–animal pattern of relationship in the domestic sphere should be based on kinship. Particularly to those who do not keep pets or interact regularly with animals, it might appear as if people who keep animals are lonely people who displace their longings for human interaction and family life onto their pets; and indeed, ordinary people often share this notion with some students of human–animal relationships. People might say, for example, that animals replace friends or children for some individuals. As Serpell points out, however, the 'displacement' view is inconsistent with an abundance of documented evidence that the majority of pet owners are families rather than isolated individuals, and families presumably do not have a greater need than single people do for affiliation with an animal *as a stand-in* for another human being.[17] A more substantial answer must lie elsewhere.

The Nuclear Family and the Privatization of Feeling
Recent scholars of the modern nuclear family and its proliferating variants in contemporary society view the history of Western capitalist society as one of progressively separating and differentiating the kin-

ship system from all other kinds of social institutions and relationships. It is a history of the removal in succession of the political and economic functions from the family domain, and the simultaneous suppression of bonds of intimacy, affection, and affiliation in other spheres of life, particularly community and worksite. The result has been the progressive privatization of the family and, with it, the privatization and increasing confinement of emotional relationships to the domestic sphere. As Marxist cultural critic Joel Kovel has noted, the other side of the growth of the personal sphere is 'the iron requirement of capital for a depersonalized world.'[18] In much of the West, and particularly in North America, it is virtually only in the domestic sphere that a relatively unrestrained 'public' display of love is allowed to occur without censure. The modern nuclear family in all its contemporary manifestations – the product, consumer, and reproducer of capitalist culture – has become the one truly legitimate domain for freely expressing affection, affiliation, and intimacy. We might say, paraphrasing Marx, that the private world of the modern family is the *only permissible locus of the relations of the production of emotional life.* 'Love,' says David Schneider, 'is what American kinship is *all* about.'[19] (This, of course, is not to describe everyday experience, but rather a deeply held cultural ideal.) The display of such emotions is otherwise highly restricted in a culture driven by a capitalist ethic, which isolates and divides people and promotes competition and consumption and the unending pursuit of the fulfilment of desire. Love, affection, and attachment are antithetical to the spirit of acquisition, competition, and consumption necessary for the eternal re-creation of a market culture, whose one end is the 'economization of reality: a set of practices essential so that the world becomes a market out of which commodities can be made.'[20] While it is undesirable – and impossible – that the affiliative emotions be completely eliminated, it is highly desirable that they be contained. To a great extent, the domestic sphere in the Western world has succeeded in doing just that.

Biophilia and the Domestic Domain
If biophilia, the attraction to other life forms, is a ubiquitous and profound, if unplumbed and ill-articulated, emotion in human life, as I argue in this book along with Wilson and others (while putting aside the issue of biological determinism as an unnecessary and simplistic 'explanatory' principle), and if the domestic domain is one of the very few legitimate contexts in our society in which people may express

emotions of affection and affiliation with minimum constraint, then the expression of biophilia, or totemic imagination, would have very few outlets in capitalist society outside the sphere of the family. We can therefore speculate that it is not so much that animals are loved because they are pets, but largely the opposite: *animals are made pets so that human beings can continue to experience and play out the bonds of biophilia, of totemic connection.* What Schneider says with respect to human kinship systems is apt, I believe, between species too: Love brings opposites together into a single unit while holding together those things which are moving apart.[21] Not all animals, however, are able to fit easily into the narrow niche of post-industrial urban Canadian family life; those that do are the ones we make our pets.

Thus, the kinship metaphor for human–animal relations in Western culture is not accidental. One of the few places in these societies allowed a legitimate and unhampered expression of love and care across species is the privacy of the home. The cultural model of kinship proves to be just about the only one available in contemporary Western life for allowing the full and relatively free expression of biophilia. Therefore, if a totemic sensibility is allowed to manifest itself anywhere in everyday contemporary urban Canadian life it is primarily in the domestic domain, in the activities of pet keeping, as organized by the metaphor of kinship.[22]

Given that a bond of emotional ties clearly exists in the human–animal relationship – at least from the point of view of the human respondents I interviewed – and given that this bond is not diffuse but is largely structured according to a kinship metaphor, let us now ask that most typically 'anthropological' of questions, How is this relation sustained and reproduced?

REPRODUCING THE KINSHIP METAPHOR

Animals and humans both undergo socialization and other formative processes in the creation of the pet relationship, and the relationship itself is sustained through the micro-practices of everyday behaviour. The practice approach in social theory, as developed by Pierre Bourdieu and others, seeks to comprehend these very micro-practices – the repetitive, routine, common-sense, often less-than-conscious levels of thought and action – as principal loci for the expression of culturally modelled habitus. As Sherry Ortner describes it, the practice theorist pays 'close attention to the little routines people enact, again and again, in working, eating, sleeping, and relaxing, as well as the little scenarios of etiquette they play out again and again in social interaction. All of these routines and scenarios are predicated upon, and embody within themselves, the fundamental notions of temporal, spatial, and social ordering that underlie and organize the system as a whole.'[23] Lave's concept of 'just plain folks'[24] succinctly captures this basic assumption that nowhere can one better observe the workings of a particular culture than in the unideologized, seldom verbalized micro-practices of everyday life. Ordinary people – people going about their everyday, not their 'expert' business – are, in terms of practice theory, the supreme culture-bearers.[25]

'In enacting these routines,' Ortner goes on, 'actors not only continue to be shaped by the underlying organizational principles involved, but continually re-endorse those principles in the world of public observation and discourse.'[26] It is thus in the *enactment* of an interspecies relationship in the domestic domain – the pet relation being formed, and the repetitive human–animal interactions that support it – rather than in any voiced ideology, that the kinship metaphor manifests itself most forcefully as a metaphor we live by.

Along with socialization, I want to investigate two other significant mechanisms for reproducing the kinship metaphor: *routinization* and *muting*. Routinization is, in Bourdieu's succinct phrase, 'making natural what is in fact tradition.'[27] Muting is the suppression from cultural acknowledgment – and sometimes from the natives' awareness altogether – of various aspects of experience apparent to outsiders. Both mechanisms are largely unreflective, and are based on what Bourdieu calls 'learned ignorance,' or selective, culturally imposed forgetting. Both mechanisms are means of maintaining and reproducing order in the world. We will see that 'kinship' is an organizing metaphor that provides guidelines for enacting the recurring details of socialization, routinization, and muting, and that it is in these repetitive enactments that the metaphor we live by, 'animal is kin,' is recreated and sustained.

Socialization

Bourdieu's complex but important concept of habitus, to which I referred in chapter 1, captures the notion of the reproduction of culture through the more-or-less thorough and largely unconscious enculturation and socialization of each individual – body, mind, and emotions. Habitus, you will recall, is the cultivated or learned disposition, 'inscribed in the body schema and in the schemes of thought,'[28] to behave in certain ways that are generated by the culturally mediated material conditions of life in a particular place and time. In the human–animal pet relationship I have been describing, both humans and animals experience various learning processes, mostly carried out at the level of practical consciousness, that work to mutually adapt the species to living together as 'kin' in a Western household in an era of advanced capitalism. (I will examine more overtly manipulative procedures, aimed at quite literally inscribing the body schema, in the next chapter.)

Animal Socialization
There is every evidence that a significant degree of animal socialization to the demands of the human environment takes place, as the pet-owning respondents in my fieldwork, as well as animal trainers,[29] are quick to point out. Social animals (and most of the animals adopted as companion animals are social animals, even those, like cats, with quite a different reputation) can and do learn how to interact with humans and behave 'acceptably' in a particular culture and society. What is particularly worth noting is that most socializing efforts are either deliberately calculated for, or 'just happen' to result in, *the enhancement of the 'humanness' of the animal*, traits that are most familiar to us as a species.

The first stage in an animal's social learning that will allow it to adapt to a human environment involves separating it from its mother and having humans handle it at an early age. This encourages a modicum of imprinting on humans, a fine point not lost on livestock retailers. In a pet store, the staff are instructed to handle and pet all the animals frequently. A clerk told me that the animals destined for younger children – hamsters, guinea pigs, rabbits, and the like – are handled even more often, to get them used to the constant and enthusiastic fondling of their child owners.

Once a pet is acquired, people do several things that result in establishing the animal's social identity and acceptance into the human world and family life. One of the first is finding out their pet's sex. Few pet owners I talked to ever said 'it' about their own pets, particularly their cats, dogs, or birds; they usually specified 'he' or 'she.' In my fieldwork I noted that whenever a pet was given a human name, and many were, such as Casey, Max, Prunella, Cleo, Hazel, Jake, Zach, Pushkin, Augustus, Rita, Herbert, Xena, Georgia – the list is as varied and as fanciful as a compendium of baby's names – that name always conformed to the animal's sex. David Schneider makes the telling point about American kinship that human infants are identified as male or female immediately upon birth even though they will not be sexually mature for many years. As soon as they are born they are assigned expectations and roles on the basis of gender that go well beyond the borders of biological make-up – everything from tempera-ment, stamina, and aptitude to the occupational niches they can and ought to fill when grown up.[30] Paralleling this tendency, Canadian pet owners, particularly dog and cat owners, persist in attributing 'gender-specific' behaviours to their companion animals; more often than not, these expectations are derived from Western human social life rather than from any knowledge of species-specific sex-linked behaviours.

People also always name their pets. To name an animal is to accord it subjectivity and a relationship with oneself: a person names an animal and calls it by that name. One informant called her pet cat 'no name' because she wasn't sure whether she would keep him after he was born. But he stayed around, and as time when on, 'no name,' with use and response, became 'No-Name,' the name that both human and cat identified with this being and no other. Even if the name bestowed is 'Bird,' 'Dog,' or 'Horse,' this is never a generic name. It is always deliv-ered in a particular tone of voice and with a certain emphasis, or in a diminutive form, such as 'Kitty' or 'Tigger,' or even in another lan-guage (for instance, 'Ferdeleh' or 'Ketzeleh' are Yiddish names for 'Horsy' and 'Kitty'). Such names, although apparently non-specific, in reality belong to only one particular animal.

Clerks in pet stores give private names to some of the pets that remain unsold for any length of time. These are often playful, since the animal is meant to be truly named by the family or person who buys it. But in some cases the names are taken more seriously, as if imbued with a feeling for the animal's particular subjectivity. One clerk told me with some pride that he had special charge of Jamie, the macaw. I had heard that a bulldog kept in a cage was called 'Ethel,' and when I asked whether that was really her name, he grinned and said the employees had given her that name as a laugh because she had been around the store for a while. But the macaw's *real* name, he insisted, *was* Jamie. In another store the clerk brought me over to the parrots, where she greeted Lucy and Blue, and pointed out Cassius, her favourite.[31]

Creating an identity for a pet goes further than naming, however. If

the animal is purebred, its pedigree is registered. It then has a legitimate ancestry or family tree. In certain jurisdictions it must be registered civilly as well, complete with license and identification tag.
Through a system of private veterinary physicians and public clinics, it
is immunized and its health is assured. Health insurance is now
widely available for companion animals. The animal is introduced to
its accommodations and given a place to sleep, eat, eliminate, and so
on. One pet owner put it this way: 'Zack knows things like what rooms
he can't go into, and if you say get out of a room, he'll get out of the
room, or if he's upstairs and you tell him to go downstairs, he'll go
downstairs. It's stuff you don't think about, but when you do think
about it, you realize what a repertoire he has.' And when one thinks
about it more, a pet gets socialized into urban living in ways that
humans are not even cued into unless one observes very carefully.
Another family described how their cat would wake up every morning
with the sound of the timed thermostat coming on, and would go from
one favourite air register to another to stretch out and warm himself.
At the sound of the alarm clock he would enter the parents' bedroom
and lick the face of the person who wasn't up yet.

In contemporary urban society, socialization must take on dimensions specific to the urban environment. Zack's owner, for example,
believed that 'a well-behaved dog is more fun than a wild animal ...
When I'm tired of Zack I say, "Leave the room" and he leaves, and
when I want the company, he's there.' More and more urban pets,
especially dogs, are sent to obedience schools for the extensive formal
training considered necessary to fit them for urban life. The purpose of
obedience training, according to a contemporary pamphlet, is 'to teach
the dog to be a better member of the human family.'[32]

Human Socialization
Socialization goes both ways. People too must be socialized into the
appropriate behaviour for urban pet keeping. Sociologists Lucy Hickrod and Raymond Schmitt have studied this process in depth. They
believe that one can distinguish several stages in the socialization of
humans into this unique interspecies relationship. The stages range
from the animal's first entry into the home space on a probationary
basis, through to engrossment in the animal and the realization that
bonding has taken place, and on to final separation. While each stage
must be attained before the next can occur, the process can stop in any
phase. Once a certain point is reached, however, the pet has, often

imperceptibly, come to be considered a family member, enjoying close and enduring ties of affection and care. This connection can only be effected in practice, however; it is not a purely cognitive attainment. For true socialization to occur, each stage must be *enacted* and *experienced*.[33] Here is how one of my own informants described the entry phase: 'Slowly the cat moved from the garage into the corridor between garage and basement, and we fed it and gave it a litter box ... And then winter came again, and the cat went back inside and that year she lived in the corridor. And then in the third year she lived in the basement. In the fourth year she was living in the entire house.'

While the idea of human domestication and its consequences may be viewed with some alarm in scholarly circles,[34] quite a number of my respondents speculated seriously but not in the least unhappily that in the human–animal relationship, humans may be as domesticated as their pets. People appear to be anxious to respond to as many of the creature's needs as they can understand. They spend a lot of time, effort, and money on the care of their animals. They organize their space, schedules, daily activities, and long-term plans to adapt to the animal's needs. People seek out their pets' company very frequently. One veterinarian suggested to me that humans may in fact be far more socialized and domesticated in this relationship than the animals are. It was hard to turn this thought aside when, from the warmth and safety of a bus window-seat early on a cold, wet, windy, and thoroughly disagreeable fall morning I watched a middle-aged man, dressed impeccably in a three-piece suit, top-coat, and hat and struggling with a half-opened umbrella, being pulled vigorously and impatiently off his feet along the sidewalk by an exuberant dog. The two, you will have guessed, were joined by a leash.[35]

Routinization

A father described the following routine in his family, involving his young son (Mike) and the family cat (Max): 'Max will take Mike up to bed, and we have a little cat basket up there, and he will go up and sit in the cat basket and wait for Mike to go to sleep. And sometimes he will go up on the bed with Mike and stay there for an hour or two after Mike is safely in bed and asleep. And he will come downstairs and stay with us.' Practice theory in anthropology emphasizes how important repetitive, routine, everyday behaviour is in reproducing the cultural systems we live by. Social theorist Anthony Giddens, believing

that most of the vast accumulated knowledge of any culture is incorporated in the recursive routines of its everyday life, calls most such
knowledge 'practical'; that is, 'it is inherent in the capacity to "go on"
within the routines of social life' without the native necessarily being
able to describe in words what he or she is doing or why. Giddens calls
this form of unwitting knowledge 'practical consciousness.'[36] People
are usually quite unaware of the competence with which they carry
out the culturally mediated routines through which they reproduce
their lives. As we see from the anecdote with Max and Mike, animals
can be astonishingly competent partners in this reproduction as well.

Human–animal relations in the domestic domain are unreflectively
carried on with animals as fictive kin in many ways, such as the recursive activities of nurturance, touching, and communicative interaction,
and the weaving of family histories and myths through storytelling.
These repetitive interspecies acts are not ritualized or set apart from
the rest of family life; they are, rather, casually homespun into the fabric of everyday behaviours.

Nurturance
Feeding is a basic activity that continually reinforces both the companion animal's dependence on humans and a human desire to nurture in
this relation. One woman said: 'I routinely respond to Tabby's need for
food. Just as I do to anyone that's hungry, to the kids. It's incorporated
into my general repertoire of behaviour.' For most people this is not a
disagreeable drudgery. In pet stores I noticed the persistence with
which patrons of all ages attempted to feed the animals, and how
readily and uncomplainingly the clerks nurtured them as well. I saw
very young children trying to feed the rabbits and gerbils through the
wires of their cages. With extraordinary patience, they would offer a
bit of a food pellet in outstretched palms, waiting motionless for the
twitching mouths to approach. The animals did not often accept food
in this way, but the children did not tire of trying. When an animal
actually did take something from a child's hand, the child would beam
with pride and call a parent or sibling to see. In another area of the pet
shop I watched as an adolescent girl patiently fed seeds to a macaw
through the wires of its cage, the bird picking up the small seeds from
her fingers one by one with its sharp beak and fleshy tongue. The girl
crooned and clucked softly, calling the macaw 'pretty bird.' On another
occasion a pet-store clerk I was interviewing stirred a powdered vita-
min fastidiously into a parrot's drinking water and gave it mixed nuts

as she spoke with me. 'He's very messy,' she commented indulgently. 'Peanuts are his favourite.'

People seem to feel that they have accomplished something important, formed or renewed a connection between themselves and the animal, when the latter accepts food offered. It is a bond people value. A number of my respondents echoed what these two informants said about feeding animals: 'If an animal is hungry, you don't have to feel so helpless.' 'Yeah, it makes you feel nice. You give them food and they appreciate it and you feel nice about it.'

Touching and Communication

Touching and communication are important aspects of routine interaction between humans and other animals. The first thing almost any pet-store visitor does, most especially a toddler when hoisted up by its parent to see better, is to reach out to touch. Children are always poking their fingers unselfconsciously into whatever cages they can reach to feel the animals. In both public and private circumstances, pet owners of all ages readily stroke and fondle their pets. I watched as a clerk in a pet store let Cassius, her favourite parrot, out of his cage and stroked his feathers and the nape of his neck. Cassius snuggled into her shoulder. She said the bird would not let himself be so easily handled by the rest of the staff. 'He likes me,' she said, with evident pleasure and pride.

As a highly social species, humans are fundamentally responsive to the actions of others.[37] With continued interaction, people learn to recognize certain signs, sounds, gestures, and postures of their pet that can give some indication of the animal's state. According to his humans, family dog Zach will ask to be followed by looking alternately in the direction he wants to go and at the person, his tail down, his eyes staring steadily, keeping up this behaviour until some response ensues. Hazel, his adopted sibling, will demand to be let out to relieve herself by continually moving toward and away from the door to the backyard and sometimes barking, a manoeuvre called the 'pee-pee dance' by the household. At human mealtimes, both animals will sit by patiently but obtrusively, staring with large glistening eyes at the diners and their food. All these routines appear to induce responses in their human companions, whether behavioural or emotional, or both.

Interaction and communication are continually sought after by human owners, and what is taken to be interspecies understanding is greatly prized. Said one once-reluctant pet owner: 'It's like the way I finally became attached to the cat. You begin to see their habits ... And you begin to relate to them as more than just sort of things. There's behaviour – it's meaningful behaviour.' People show pride and a sense of achievement in feeling that they have correctly fathomed what their pet is communicating. The young boy Mike explained carefully and precisely to me: 'Whenever Max thinks something is wrong, his tail will move back and forth. [When he's happy] he just purrs ... or he usually closes his eyes as well.'

The Telling of Tales

The telling of tales is another common way that people reiterate and routinize the relations between humans and animals in the domestic domain. A man said to me, 'Let me tell you a story,' and he proceeded to impart, with much interruption and clarification from the rest of his family, an apparently oft-told tale: 'We were playing a little game, it's a dice game called Shut-the-Box, and you have this little box, and you throw the dice into the box. We were playing with the dice, and – the cat! The cat went off and came back and brought back his own die and started playing!' His wife added, 'Yes, he watched this game, he wasn't part of it and he just watched and watched, and he went off and got his own.' Another informant told the story of her father's last hunting expedition. When she was a child, she said, her father shot a wild rabbit and discovered that this was the mother of seven now-orphaned infants. He brought the baby rabbits home, and he and his family fed them until they could be released back into the wild. After that, she ended, her father never hunted again.

Such cherished tales were common. Often the children were encouraged to tell the stories, even if they had not been a direct witness to the exploits themselves. One teenaged daughter told of how, early in her parents' marriage (as she had been told the story), her father absent-mindedly persisted in bringing his wife gifts of kittens even though both were self-professed 'dog persons' and neither had any predilection they knew of for felines. A boy repeated to me the tale of the 'jealous cat.' When the boy was born, it appears, his parents' Siamese cat became so distraught with sibling rivalry that they had to give the cat away.

In this storytelling way, significant human–animal events are woven into family histories, mythologies, and sagas, becoming in their own time, through recursive narration, templates and expectations for the relations between the species. They become metaphors for the next generation to live by.

Muting

Sometimes organizing metaphors, metaphors we live by, must create order by negating certain 'truths.' People tend to suppress from cultural life, and sometimes from psychological recognition as well, selected aspects of their own experience. I would agree with Ortner's contention that action is constrained most deeply and systematically by the ways in which culture controls the definitions of the world for people, limiting their conceptual tools and restricting their emotional repertoires.[38] As Kovel puts it, consistently ignoring truths is 'a kind of labor, highly rewarded and contributory to the given structure of the world.'[39]

A group discussion I attended brought out, from the depths of each participant's practical consciousness, a paradox hitherto out of awareness. One woman said: 'It's interesting what we do to animals, to domestic animals, to make them domestic. You've got to neuter them, you have to declaw them; perverting very basic drives. You're disarming them. You're making them less of what they are, less animal.' Added another: 'More civilized.' A third participant countered: 'What do we do to babies? What do we do with human beings? It's the same thing.' In the kinship metaphor that organizes human–animal relations in the domestic domain, it appears that what is most actively suppressed is *an acknowledgment of the animal in pets and in human beings.*

Muting the Animal in Pets
The more obvious efforts to minimize the 'animal nature' of pets – genetic engineering (which we will pursue in another chapter), neutering, declawing, 'debarking,' wing clipping, tail docking, obedience training, and so on – affect the animal directly. Other muting mechanisms are of particular interest from an anthropological and a practice perspective because, being largely dependent on unreflective behaviours that actively and recursively constrain the conceptual tools of the society's members, they work by affecting people's perceptions of the animals in their care. Muting mechanisms of this sort that I was able to discern in fieldwork include minimizing the pet as another species, disguising animal needs, and defining animal traits as 'polluting.' Let us look more closely at these mechanisms now.

Minimizing the Pet as Another Species: Pet owners usually acquire their animal charges singly, and only when the latter have been weaned. Consequently, they do not often have the opportunity to observe their pet interacting 'naturally,' with its mother, its litter-mates, or other conspecifics. Pet owners thus have little, if any, exposure to their pet as a member of a nonhuman species, and therefore little appreciation of their pet's intraspecific relations outside the realm of the human domestic domain (or other human domains such as a zoo or a pet store).

Furthermore, in acquiring a pet, people are neither required nor consistently encouraged to be informed about its animal ancestry and behaviour, or its special needs as a nonhuman animal. Indeed, such needs are unclear to most pet keepers. I joined a group of informants as they were discussing the requirements of a house pet for a minimum territory. One claimed that a pet needs a lot of space to roam in, another opined that it can live comfortably within the confines of a small space. In the end the group agreed that they really had no idea of the true territorial or social needs of a domesticated cat, dog, bird, or fish (and neither did I). I noted with interest the relative absence of distress over this ignorance. While not knowing was fleetingly exasperating for the debaters, only a few individuals considered that the lack of this knowledge might be of vital significance to the well-being of the animal. Most pet owners seem to be far more interested in obtaining information that would ensure the animal's smooth adaptation to a human domain.

People also tend to ignore, to minimize, or simply to be unaware of the importance of those animal features that human beings do not share in the same degree, but that may be vital to the animal's meaning system, such as a powerful sense of smell, hearing, touch, or taste. Toronto journalist John Bentley Mays relates a remarkable personal experience that bears on such alternative meaning systems. He was recovering from minor surgery when his hearing suddenly changed. He writes that during the weeks of convalescence, 'the walls of my house seemed to evaporate, and my hearing briefly became astonishingly, painfully acute.' He heard not only the sounds of cars, garbage trucks, and shrieking children playing in the streets, but also and more agonizingly for him, 'ambient noises with permanence and opacity, like that of brick and cement – the steady whine, never louder and never softer, emitted day and night by the toilet factory a block away, for instance,' or the 'high-pitched wheeze' of the microwave oven. The experience, while thankfully short-lived, remained memorable for him 'inasmuch as it made the invisible architecture of urban sounds present to me for the first time – as tangible and complex as the solid architecture of streets and buildings that comprise the central visible fact of our urban dwelling.'[40] This reminiscence of an unsettling bout of aural acuity and the 'sonic city' it unveiled (or rather, unmuted) for Mays encourages us to imagine how different the alternative realities of beings with different sensing and meaning apparatuses may be from ours.[41]

Some people I interviewed did appear to have engaged in a desultory study of the animal nature of their pets. One family, for instance, extolled the virtues of their Siamese cat as a breed of animal that, they believed, has retained many feline traits found in the wild and that they thought was less domesticated than other pets. The 'wildness' they attributed to this animal was a prized characteristic for these pet owners. However, even where such interest was evinced, the value of this knowledge, in the sense of value as a 'vector for action,'[42] appeared to be minimal. While one might be interested in knowing something about the nocturnal hunting instincts of cats, the propensity of dogs to follow a leader, or the mating song of finches, I met few people who felt compelled to acquire such or other knowledge with the express intent of adapting their practices for the sake of good pet keeping. Knowledge of the 'dogness,' 'catness,' or 'finchness' of the pet was far less emphasized than evidence that the animal was successfully socialized into the human domestic domain. Among my respondents, at least, there seemed to be a general sense that all one really needed to know about the animals in their care related specifically to the pet in its guise as human kin.

Bateson has said that if humans are attempting to interact and communicate with other animals they need to learn to understand, to the degree possible, the metaphor system of other animals.[43] But in order to be able to do so, pet owners would have to know something about the behavioural life cycle of these animals in their natural groupings. Only then could they translate or interpret similar behaviours transposed to other contexts such as the human domestic domain. In other words, humans can only guess at the metaphors their pets live by – such as a cat's 'kneading behaviour' on a soft surface – without knowledge of their original animal referents: in this case, the infant kitten's stimulation of its mother's milk glands. Significantly, most pet keepers do not appear to consider information of this kind necessary for the proper care of their pets.[44]

Disguising Animal Needs: Another muting mechanism involves disguising a pet's animal needs. If you walk into a North American pet store for the first time, many of the products will seem completely familiar, even though they are meant for ultimate consumption by species other than humans. Among the commodities sold for small mammals such as guinea pigs and gerbils, for example, you might find a 'Complete Exercise Centre,' 'Mini-Gym,' 'Sky Restaurant,' and 'Den-Add-On': all basically treadmills, yet all evoking by their names and shapes essentially human preoccupations in the Western world in an era of advanced capitalism. They are all made of the same sturdy, brightly coloured plastic from which many toys for newborn human infants are fashioned, and at first are indistinguishable from such human 'infant stimulation centres.' Also available are vitamins, food supplements, and 'stress compounds' for birds and other animals. There are coats, sweaters, and other clothing for dogs. Toys for dogs include brightly coloured rubber monsters and robots as well as the more familiar shoes and bones. A special toilet-seat attachment for cats purports to lure the pet to eliminate in somewhat the same way as human toddlers in the West are taught to do. Animal 'treats' are unabashedly packaged to appeal to humans: 'pet checkers' and 'pet cocktails' meant for guinea pigs look like bite-sized (human bite-sized, that is) appetizer biscuits. A bird 'sandwich' turns out to be a seed combination made to resemble two slices of bread held together by a filling. All of these commodities tend to make one forget that they are meant for use by animals and greatly encourage the idea that the pet is really a human being.

Defining Animal Traits as Pollution: While browsing through a pet shop, I was intrigued by a line of prominently displayed products in elegant black and silver packaging, called 'Four Paws.' The line had a 'pet cologne' as the star attraction. I sprayed the test bottle, fully expecting it to smell like an animal. Instead, I found that the odour, far from being animal-like, was rather more like a discreet home deodorizer. This small episode, coupled with the truly remarkable range and abundance of deodorizing, spot-removing, and cleaning materials for sale in pet stores, reminded me once again how constant a theme in human–animal relations is *pollution.*

Many people, pet owners and non-owners alike, readily confessed to a distaste for certain features of pets: excrement and urine, sloughed-off feathers, fluff or hair, fleas, saliva, and other excretions,[45] and above all, it seems, odours. For some people this distaste for animal leavings and emanations amounts to a disgust verging on revulsion and nausea: 'I couldn't stand the smell, I–could–not–stand–the–smell,' one woman repeated, her face screwing up against some noxious assault she remembered from more than a decade past, as she recounted a time working near the animals on an Israeli kibbutz farm.[46]

As Mary Douglas has shown us so well, dirt is not an entity that stands alone. It is substance perceived as disordered or anomalous *in an ordered system*. 'Dirt,' she asserts, 'is the by-product of a systematic ordering and classification of matter, in so far as ordering involves rejecting inappropriate elements.' She goes on to sum up dirt as 'all the rejected elements of ordered systems.'[47] Furthermore, in Douglas's notation, the traces of discernible animal presence would be considered *dangerous dirt*: as long as they retain some of their original identity, they defile by being 'matter out of place,' or matter that must be excluded if a pattern is to be maintained.[48] In the organizing metaphor that orders human–animal relations in the Canadian domestic sphere, 'bothersome' vestiges of animal being are, precisely, 'inappropriate elements' that must be rejected for the pattern of animal as human kin to be sustained and reproduced. That this active muting process is vigorously carried out is freely evidenced by the booming business sector devoted to pet deodorizing, cleaning, and grooming.

Muting the Animal in Human Beings

Once I kept a six-month diary while observing a cat with her two kittens. Here is one entry:

> To see the mother cat so sure, so attentive, benignly neglectful yet alert at appropriate times; relinquishing her food to the greedy young ones; very patient with the kittens jumping all over her and chomping on her tail or nursing; watching her as she firmly holds her rambunctious babies down with her paws or even sits on them while she cleans and grooms them, ignoring their protesting cries; seeing her gentleness yet firmness – it all brings home the fact that we usually don't get to see this extraordinary relationship among animal kin. It has taken me three months of observing this mother cat and her kittens to realize that my extreme absorption and fascination in watching them stems not from some obscure 'prurience' but from the real rarity of any opportunity to observe this intimacy in our society, among animals *and* among humans.

What was so striking, so 'extraordinary' in this interaction, I thought then, was its similarity to human maternal behaviour. I noted down in amazement, 'How *human* this cat mother is!' It was only later that I understood that I had put the emphasis in the wrong place. What I came to sense eventually was not how human this cat family was, but rather how catlike human family behaviours are; in other words, how similar are many human and other mammalian interactions. My original 'inversion' was an example of how we tend to mute the animal in human being. And, along with this Western penchant for ignoring continuities in interspecies behaviour between humans and other animals, we also engage in muting the animal in human beings more actively through ideology and through the adoption of powerful cultural blinders.

Ignoring Continuities in Interspecies Behaviour: I revised my assessment about the 'humanity' displayed by the mother cat in my diary observations in a small but paradigmatically important way after a discussion I had joined as an ethnographer turned to humans and animals. One woman related this incident: 'The other day my baby had some food on her face and I actually found myself licking it off ... And then I started thinking about animals who clean their babies by licking. Then I thought that maybe it was a more natural thing than I thought, and that any kind of natural feelings we have have all been civilized out of us. You "don't do" these things; it's not really considered appropriate behaviour.' Another woman revealed how her husband had admitted to a great urge, on each of three separate occasions, to lick their newborn babies as they emerged from the womb. A third told how powerfully affected she was when she came upon her sister, a new mother, suckling her baby at her breast while their youngest sister, a girl not yet in her teens, sat gazing intently yet dreamily at the pair. What each informant in turn was giving voice to was an episode of sudden, unmediated recognition of the *animal nature* of human maternal behaviour.

In the metaphor 'pet is human kin,' the animal is 'humanized' while the human is concomitantly 'de-animalized.' That is, human animal nature is, to the extent possible, suppressed from public display and repressed from consciousness. Ultimately, putting together the animal and human incidents I have narrated here, we can see that what is called for is not a notion of similarity in behaviour between the species, but one of continuity. These glimpses of animal and human behaviour are striking vignettes of the essential unity of mammalian maternal activity, striking because so clearly recognizable, even in small details. They are not metaphoric of each other, they are equivalent to each other; not analogous, but homologous. Yet in humans most of these 'animal' behaviours are consistently minimized or ignored: they are still infrequently displayed in the public sphere (and seldom, as attempts at breastfeeding in public places has shown, without contention), rarely if ever noted or discussed even within the most intimate confines of family life, and never in my experience in or outside the field referred to as 'animal' behaviours. Said another person in the group: 'This has begun to strike me very much, that we no longer know what constitutes the natural.'

Muting the Animal in Human Beings through Ideology: An avid outdoorsman told me that he always had a different reaction when glimpsing a moose standing in the woods beside a railroad track and when encountering one deep in the trackless forest. The first moose, being associated with the works of human beings, he experienced as 'not natural,' whereas the second moose would feel 'pristine' and 'natural,' and decidedly more valued. Quite a number of my informants expressed the sentiment that anything that appeared to be 'touched by human hands' was 'not natural': 'Where man is,' another summed up, 'that's not-nature.'

Philosopher Mary Midgley reminds us in her inimitable, cleansingly acerbic way that human beings 'are not tourists here ... we are not fit to live anywhere else.'[49] Yet, from the Renaissance until the last quarter of the twentieth century, humanity's 'right' to conquer the material world remained a constant theme in Western ideology, stemming from Man's privileged position outside of and up against raw (*pace* Lévi-Strauss) nature. The effects of this ideology remain with us still in the entangled ecological and economic management practices we engage in despite manifestly moderating public beliefs and attitudes. In much of the contemporary counter-ideological literature on human relations with the environment, human beings are still defined as outside of nature, but the valence has shifted: from Man the master of nature to humanity as the suspect, destructive, 'unnatural' species. Thence, all that humanity affects becomes in turn tainted with the epithet 'unnatural.'[50] Within anthropology itself the manner in which the nature-culture debate has been cast – as one domain *in opposition* to another – plays its non-negligible role in perpetuating the notion of the separateness of humanity from the rest of the natural world. This commonplace ideological posture, whether presented in its positive or negative form, acts, intentionally or not, as a further muting and obscuring force against our ability to recognize and experience our inherent biological being. It tends to stifle any stirrings of the totemic imagination.

Nor have some proponents of human–animal continuity helped the argument, as critics of sociobiology and some popular ethology have been quick to point out. Many proponents of sociobiology, for example, have made the ineradicable founding error of assuming that all animals apart from humans are inherently simple, driven by simple genetic determinisms, devoid of complex internal life or external agency, and then transposed this diagram onto human behaviour. The extremely reductive arguments such writers have put forward for both humans and other animals have amounted, in the eyes of their critics, to major distortions that have discredited the whole of their hypothesis. The resultant picture, so obviously missing the 'heart' of what it is to be human, has turned many thoughtful people away from *any* consideration of human–animal connection.[51]

Another Side of Muting: Human–Animal Relations as Releasers
At this point let me introduce an intriguing series of fieldwork observations. Although they merit a great deal of further investigation and elaboration in their own right, I will only touch upon them briefly in this book as an example of the way in which cultures as ordering systems so decisively constrain human practice at the level of cognition. The behaviours I describe consist of a paired set: first, the repeated demonstration of 'non-normative' conduct, and second, what might almost appear to be a code of public silence over the anomalous practices observed.

Human–Animal Interactions as Releasers: In a pet store I watched a father showing the animals to his small son: 'See the birdie? See the birdie?' shrilled this tall, lanky man in the peculiar, distinctive, high-pitched telegraphic language we know as 'babytalk' or 'motherese.' Many otherwise well-behaved fathers of young children were overheard in pet stores to exclaim repeatedly in falsetto over 'bunnies,' 'birdies,' 'doggies,' and 'fishies.' Perhaps this intimate form of speech was meant in part for the children they had with them, for it might be assumed that the presence of very young children would facilitate this kind of specialized talk. However, younger males, boys without babies in tow, were equally unselfconscious about their automatic lapses into motherese and displays of nurturant care when in the presence of animals destined as pets. Indeed, it appeared to me that in such instances males and females behaved in quite the same manner. Without forgetting that much pet-store livestock is bred for neoteny – that is, the retention of juvenile features into adulthood, which appears to act as a powerful releaser of nurturant behaviour in human beings – it is virtually never remarked that *when the object is an animal, this releaser acts as powerfully on human males as it does on females.* Similarly, in a study of human–animal interactions in the waiting room of a veterinary clinic, psychologist Aaron Katcher found that, as might be expected, pet owners frequently touched their pets, but further, there was no difference in the frequency, kind, or amount of pet touching between male and female owners. Males pet, stroke, pat, hug, and kiss pets as much as females do,[52] and far more than they may do to other humans, certainly in public.

It is interesting that in many two-parent heterosexual households, men take on the primary responsibility in the family for the basic care, feeding, grooming, medical care, training, exercise, and play of the family pet, in a mirror image of the primary responsibilities and traditional roles still expected of women with respect to their children in this society. Two respondents described the extraordinary lengths to which one of their husbands went to save the lives of some abandoned kittens. Said one: '[My husband] decided he was going to nurse [the kittens] and he did. There were three of them and he was just like a mother to these kittens for a long time.' Her friend added: 'Do you remember he was trying to figure out how to get them to use the litter, and he had them in a box and made a sort of split-level little house, and they had to go through this little door to another little spot where the litter was. He was trying to train them ... and if he gives them a few clues, the way the mother usually does ... His parenting instinct, I think, coming very strong, like a mother.'

The copious, unselfconsciously nurturant and intimate mothering behaviours that many human males display privately and publicly when the object is a pet are rarely seen in public when the object is another human being, except perhaps where the object is a baby – and even in that case, with some circumspection. It is likely that socialization can mask certain fundamental, more universally built-in behaviours or potentialities that the society considers inappropriate for certain members to display toward other members of that society. In North American societies, perhaps the socialized prohibition against the male display of effusive caring in public is not operative when the objects that elicit this behaviour are not quite human, but are rather metaphorical humans: that is, pets. Human–animal interactions appear to permit the mask of socialization to slip sufficiently to allow us to see not only the capacity of human males for nurturant behaviour (for this in itself is not the great surprise), but more important, the *largesse* of that caring, the unrestrained, superabundant, and persistent quality of it, which Western society more readily associates with female behaviour.[53]

The Muting of Cultural Anomaly: This is but half the story, however, for paired with this profligate display of unmasked male nurturance is the singular lack of comment about it. People rarely call attention to this behaviour as unusual, anomalous, or even just plain different. Indeed, it is usually not mentioned at all. No one even seems to notice these often flagrant lapses from the cultural norm, or if they do, as my two informants did who described how a man's mothering instinct came out when confronted by orphaned kittens, they do not tend to compare this behaviour with intra-human patterns, or try to draw some conclusions about the latter.

Thus, while these caring male practices succeed in strengthening the animal-as-human-kin metaphor, they also operate to simultaneously reveal and mute a traditionally unacknowledged aspect of the human male repertoire, acts of which males are sometimes still considered to be constitutionally, or 'naturally,' incapable. We can but wonder at the force of learned ignorance that simultaneously allows us to observe and prohibits us from *seeing* what is enacted routinely before our very eyes. This is an instance of deep and tenacious cognitive constraint, one of the many forms of learned ignorance necessary for the maintenance of ordered systems.

Reproduction and Privacy

We have seen that animal-as-human-kin is a primary organizing metaphor guiding and shaping human–animal relations in the domestic sphere in Canadian, indeed North American, urban society, and that socialization, routinization, and muting, as positive and negative forms of cognition-in-practice, actively preserve and reproduce this metaphor we live by in powerful ways. We have also seen how much these positive and negative modes of cognition-in-practice depend on learned ignorance, or culturally influenced selective inattention. This brings us back to doxa, beliefs that are taken to be self-evident and remain, therefore, unquestioned. Outside the world of doxa lies not merely the improbable, but the inconceivable. Cultural reproduction must rely a great deal on such taken-for-granted, unquestioning attitudes in order to be able to continue without undue fitfulness. It is therefore most successful when it is carried on in those areas of life where action usually proceeds with little reflection. Bourdieu writes: 'The instruments of knowledge of the social world are ... political instruments which contribute to the reproduction of the social world by producing immediate adherence to the world, seen as self-evident and undisputed ... The political function of classifications is never more likely to pass unnoticed than in the case of relatively undifferentiated social formations, in which the prevailing classificatory system encounters no rival or antagonistic principle.'[54] In complex societies with highly differentiated social formations, these 'political instruments' are least likely to encounter rival or antagonistic principles, and are therefore most likely to function effectively, in those arenas of life that are most private. In urban North American society, the home front is one such domain. It is in such private arenas, as practice theorists maintain, that 'much of the conservatism of a system tends to be located.'[55] Privacy is of utmost importance for the successful reproduction of the kinship metaphor that guides human–animal relations in the domestic domain, for it permits the recreating routines of everyday life to be performed without reflection or interruption: it permits the contradictory to go uncontradicted, the muted to remain unvoiced, and the metaphor to be lived as if it were real. Privacy permits and encourages the closed system of doxa, the unconsidered round of life, and it is largely in this way that human beings and other animals reproduce the system that sustains them.

LIMITS TO THE KINSHIP METAPHOR

At the beginning of this chapter I argued that the kinship metaphor for human–animal relations is not accidental. The domestic domain – virtually the only legitimate field for encountering all together the sustaining intimacies of life: nest, nourishment, communication, touch, and affection – provides one of the few permissible settings in our culture for expressing relational ties with living beings other than human beings. In modern urban Western life the totemic imagination, or biophilia, takes as one of its most widely shared forms the pet relation with its cultural model of kinship because it is largely restricted to this form in modern capitalist societies. Once adopted, however, the metaphor as cultural model must be served. As we have seen, innumerable activities – the repetitive micro-practices of everyday life – go into its reproduction.

As-ifness

At the same time, there are limits to the kinship metaphor. The essence of metaphor, as noted elsewhere, is its *as-ifness*. Metaphor is not complete identification. People know, at some level, that one thing is not 'really' or completely another. When metaphors we live by act as ordering devices shaping behaviour, or cultural models, certain key attributes that foster this as-ifness are constantly reiterated while other attributes, which either do not foster similarity or may not foster the particular similarity that has been chosen for emphasis, are recursively muted through the daily activities of living. Since as-ifness is not complete identity, a metaphor is inherently self-limiting. In human–animal relations the kinship metaphor goes only so far. My informants manifested this appreciation of the limitations of the metaphor and recognition of the otherness of the animal in countless small ways. A youngster of six, for example, knew that his pet was not human, and listed some of the things his pet did not do that human beings did: eat with a knife and fork, pick up his milk bowl when he drank, go on vacation, play in the same way that he did with his friends, and so on. 'I think,' he said, 'that [my cat] kind of just acts like he thinks he is one of us, but if he really thought he was one of us, I think he'd want something covering him overnight instead of just lying in his bed with nothing over him ... If he really thought he was like one of us – he has seen us lots of times – I think he would try to do the same things as us.'

Despite the muting that goes on all the time, people's ultimate recognition and appreciation of the otherness of the animal – its own subjective existence apart from human interest – provides strong clues about the biophilic substrate underlying human–animal bonds. The pet relation can be thought of as the domestication and circumscription of the human totemic tendency to identify more closely with other beings and make common cause with them. As we saw, the containment of this thrust, so necessary to a capitalist culture, is ensured by locating the affectionate human–animal relation in the privacy of the domestic sphere and minimizing the otherness between the species through mis-recognizing the animal natures of both. Human attachment to the rest of nature is thus achieved (or permitted to happen) in a disguised way by enculturating the connections and continuities of nature in the pet relation.

Liminal Domains

In line with my emphasis on the critical impact of context on cogni-tively and ideologically implicated activities, the kinship metaphor appears to be most fully activated in the domestic domain. But, as any visit to a pet store will demonstrate, it is strongly activated in this latter realm too. The pet store is an anomalous domain in North American society, an arena where two powerful metaphors we live by intersect. In this ambiguous sphere, animals are treated simultaneously as if they were potential kin and as if they were articles for sale – live–*stock*. For this reason, the pet store might well be thought of as a transitional domain between marketplace and home – transitional, that is, for the reader, but liminal, in the transformative Turnerian sense, for the ani-mal. In the next chapter, entering by means of this liminal world of the pet store, we will explore another widespread pattern of human–ani-mal relations in the West, shaped and fuelled by another key cultural model. We will examine the themes of animal design, manufacture, use, and exchange under the organizing metaphor of the animal as human creation, or *artifact*.

Chapter Four

Manufacturing the Natural Order:
The Factory Domain

For we are to understand that it is the deconstruction of sentient tissue that is taking place ...

Elaine Scarry (1985)

BIOPHILIA AND THE MARKETPLACE

In the shopping-mall scene that opened the last chapter, the clerk–puppy duo's task was not meant merely to elicit emotion from passersby. Their task, as the clerk told me, was to attract customers into the store. The 'entranceway scene' is a deliberate marketing ploy enlisting the animal in attracting human shoppers to buy the store's products, the animal itself among them. In other such instances, store managers place cages of young puppies, kittens, ferrets, or rabbits just outside the shop to perform the same duty. They also rely on the colour and movement of tropical birds placed in storefront windows. People's urge to look, to touch, to cradle and protect proves irresistible to many passersby, and these cages and windows are seldom without humans milling about, some lost in contemplation, others actively trying to gain the creatures' attention.

Mixed Metaphors

When people enter a pet store in an urban North American shopping mall they cross a threshold into a curious world. Other mall emporia sell 'goods' or 'articles.' A pet store also sells 'livestock.' Assailing patrons with a riot of smells, colour, noise, and movement, sensuously insistent, it is a marketplace of beings. Indeed, a pet store is primarily in the business of selling *being*, and the human urge to connect with other life is its most compelling marketing tool. As Kovel reminds us, '[W]e would miss much of what capitalism is all about if we overlook its role in restructuring and marketing desire and impulse themselves.'[1]

'Through all historic time,' says historian Gerald Carson, 'man has oscillated between acknowledging his kinship with the natural world or denying it.'[2] Nowhere is this oscillation so immediately and poignantly experienced as in a pet store. It is a liminal world with ever-shifting boundaries, with contradictory forces and tendencies pulling at the same time. Indeed, the term 'pet store' itself, as well as managerial references to livestock, epitomizes how intricately two literally equi-vocal organizing metaphors – at once connoting priceless intimacy between species and the price-driven forces of the market economy – make their competing claims on hapless customers. My own reactions on entering such domains were mixed, with strong positive responses to the creatures combined with a feeling that all of this variable life was, in this setting, merely stock to sell. This latter impression was less pleasant to think about, and, indeed, I did not spend much time engaged in this sort of thinking.

Pet-store management and staff understand the force of this equivocality and put it to effective use, prominently displaying animals huddled together in cages, apparently uncomfortably, while clerks talk of how long the creatures have been in the store, and how much they wish to see them 'adopted.' The clerk with the puppy in the doorway, for example – the 'Front Lady,' as I came to think of her[3] – told me that the puppy had been in the store for two weeks and she hoped he would be sold soon because he needed a good home. She didn't want him to go, she said, but she felt that he had best go to a good home. Kinship sensibilities notwithstanding, pet-shop staff are paid to sell consumer goods, and in this arena, consumer goods are what these animals predominantly are.

Like most other commodities, pet-store livestock are also made, in the sense of human intervention and control in their coming to be. This chapter looks at animals as objects of human creation, or artifacts, for human use or exchange.

ARTIFACTS AND THE FACTORY DOMAIN

The manager of an animal shelter compared her work to pet sales, saying: 'I would find it rather frustrating, working retail. In the situation we're in here, we're adopting out animals. We're screening people to make sure that the person and situation fit the animals that they're interested in. When you're in the business of selling animals, you sell an animal to whoever wants it – like a pair of shoes: you sell a person a cat, or you sell them the dog.' Unlike 'adoption,' a procedure that refers back to and is culturally situated in the domestic domain, when an animal becomes a commodity, like a pair of shoes, even though much of its saleable charm may lie in its living, creaturely being, insofar as humans relate to it it takes on many of the attributes of an unalive thing, an object.

Artifact as Organizing Metaphor

An object made by a human being is an artifact. In its simplest denotative sense an artifact is an object showing human workmanship or modification or, as *Webster's Collegiate Dictionary* notes, 'a product of artificial character due to extraneous (as human) agency.' Unlike 'found' objects, artifacts are intentional: they are made by human beings for a specific reason. Different purposes are possible: they may be meant to be commodities for sale, tools, or objects of art or design. When animals are treated like artifacts, they may be intended for any of these purposes.

In order to understand the special nature of the human–animal relation subsumed under the metaphor 'animal is artifact,' it is essential to grasp the importance of the human hand and mind in the creation of the artifact and in the enactment of the artifact metaphor. The word itself stems from the Latin *ars*, skill, and *facere*, to make. Making things is as fundamental an activity for human beings as speaking, as basic as flying is for other animals and burrowing for still others. As Marx understood so well, to be human is, in large measure, to make. By making things, human beings alter the world, a little bit or a lot; we order the world to suit our own needs. In enacting the organizing metaphor animal-as-artifact, we are thus engaged in ordering the natural world.

In Western cultures the status of artifact carries with it a particular cluster of concomitants. In addition to being created by human beings, artifacts are not considered to be sentient, they are eminently discardable, and, apart from their status as property, they have no moral standing in the human community. What evidence is there to support my claim that the cultural model animals-are-artifacts does, in certain settings, actually organize practice in human–animal relations? Let us investigate these features of the artifact as they relate to the human–animal relation.

Animal-Artifacts Are Made

People have interfered with the reproductive capacities of particular animal species for many thousands of years, usually to enhance features considered to be of some material benefit to the society involved: for food, transportation, herding, and so on. As is well known, a significant impetus to Darwin's intellectual development was his familiarity with and respect for the ancient craft of selective breeding.[4] In the case of the manipulation of pets – as domestic animals kept for pleasure rather than utility – elements of creativity, control, and play rather than mundane advantage appear to be strong motivating factors. Pet-store managers say they do a steady trade supplying fish, birds, and other animals to their customers for hobby breeding.

Pet shows are instructive settings for discovering how human beings manipulate animals genetically, phenotypically, and behaviourally. In fact, a major purpose of a pet show is to demonstrate these skills and their products. Visits I made to dog shows revealed how malleable even flesh and bones can be under human control, and how fancifully humans can alter other living beings. There were one hundred and forty-five breeds of dog recognized by the Canadian Kennel Club during the period I made my visits – large, small, and 'toy'; long-haired, short-haired, wire-haired, and hairless; dogs bred for plain, swamp, mountain meadow, or lap; and for hearing, smell, or sight – a striking diversity of animal types that can be classed under one species, all created by human ingenuity. A pamphlet describing 'How to Understand and Enjoy a Dog Show' informs us: 'Man never seems to be satisfied with anything. No sooner has he developed a breed than he tries to make another variety of the same breed.'[5]

A dog or cat show presents pets primarily as objects of visual and sculptural design. In breeding, every effort is made to match the animal to a physical and behavioural aesthetic ideal, and then to improve on that ideal. People at a pet show are there to appreciate this design and the process of its manufacture. At one 'feline fancy' show I attended, the judge took each cat out of its cage and, handling it firmly but gently, stretched its body out to examine its length and proportions and the length and features of the legs. Tail, skull, ears, muzzle, coat, and markings were all important in the judging. By teasing the cat with feathers and toys to get it to leap or pounce, the judge also seemed to be evaluating the swiftness and gracefulness of its movements.

The animal on show at such events is not considered to be a being that has grown beautiful or interesting; its main attraction is as a thing that has been made so by human intervention. Caretakers pay an extraordinary amount of attention to barbering and grooming the animals, a way of engineering the phenotype to particular standards once the genotype has been manipulated. I watched as pet owners at a dog show endlessly combed and feathered long manes and bushy tails, plaited locks, and applied ribbons and bows to their pets. In the washrooms some of the sinks were occupied with dogs up to their noses in bubbles, patiently still and almost uncannily silent as their owners scrubbed them for their big performance.

The aesthetic standards seem to be highly arbitrary. One dog-show informant explained that among the criteria of excellence for the setter class – dogs originally bred to assist in retrieving game – is a luxuriant growth of hair along the dog's underparts, from chest to tail, with long, feathery tufts on the legs. While this undercoat is much admired by dog-show audiences and judges (and I thought it quite beautiful myself), this very feature, I was told, is inhibiting to a dog that actually does hunt because the undercoat gets tangled, muddied, and matted in forests and swamps, slowing the animal down considerably in performing its tasks.

Aesthetic compositions sought by pet designers include the bizarre, the comic, and the grotesque as well as the beautiful. At one show I saw a tiny 'toy' poodle that had just recently come under the topiarist's shears. It was shaven to its pale pinkish-grey skin everywhere but for curly white pompons left *in situ* at intervals along both sides of its thin, trembling body and above each paw, one pompom bobbing absurdly on each haunch with every step the animal took on its matchstick legs. A long-haired spaniel had its coat cut to resemble an over-large sweater, with four sleeves dragging below its paws. I wondered how easily this rollicking animal could manoeuvre its 'outfit' as it bounced about: was it likely to step on its own coat and trip? The shar-pei, a dog with many folds of loose skin, a dense coat like deep-pile carpeting, and a 'hang-dog' expression, is offered by geographer Yi-Fu Tuan as an example of the canine grotesque. He quotes an American newspaper article: 'Fawn II, a one-year-old Chinese *shar-pei*, took top prize at the

Ugly Dog Contest ... in Petaluma, California. The judges voted Fawn, who looked not unlike an unmade bed, the "ugliest dog by any standard."[6]

The creations of pet breeders do not often raise a public eyebrow, even when some purebreds, bred not with the whole animal in mind but only for particular traits – and the products, if fragile but liked, kept alive through human intervention – are prone to particular diseases and disabilities because of careless, misguided, or simply whimsical design. Historian Harriet Ritvo documents the transformation of the 'British bulldog' in Victorian England from a canine not much distinguishable from a mastiff to the dog we know today, 'well out at the shoulder and with a good broken up face,' as the Kennel Gazette reviewer of the time (1891) phrased it. The shoulder feature was, in fact, a crippling deformity, making it difficult for even a champion dog to run for more than a couple of miles. Had the dog still been used for bull-baiting, which was no longer the case by later Victorian times, the now-familiar pushed-in muzzle would have permitted the bull to get off scot-free. Tuan describes a variant of goldfish prized in China and Japan called the 'Telescope goldfish,' bred with eyes so disproportionately large and protuberant for its body that it is likely to injure them while swimming against hard objects (such as a glass aquarium), and it not uncommonly blinds itself. Other expert sources tell us that the shar-pei is prone to skin diseases largely because of the desirable trait of its many folds of skin, which may harbour parasites and bacteria in snug abundance. Through lengthy breeding, Siamese and Persian cats often have inherited defects in hearing and vision. The tailless Manx cat is known for a susceptibility to spina bifida. A highly respected handbook on cats sums up the general problem for all pets: 'There is no amount of inbreeding that is without risk of increasing the incidence of birth defects.'[7]

Yet this kind of manipulation is a comparatively benign variant of the most extreme and controversial example to date of how far animal-as-human-creation can be taken as a metaphor to live by: the 'patented animal.' In 1980 the United States Supreme Court, by a narrow margin, granted a patent to the General Electric Company to produce a microorganism that would eat up oil spills. Since 1987 the United States Patent Office has permitted the patenting of all animals, provided these animals demonstrate some significant change engineered by genetic manipulation. These permit mean that the holder owns the animal's 'blueprint,' so to speak, and to date extend to every species except *Homo sapiens* – while not excluding human genes, cells, tissues, embryos, or fetuses.[8] Thus, human beings can 'invent' and patent a complete animal and profit from both the process and the animal itself, as with any other invented artifact. By American law, this makes all living beings aside from humans into potential objects or products (or even 'factories,' producing substances of use to humans), and by implication protects the right of humans to continue to manipulate them virtually at will. In 1988 Harvard University received its American patent for the 'Oncomouse,' a genetically defective mouse susceptible to lymphomas and skin, bone marrow, breast, and spleen cancers that is bred intentionally for medical research. Canada's Patent Office denied Harvard a Canadian patent in 1995 after ten years of investigation on the rodents. As reported in the *Toronto Star*, the Patent Office board's decision to reject the American bid did not involve an ethical dilemma: 'The board's job, said [a member of Canada's patent board], was not to answer whether anyone can, in good conscience, patent life forms. Rather, members had to decide if a life form fits into the Patent Act's definition of invention.' The case has been appealed and at the time of writing is still before the Canadian courts.[9]

Animal-Artifacts Are Not Sentient

In addition to being made, real artifacts are by definition not sensate. What about animal-artifacts? A veterinarian described her father's reminiscences about the establishment of factory farming in Canada after the Second World War: 'Every veterinarian who did large animal work in North America didn't see anything wrong with lining up six sows in a pen, because you get brainwashed. It's a commodity. You don't view them as living, thinking, feeling animals.' In today's parlance, farm animals are supposed to be treated as 'biomachines.' Thus, we get the following modern-day advice to pig farmers in *Hog Farm Management*, an American pork-industry journal, as reported in the *Toronto Star* in October 1990: 'Forget the pig is an animal. Treat it just like a machine in a factory. Schedule treatments like you would lubrication. Breeding season is the first step in an assembly line. And marketing like the delivery of finished goods.'[10]

In medical or other laboratory research, where animals are used as tools, they are often referred to as if they were complete abstractions – 'living systems,' 'standardized research material,' or 'animalwork' (analogous to 'paperwork') – thus eliminating any hint of the animal as a living, feeling being. British moral philosopher Mary Midgley, who has written extensively on the relations between humans and other animals, notes that in the laboratory the rat is 'simply a standard object, a piece of laboratory equipment with the function of being used to test hypotheses, a kind of purpose-made flesh-and-blood robot.'[11]

The animal's sentience is not always considered to be of consequence even in more cordial settings. People will often enter a pet store, for example, solely to be entertained. A multisensory event, the shop is a vibrating canvas of exotic colours and intricate patterns, a chaotic choreography of darting, sinuous, or playful movements, a cacophony of assorted munchings, squawkings, songs, and sighs, a luxuriance of thick, furry coats or silky iridescent feathers one longs to reach out and touch; and everywhere, layers of ambiguous, faintly reminiscent (and among them, long-repudiated) odours. With all senses assaulted at once, pet-shop patrons move from one 'scene' – aquarium, cage, or perch – to another, examining and commenting on the animals as they go past. In these instances, the primary function of the animals is as *spectacle* (in the broadest possible sense – auditory, haptic, and olfactory as well as visual) for the aesthetic delectation of humans. In a similar vein, art and cultural critic John Berger has this to say about zoos: 'In principle, each cage is a frame round the animals inside it. Visitors visit the zoo to look at animals. They proceed from cage to cage, not unlike visitors in an art gallery who stop in front of one painting, and then move on to the next or the one after next.' As an object of art, entertainment, or spectacle, the animal's sentience is minimized; as far as human beings are concerned, the animals do not register them. In the 'ideology of the spectacle,' as Berger puts it, 'the animals are always the observed. The fact that they can observe us has lost all significance.'[12]

Animal-Artifacts Are Discardable

Made by human hand and devoid of sensation, artifacts in our consumer society are also characterized by their discardability. This characteristic also inheres in the metaphor shaping the human–animal relation. Pet shops, for instance, have a vested interest in fostering notions of product replaceability as one facet of return trade. They are greatly assisted in this by the fact that many of the animals they sell are toylike in character, a quality stemming from the marked neoteny bred into the mammals. This toylike quality, in turn, is abetted by another thriving industry turning out stuffed animals modelled on and exaggerating the neotenous qualities of infant animals. The more toylike pet-store animals appear, the greater the likelihood that the notion of discardability and replaceability can, albeit subconsciously, take hold.

These shops also sell pet 'starter kits,' items that tend to bolster the idea of a living pet as a toy or a project and of caring for the pet as something of a game. Starter kits consist of a brightly packaged assemblage of rudimentary paraphernalia for housing and feeding (and sometimes 'amusing') one's newly acquired pet fish, bird, gerbil, or hamster. When the child has used up the contents of the starter kit he or she is meant to obtain refills with which to maintain the animal. However, this kind of boxed presentation, suggesting the end of the game or project once the contents are used up, tends to encourage subliminally the notion of throwaway pastimes, muting the reality that the animal in question has a lifespan and needs of its own surpassing the limited resources in the box.

That pets are not infrequently treated as discardable was attested to by a veterinary assistant who recounted that some pet owners, faced with a costly veterinary bill, would refuse to pay for or to claim their animals, declaring that they could get another at a much cheaper price, as if the animal were an old clock whose unexpectedly high repair bill had the effect of substantially reducing its original charm. Not so different was the anecdote told to me at the Toronto Humane Society. One day a teenaged boy inquired whether he might 'trade in' his grown dog for a 'younger model' – a not-uncommon request, I was told.

Perhaps most telling in terms of the casual discardability of animals-as-artifacts is the case of animals used as tools in experimental science or teaching. 'At the veterinary schools in Canada,' said a British-born veterinary assistant, 'they will raise animals, or have animals brought in, and they will break their legs so that they can operate on them, to see how they can fix them. In the veterinary schools in England they don't do that. Over here [in Canada], they'll do a dozen surgeries on an animal and then decide they'll put it to sleep.'

Animal-Artifacts Are Excluded from the Moral Community
In discussing the patenting of animals, a researcher involved in transgenic experimentation responded this way to a radio interviewer:

Interviewer: 'Have you discussed the ethical considerations involved in this kind of research amongst yourselves?'
Researcher: 'Oh, well, we've talked about it.'
I.: 'In what terms have you talked about it?'

R.: 'In the same terms that anybody else talks about it. If we thought it was wrong, we wouldn't be doing it. It's just as simple as that.'[13]

As artifact, the animal is less likely to be regarded as having intrinsic worth or virtue and therefore has minimal claim to human obligation or respect. Rather than possessing individual subjectivity, the animal-artifact is regarded as a better or lesser specimen of a class of manufactured objects. As animals become objects and lose their separateness and sentience, they are excluded from the moral community.

To return to the relatively innocuous instance of the kennel club or cat fancy show: here, animals are awarded points and prizes for the degree to which they conform to rigid physical standards of breeding or to behavioural standards of obedience worked out by pet clubs around the world. Rather than acknowledging the worth of the animals themselves, however, these organizations are in the business of evaluating and rewarding human skill and ingenuity. The value of the object lies with the maker, not with the animal-thing; in this cultural arena, the dog's obedience is the achievement of the human being, not of an intelligent animal cooperating in the training. 'Every owner is proud of a dog which can be placed somewhere, and will be there when the owner returns,' declares a pamphlet that accompanies a kennel-club program. 'Any owner of a supposedly well trained dog would be properly embarrassed if his dog refused to jump some simple obstruction.'[14] Not only breeders, but ordinary pet owners express this sentiment as well. One respondent noted how proud he was to show off the good behaviour of his dog, unleashed, on a crowded downtown street. He had trained the dog himself. The general implication seems to be that since the animal-as-artifact is not part of the moral community, the trainer, or manipulator, deserves the credit for the prized results.[15]

The consequences of enacting the artifact metaphor are, of course, often more pernicious than this for the animal. Anthropologist and philosopher Barbara Noske suggests the grotesque degree to which this metaphor may cloud moral sense and basic logic in her story about two Danish doctors with Amnesty International. They were said to have performed torture experiments on pigs in 1977–8 as a way of gathering data for Amnesty International's cause of eliminating human-rights abuses, chiefly torture, around the world. Although Amnesty had not asked that the experiments be done, they gratefully accepted the results. Pigs were used because of their physiological similarity to human beings. Thus, even though the research design made no sense unless based on a presumption of human–animal kinship in the first place (at least at the physiological level), 'the anti-torture ethics these doctors undoubtedly stood for was not extended to the pigs!' writes an incredulous Noske.[16] Animal-is-artifact, it appears, is sometimes an imperious metaphor that brooks no alternative constructions.

Creator-to-Artifact: A Metonymic Relation

While the metaphor we are exploring here is the animal-as-artifact, the human–animal relation itself is not, strictly speaking, metaphoric in the sense of a symmetrical, 'A is like B' relationship. As many of the instances we have looked at illustrate, in the grip of the animal-is-artifact metaphor, we often perceive humans and animals as having complementary rather than analogous roles. The interspecies interactions recorded here describe an asymmetrical, hierarchical relation of creator-to-created thing. As we move from the liminoid and equi-vocal world of the pet store to other arenas in the production and market sphere of Western culture – the 'factory domain' – the human–animal relation that increasingly obtains is a univocal relation, one of metonymy. Metonymy pervades the human–animal relation shaped by the artifact as a metaphor we live by. This relation is characterized by the reduction of an entire being to one or a few selected components or attributes useful to the human manipulator, while the 'rest' of the animal,[17] or the animal as a whole and complex being, is ignored or actively suppressed. The animal is reduced, in practice, to the metonymic attribute that stands for it. Historian Ritvo provides the example of a reputed English breeder, Robert Bakewell, who developed strains of sheep and cattle for the prevailing tastes of the market. Bakewell's motto seems to have been that an excellent cow or sheep was 'the best machine for turning herbage into money.' Although well known for his kindness to his animals, he nonetheless bred them with a view to minimizing worthless bone and offal and maximizing the animal's marketable parts. His most elaborately engineered creatures, Ritvo tells us, were relatively large in the expensive rump cuts and smaller in the cheaper shoulder ones.[18]

A veterinarian informant's description of the old-time Canadian farmers' understanding of their relation to their animals highlights for us how both metaphoric and metonymic aspects can be operative simultaneously: 'Survival is just as hard for the farmer as it is for the animal. So you're on equal footing. I mean, the animal has to pay its way, because you're paying your way too. Nothing's free in this world ... When we only had horses and not automobiles, let's face it, that horse *was* your automobile. And you drove it until it died.' While, on the one hand, the lot of both farmer and animal may be perceived as symmetrical (they both have to pay their way in this world), that same animal is also perceived as being there primarily for the farmer's use. The converse, however, does not hold. The farmer is not understood to be there primarily for the horse's use. The actual, enacted relation is thus not analogous but asymmetrical, complementary, and vectored: the horsepower of the animal is harnessed for the use of the human being, and the horse is reduced essentially to a means of transportation.

Both metaphor and metonymy are ways by which human beings create order in their worlds. As with metaphor, metonymy is part of the ordinary, everyday, often out-of-awareness way people think, act, and talk.[19] As a verbal trope, metonymy can enlarge discourse by nudging the listener into a memory of the whole to which it refers. As a trope we live by, however, as a way of thinking and perceiving that organizes action in the real world, metonymy invariably becomes a reductive process. It inevitably makes a part out of a whole. Metonymic processes cannot but become reductive as people live them and practise them. This human cunning for turning complexity into simplicity, whole into part, being into artifact, carries within it a zealous tendency to diminish the wholeness and complicatedness of the Other. And the invariable result is to be expected. As Edward Wilson observes, '[A]rtifacts are incomparably poorer than the life they are designed to mimic.'[20]

Epitomized in the refinements of Western scientific and technological pursuit, the metonymic faculty is the human talent modern Western civilization has most admired and most relied on – the capacity to simplify and reduce and, in consequence, to objectify and diminish. This same faculty always has been and is still the mainstay of the 'factory domain,' the general label I have given to the production- and market-driven arenas in the Western world. The metaphor 'an animal is an artifact' and its associated metonymic relation organize human–animal interactions in virtually all of these arenas.[21]

The Factory Domain

As I have argued earlier, cultural context has potent effects on the cog-

nitive and behavioural patterns our relationships take in particular settings. Since cognitive practice is inextricably enmeshed in – simultaneously constituted by and constitutive of – its context, this context
must be understood as 'space-in-time' organized physically, socially,
economically, politically, and conceptually. It is a cultural and historical
moment in the life of a society and thus, inevitably, ideologically satu-
rated. A foray into the factory domain in contemporary Western culture provides insight into what it is that evokes the artifact as a central
organizing metaphor for human–animal relations in this context.

The following impressions, recorded early in my fieldwork, have
retained their resonance for me over time:

> It is a grey day in mid-winter. I am on my way to a dog show being held
> in the Industry Building on the grounds of the Canadian National Exhibi-
> tion in Toronto. The only way to get here is by car or public transit; it is
> not an easy or pleasant walk from any part of town. The setting is all mul-
> tilane expressways and tramlines and traintracks cross-cutting each other.
> There is not a tree in sight. It is built environment at its most utilitarian,
> disclosing the unlovely workings that keep a great metropolis moving.
> Lake Ontario, which is nearby, cannot be seen.
>
> The building itself is a huge concrete shell the length of a city block and
> almost as wide. The floors are cement. Everything seems to be painted
> grey. The layout for the show is precisely planned in neatly demarcated
> sections, like a factory floor. The indoors of the Industry Building with its
> grey colour and straight lines mirrors the outdoors on this grey day –
> planned, built, inorganic, unalive.

It is no accident that the largest kennel club in Canada holds its
annual dog show in an industrial trade-show arena. For this enterprise
lies well within the boundaries of the manufacturing, market, and reg-
ulatory context called here the 'factory domain.' By this term I mean
public arenas and settings for the making, marketing, and managing of
things chiefly for exchange and profit. In its narrow sense, this term
comprises every work setting: the factory or workshop, market outlet,
and trade fair; and also the world of technology, the research and
development sphere for the invention of artifacts, processes, and tools
– in technology critic Langdon Winner's phrase, 'all of modern practical artifice.'[22]

However, by factory domain I also want to convey a particular *ambi-
ence* or cultural medium. Evernden comes closest, perhaps, to articulat-

ing this sense when he describes Martin Heidegger's notion of technology: '[T]echnology to [Heidegger] is not simply the creation and utilization of tools and techniques. It is rather the encountering of the world as a field *for* the use of tools.'[23] The factory domain must similarly be understood: as a form of 'life field,' culturally and historically specifically conditioned for encountering the world *as a medium for the making of things*. Thus, the factory domain encompasses the entire human enterprise of making – 'transforming nature,' or 'world alteration'[24] – as it is institutionalized and industrialized in Western society for economic ends.

As noted in the last chapter, the efflorescence of a privatized, nuclearized, and intensely emotional family domain is the other side of what Kovel calls 'the iron requirement of capital for a depersonalized world,' a world from which feelings of intimacy, affiliation, and affection must be banished. For, as we know so well both from ideology and experience, the domain of public work life in capitalist society is itself ordered by means of that most compelling and imperious metaphor of the modern age, the machine. Here is George Stocking recreating a scene in the Crystal Palace, at the 'Great Exhibition of the Works of Industry of All Nations' in the London of 1851: 'There, in the rooms filled with machinery in motion, one could watch the power looms, the model locomotives, the centrifugal pumps, the horizontal and vertical steam engines – 'a thousand iron monsters snorting and clattering.' Foreign visitors were overwhelmed, and English farmers, dusty from the distance they had come, stood with mouths agape, as the British Industrial Revolution, pandemonic in its noise, but cleansed for the moment of its pain, went twirling and thrusting away before their very eyes.[25]

Of all arenas of shared life, it is the domain of fabricating, of world-alteration, that has most completely embraced modernity's mechanistic world-view and turned it into a metaphor to live by. Since the industrial revolution, observes Lewis Mumford, the West has come to adapt its entire mode of life to the pace and capacities of the machine. In his book *Discipline and Punish*, Michel Foucault shows that the machine metaphor, with its fragmenting of projects, bodies, tasks, time, and space, was actually active well before the industrial revolution. Indeed, he believes that its enacted presence in clerical, military, educative, and other domains in the eighteenth century in Europe significantly helped shape human compliance to the industrial revolution's factory model, thus easing its rapid spread throughout Europe and America, and eventually the world. [26] Today, the factory domain still organizes people, materials, and equipment according to the model of a rigid, impassive mechanism made up of interacting parts. All entities – humans, other animals, minerals, plants, instruments, engines – are treated like embodied metonyms, each but a fragment of some distant 'whole,' just a part with no independent use or meaning outside its place and function in the entire mechanism-enterprise.

In this domain human labour is made from the raw material of persons: their tasks divided, analysed, quantified, and unhinged from the end-product, their functions specialized to the point of extreme deskilling, their needs suppressed to the greatest extent possible. Tuan observes that it is not uncommon for workers to be made to feel 'that they are the weak and undependable parts of an otherwise beautifully running machine.' The human being is reduced to a thing whose meaning is attached to the greater meaning embodied in what Herbert Marcuse calls the 'omnipresent apparatus.' Taken to its logical extreme, the ultimate goal of the capitalist organization of labour, whether state or individual, local or global, is the reduction of a person's subjectivity to what Kovel calls a predictable, controllable, and quiescent object.[27]

Once the aim of the factory domain is conceived as the objectification of all things and beings, including humans, into artifacts – whether raw materials, tools, or commodities – then the minimization of the labourer's sentience, the workforce's discardability, and its limited voice in the moral community[28] are all easily perceptible. Mumford believes that capitalism 'turned people from tangibles to intangibles.' As Kovel puts it, the machine metaphor both encourages and flourishes in a domain that consigns all spiritual being to a second-class existence. Everything possible is done to shed *bios* from the factory domain, to 'remove all sensuous immediacy from the object, who is thereby deprived of the basic mark of humanity, and prepared for profit or extermination, as just another "thing" in the world.' In order to make a market of the world, he comments, capitalism needed to create a mass of propertyless, mobile wage labourers, a discardable workforce of interchangeable parts whose fortunes did, and continue to, dangle at the whim of their capitalist owners. People treated like objects are 'outside the web of care,' things without value, having 'position in time and space, and nothing else.'[29] And so the perfect factory domain is modelled as closely as possible on the perfectly insensible, replaceable, non-moral world of the machine. Indeed, the model has taken hold so well that it is quite difficult to imagine alternative 'making' – technological – metaphors that we could feasibly live by.

As a medium for the making, marketing, and regulating of things, the factory domain remains extremely vigorous. It pervades all of institutionalized work life, affecting in the same ways the shop floor, the office, the government bureaucracy, the educational institution, the food service industry, the human service industry, even the small corner in a home reserved for piecework, on scales local and global. Today we have begun to see some of the effects of the movement toward completely replacing imperfectly controllable human beings with perfectly manageable machinery in entire workplaces (a dream already expressed by technophiles in the nineteenth century). The wholesale downsizing of all but the top of the workforce hierarchy in the 1990s in most economically advanced Western societies is just one recent example.[30] It is not surprising, therefore, that other animals in these settings are also treated like parts of this great machine.

The factory domain is not, however, a *machina ex deus*. It is neither a self-running nor an inert environment. Fundamentally, it is people engaging in a set of social, cultural, and cognitive-ideological practices-in-context. It is a multiply-motivated web of human activities, exploitative and cooperative, interactive, reactive, and counteractive, all conspiring in the end, whether with active intent or not, to render object out of being, machine out of *bios*, quiescence out of vitality.

MANUFACTURING THE ARTIFACT METAPHOR

The Transmutation of *Bios*

What an extraordinary feat it is to make inert yet not-dead things out of living, breathing, motile, behaving creatures. As Evernden points out, we do not, after all, start out thinking this way: 'Children are prone to assume that the world is, like themselves, alive and sensate. Only age and education can "correct" their view.'[31] In the factory domain the practice of transformation, or more accurately, trans*mutation*, includes a privatized reiterative practice similar to the one characteristic of the domestic domain. But here the process is neither as straightforward nor as completely unexamined as that one. Making an artifact of a sentient being entails a lot of work and a number of steps. As we saw in the formation of the human–animal kin relation, in order to successfully transmute, it is first necessary to mute. Further, in the factory domain, to maintain and reinforce the perception that the sounds and movements of living creatures are, in fact, the silence and inertness of unalive, although admittedly un-dead, artifacts, it is necessary to periodically engage in (semi)-public enactments of category change, or *performances of denial*. Let us explore how human beings transform the natural world in the factory domain through muting and through such performances of denial.

Muting

Muting an Animal's Repertoire as a Living Being

Everywhere in the factory domain, animals are restricted. They are often physically restrained and behaviourally deskilled, their body tissues altered, their social worlds obliterated. The aim is to extract a part out of a whole and, as much as possible, to disregard the waste that is the rest. The task at hand is to mute the animal's repertoire as a living being. Here are some of the ways this is done.

Confining and Crippling Animals: A veterinarian respondent continues her description of the rise of factory farming in Canada: 'In the sixties, intensive farming probably reached its height with, like, six sows tethered in a room no bigger than this [she gestures around a very small examining room]. And I mean tethered: that's where they were born and they grew up and they died. With a collar around their necks. And the dairy cattle business. And intensive poultry farming, with six or eight pullets in a cage. Never saw the light of day. That's all they did until four or six months of age. Then off to have their heads cuts off.'

Historian Keith Thomas reports that battery farming was practised widely in England long before the industrial revolution. In Elizabethan times, for example, 'the usual way of "brawning" pigs was to keep them "in so close a room that they cannot turn themselves round about."' Poultry and game birds were often fattened in darkness and confinement, and sometimes blinded. Some farmers in seventeenth-century England cut the legs off living fowl, believing that it made their flesh more tender. Dorset lambs were specially reared for the Christmas tables of the wealthy by being imprisoned in small dark cabins.[32] Similar practices continue today, but the scale is now so vast and the technological and corporate takeover so complete as to render the operations virtually – perhaps we should more truly say 'culturally' – incomparable.[33]

Muting itself – removing the voice – plays its part in unmaking being, as American literary analyst Elaine Scarry demonstrates in her indelible study of the political and perceptual implications of human pain and torture, *The Body in Pain: The Making and Unmaking of the World*.[34] She shows how a human being's subjectivity collapses in the face of great pain by rendering the person's vocalizations progressively inarticulate – 'sounds anterior to language that a human being reverts to when overwhelmed by pain.'[35] In the case of animal distress, it has sometimes been found necessary to cut the vocal cords entirely.[36]

Desocializing Animals: Intense pain need not only involve active wounding. For social species (as human beings continually struggle to bear witness),[37] there are unspeakable agonies to be endured in boredom and isolation or in suffering unendurably close quarters. Noske observes that, like us, most domesticated animals are highly social creatures for whom the importance of communication, skin contact, social play, social learning, and exploration of their environment is as well known as their need for territorial identity and optimal space. Yet in the factory domain, especially in research laboratories and factory-farm settings, animals are often either completely isolated from one another or jammed together in intolerable proximity; or, perhaps worse, as in industrial hog farming, completely isolated from one another physically in almost immobilizing cages while able to see, smell, and hear sometimes thousands of their sisters and brothers.[38] In the ever-diminishing instances of human–animal interaction in such settings, the contact, as described earlier, is equivalent to the human manipulation of tools, things, or embodied abstractions.

Deskilling Animals: Domestication involves shaping animal behaviour toward ever-increasing docility. It is not desirable, for example, that companion animals have too much vigour and initiative: 'The pet,' notes Tuan, 'if it is to find acceptance in a well-run household, must learn to be immobile – to be as unobtrusive as a piece of furniture.'[39] A number of animal owners I spoke to boasted about their pets' tractability and self-restraint – and might sometimes slyly refer in passing to their neighbours' animals' lack thereof.

Whereas true domestication, that is, changes in the animal's genome through human intervention, fosters a general leaning toward docility and malleability in the animal, obedience training shapes its conduct in specific ways. Dogs are taught to 'heel,' that is, to walk at the human being's left side and to sit immediately at the handler's left heel when the latter stops walking.[40] They are taught when wandering to return promptly upon being called, to sit and lie for extended periods of time, to retrieve projectiles over different terrains, and so on. One might argue, as does philosopher and animal trainer Vicki Hearne, that an animal's behavioural repertoire is enlarged and enriched by this training.[41] Gregory Bateson, however, counters that a primary rule of animal trainers is that once an animal has been made aware of the choices it has in a given context, it must be *prevented from exercising those choices*. Above all, it must obey the trainer. In certain circumstances, for example in circus acts, the animal must entirely abrogate the use of certain higher levels of intelligence.[42] The result is a severe form of deskilling, of restricting the animal to behaviours deemed appropriate by someone located outside the experiencing subject, and no others.

Together, these practices serve to minimize and distort the being of the animal, to diminish it and transmute it into artifact. Another set of practices, acting to *mute human perception and emotion*, closes the circle.

Muting Human Perception and Emotion

Scarry's central question in *The Body in Pain* concerns us here in the examination of relations between humans and animals: 'How is it that one person can be in the presence of another [being] in pain and not know it – not know it to the point where he himself inflicts it, and goes on inflicting it?'[43] While the answer to this human mystery eludes us, there are some clues we might pursue.

Unnaming: Among the many subtle practices that contrive to minimize the individuality and subjectivity of animals in the factory domain is their unnaming. In a pet show the 'entrant' is the owner or handler, not the animal, and the animal is never officially referred to by name, but only by category: breed, class, and so on. Now, as we saw in the last chapter, almost all pets have names that have been lovingly and thoughtfully chosen; in this arena, however, it is animal-as-specimen-of-a-class-of-objects that counts above all, and its individuality is muted. In a laboratory, factory farm, or other arena of the factory domain, animals are usually not named at all; at most, they are numbered or otherwise labelled for the purpose of inventorying the commodity stock, or as data to disprove scientific hypotheses.

On Learning 'Learned Ignorance': As many writers have observed, a critical step in the process of muting animal being into artifact is the concomitant transformation of the human being into a creator and manipulator of artifacts. 'The student who enters a biology program with experience of animals as subjects,' says Evernden, 'must "unlearn" his initial understanding before he can proceed to a biology of objects.'[44] Students learn to dissociate and suppress normal sensibilities through reiterated practices, eventually coming to perform with little apparent second thought the casual brutalities that are so characteristic of much of this domain, and are rewarded for, and come to pride themselves on, a certain tough-mindedness. Those who cannot do so leave the field. The efforts of those who remain are fully supported by what is almost always a tunnel-vision training into scientific 'expertise,' a method that rewards a deep study of the part to the neglect of the whole, with an associated emphasis on statistical and mathematical thinking. Observing, recording, and reporting only what is deemed to be quantifiable has the effect of transforming the de-brained or otherwise maimed animal in front of the researcher into the ultimate metonym: a possible future point on a potential graph.

It bears pointing out that the metaphor itself helps to structure feeling and value as well as cognition and action. As Fernandez says, 'Every metaphor has its mood.'[45] Through metaphor, practice theory, and the idea of habitus, we can better understand how history informs and shapes a society's 'structures of feeling,' as Raymond Williams calls the ways in which historically informed meanings and values are actively experienced in the world, as they are being lived and felt. George Marcus and Michael Fischer put it this way: '[E]xperience, the personal, and feeling all refer to a domain of life ... in which dominant and emergent trends in global systems of political economy are complexly registered in language, emotions, and the imagination.'[46] In accordance with the artifact metaphor in the factory domain, feeling is to the greatest extent possible cast off, because feeling is merely leftover trash.

Misdescription and 'Debased Language': Neurochemist Gill Langley presents many examples of misdescription, 'debased language,' and categorical sleight-of-hand found in the practice and literature on animal research. To mention just a few: a dead cat is termed a 'mammalian preparation'; the chemical induction of pain and inflammation in a rabbit's joints is the creation of an 'animal model of arthritis'; irradiation to the head of a mouse causing such widespread and severe injury to its mouth that it leads to death by starvation becomes an 'oral radiation death syndrome model' leading to 'diffuse mucosal damage in oral cavity' resulting in 'nutritional insufficiency.'[47] In discussing the use of transgenic animals in biomedical research, philosophers Hugh LaFollette and Niall Shanks assert that the position of most researchers is that naturally occurring animals are 'weak models of human bio-medical conditions'; 'designer' animals, it is thought, provide 'strong models' of the same. In other words, laboratory animals are routinely reduced to models of human 'conditions.'[48]

Abstraction from the laboratory site to the printed document further disconnects an animal's pain and suffering from the 'information' or 'intelligence' that is reported. Midgley has noted: 'In scientific articles, experimental animals never moan, scream, cry, growl, whimper, howl, snarl, or whine; they just discreetly vocalise.'[49] Through the artifact metaphor, a being's pain and fear are *categorically* denied. 'The most radical act of distancing,' declares Scarry with respect to the torture of human beings, 'resides in [our] disclaiming of the other's hurt.'[50]

In her book *Primate Visions*, Donna Haraway describes some of the 'surrogate mother monkey' devices to repel clinging infants invented by psychologist Harry Harlow and his colleagues in an effort to study the effects of maternal deprivation on monkey young. In the words of Harlow and his co-author Clara Mears, quoted in Haraway: 'One sur-rogate blasted its babies with compressed air, another tried to shake the infant off its chest, a third possessed an embedded catapult which periodically sent the infant flying, while the fourth carried concealed brass spikes beneath her ventral surface which would emerge upon schedule or demand ...' – an instrument the research team dubbed 'The Iron Maiden.' Later in the same paper they reported: '[W]e resorted to an apparatus affectionately termed the rape rack, which we leave to the reader's imagination.' Yet another piece of equipment for use with monkeys was called the Well of Despair, an instrument so dishearten-ing that some research staff refused to continue the experiments. Com-menting on this set of experiments, Masson reports that the infant monkeys placed in the stainless-steel vertical trough for forty-five days of solitary confinement were permanently impaired. As Haraway her-self comments: 'For the historian of science trying to avoid simplistic interpretive strategies, the metaphoric translations in the Harlow lab are defeating in their isomorphisms.'[51] In some parts of the factory domain of animal-based research, we cannot but agree with Scarry that 'the question, whatever the content, is an act of wounding; the answer, whatever its content, is a scream.'[52]

It seems clear that the human penchant for metonymic or dissociative thinking lies somewhere at the ideological heart of the artifact as a metaphor we live by. But metonymic thinking is not foolproof. Indeed, it is its very fallibility that may account for some unexplained practices I came across repeatedly in my fieldwork. These are disparate practices, some of which on first sight are apparently contrary to the distancing activities I have described above, but which turned out to be not at all incompatible with the production and maintenance of the artifact metaphor. In time, I came to regard these practices as particular enactments of category change or, to use the phrase that suits the factory domain most closely, performances of denial.

Performances of Denial

Her voice trembling with outrage, a respondent described a videotape she had seen of a military experiment:

> There was an horrendous part of the movie where they took a pig that hadn't been anaesthetized, and they put him down on his side. They put a thing around his nose and they had him tied down so that he couldn't move – he could only flinch, couldn't move. And they covered him with something, like gasoline or something, it might have been something else. They took a blowtorch and kept it on his body, going up and down, up and down, for ages and ages, until he was burned through to the muscle. And this animal is awake. They do this over the whole pig's body. And it was coming up in bubbles. And I made myself watch every minute of it. I didn't turn my eyes or close my eyes. And the skin, it was just coming up in bubbles, bubbling like you would see tar bubble. And they stopped and let it cool down, and it was in pieces. It looked like lava that had broken in pieces. They took the pieces of the skin off.
>
> And what is he [the experimenter] thinking when he is doing that? He doesn't see the animal as alive, as feeling any pain. He doesn't, obviously – or, if he does, he's a monster.

I wondered why any military establishment would film such an experiment. The mystery grew, for as my fieldwork progressed I found out that most of the many videotaped, filmed, and photographed records of animals subjected to countless grim and tormenting interventions, utterly graphic and completely unambiguous (but generally hidden from the uninitiated and since appropriated and exposed to general public view by animal welfare and rights groups), are documented in minute detail by the researchers themselves. I looked further.

In another arena of the factory domain, in trophy hunting, a similar dynamic obtains. The hunter displays the outcome of the hunt – a set of antlers, a pelt, a tail, a head – in his home. Big-game hunters in contemporary North America belong to prestigious trophy-hunting and safari clubs where, as the Canadian Broadcasting Corporation television show *The Fifth Estate* reported in February 1987, the talk is about 'big guns, big game, and big bucks; it's a world in which men are measured by the size of their antlers.' Here hunters receive points for the 'quality' of the animals they 'bring down.' But most important for this discussion, the hunter gets to tell in loving detail the tale of the hunt, from initial outfitting to final mounting, a passion difficult to curb even when the hunt is illegal and the hunter risks discovery. Here is an interchange from the same program between a television interviewer and an American hunter who had been caught poaching big game in Canada.

> *Interviewer (to audience):* '[The subject] is a passionate and experienced hunter, and he has the trophies to prove it. But none is as magnificent as the illegal ram,which ranked twenty-first in the world. He registered it with the Foundation for North American Sheep and it was a shoe-in for that year's gold prize.'
> *Interviewer (to hunter):* 'Why wouldn't you just have brought that head back and put it on a wall in your house along with the others? And then no one would have been the wiser?'
> *Hunter:* 'This is what I intended to do. And you know, I would have most likely got away with it if that was what I would have done. It snowballed because of other people that did see it, and the notoriety that was caused because of it. They said, "Why don't you bring it here, show it to a few other people?" Well, now, suddenly your ego sticks out further than your head, and you forget about having taken it illegally, or you conveniently put it to the back of your mind.'

Ritvo reports that in the Victorian era big-game hunters 'reaped the spoils of the chase' twice over: once in the field killing their prey, and a second time on the book, lecture, and exhibition circuit back home.[53]

Filmed demonstrations of the meticulous maiming of animals used in research, or tales of how a wild animal was stalked, killed, skinned, and parts of its body removed for nailing on a wall, are *performances*. While participants may be unaware of their motivations, such performances have very particular aims. An important function of hunting clubs, for example, is to deconstruct the animal's living being through stories of the hunt itself, tales of how the animal being came to be the set of antlers above the fireplace. In Ritvo's description of Victorian big-game hunters, their stories provided 'a precise anatomical and ballistic analysis of how the kill was accomplished and a sentimentalized description of how the animal faced its demise ... [;] the animal was reduced to its component parts.' Scarry calls this the 'structure of unmaking.'[54] These performances display to the initiated not only the outcome, but a step-by-step process, of dismantling, disassembling, disarticulating. They demonstrate the unmaking of sentient being and the turning of living flesh into, first, a lump of manipulable flesh, and then into artifacts – tools, trophies, and those least tangible of artifacts, data. In interpreting the meaning of human torture Scarry states that the so-called 'interrogation' is not meant to elicit needed information, but to make visible the process by which the prisoner becomes mute: 'The prolonged interrogation ... graphically objectifies the step-by-step backward movement along the path by which language comes into being and which is here being reversed or uncreated or deconstructed.'[55] Performances of denial are not performances of gross demolition or heedless destruction but of *structured* de-construction, the systematic deconstruction of sentient tissue. With respect to other animals, the aim is to prove that it was an artifact all along and not a sentient being at all. As if in reply to my informant's anguished question, 'And what is he thinking when he is doing that? He doesn't see the animal as alive, as feeling any pain. He doesn't, obviously ...,' Scarry says, referring to the torturer of humans: 'It is not merely that his power makes him blind, nor that his power is accompanied by blindness, nor even that his power requires blindness; it is, instead, quite simply that his blindness, his willed amorality, *is* his power.'[56]

It may seem unlikely, but the not-uncommon practice in research laboratories of selecting an animal from among its conspecifics and keeping it as a pet acts, I would suggest, as another variant of the same impulse. As one instance, British biologist Lynda Birke relates the fate of a laboratory rat of her acquaintance whose incisors were growing in crooked, leaving it unable to feed itself properly. For this reason this rodent got noticed as an individual, unlike the rest of the research rats. The staff took to trimming its teeth on a regular basis, and eventually this animal became the laboratory pet, saved thus from the destiny suffered by its more orthodontically endowed fellows.[57] Even this benign practice can be read as a performance of denial: keeping a couple of animals as pets in a lab that conducts animal experiments does not change human relations with the rest of the rat population, it simply drives home by contrast the non-pet, object, artifactual status of the other, less fortunate, creatures.

Thus, the performance, and its reiteration on film, in story, or in routinized caring practices toward a few individuals to the exclusion of the rest, are reminders and reinforcers that the animals in this context are not what they seem to be but what they are *categorized* to be: in this case, things.

In less injurious fashion but in a similar vein, kennel clubs, animal shows, and obedience trials are showcases of deconstruction. What is displayed in these settings is the assumed deconstruction and reconstitution of an animal's innate patterns of form and behaviour. These are lengthy, ritualized performances by the initiated for the initiated, demonstrating to each other the skills and steps by which an animal's very structure and its inborn behavioural repertoire can be broken down and remoulded to human specification.

These performances are meant for the initiated. Performances of denial are rituals that act as a booster shot, a reminder-sign to the initiated that the animal is indeed an artifact, thus making the metaphor real, keeping the world in its proper order. Periodically enacted in this way, the metaphor, in Scarry's words, 'helps bring about the process of perception in which all [sentient] reality is made, no matter how screamingly present, invisible, inaudible.'[58]

As noted before, most people must learn that sentient beings can be thought of and treated like inert objects. In Western capitalist culture the apotheosis of the market – 'all the world a market,' as Kovel puts it – has privileged that learning over the prior sentiment of 'all the world a world of living beings.' Yet the later learning, with its associated artifact metaphor, appears not to be completely stable. Sometimes a shred of totemic imagination may inadvertently obtrude, a fleeting sense of connection with the animals – either in its disguised metaphoric form as animal-as-kin, or perhaps in rare flashes of unmediated understanding of our shared animality. In circumstances such as these it seems to be necessary to reiterate the cultural construct periodically through these performances. In the end the made thing turns back and makes its makers: '[T]he act of human creating includes both the creating of the object and the object's recreating of the human being.'[59] It appears, then, that from time to time the animal-as-artifact metaphor, as a metaphor to live by, must get reinforced through that group of disparate practices that re-enact and re-institute category change: performances of denial.

PRODUCTION, PRIVACY, AND SECRECY

So far we have looked at ways in which two significant patterns of human–animal relations are maintained in Western, largely urban, cultural life: one through treating pet animals as if they were members of the family and reproducing these relations in the unconsidered daily round of domestic life, the other through manufacturing animal-artifacts in a planned, rationalized, efficiency-centred, and profit-oriented work environment. While the last chapter was concerned with describing how the animalness of domesticated animals (all domesticated animals, including human beings) becomes muted to serve one metaphor to live by, this chapter has been about how, in order to serve another metaphor, the very sentience of animals (in some circumstances, human animals as well) is made to become inaudible, invisible, and irrelevant.

The factory domain – the workplace and the marketplace – has ideologically been considered the very model of the public domain, the place of 'getting and spending' theoretically open to all. In fact, it is a domain that has become progressively privatized. Nowhere is this more evident than in the trades that deal in some way with animals.[60] Access to modern animal research laboratories has always been difficult for ordinary people; now, this is becoming increasingly the case with large-scale farming operations. As doxa – the only conceivable way – flourishes in the privacy of the domestic sphere, so orthodoxy – the best possible way – must prevail in the privatized world of the factory domain. Secrecy and privacy appear to be essential to the maintenance of order in this realm. It is for this reason that much of this discussion refers to the 'initiated' – people who have learned and have accepted, however precariously, to live by the metaphor 'an animal is an artifact,' and conduct their business and thus some parts of their daily lives behind the high walls of metonymic orthodoxy.

If the uninitiated, those who have not learned to live by this metaphor (but who are nonetheless consumers of the products that animals-as-artifacts become), are inadvertently exposed to its real practices and performances, they often react with revulsion and outrage. Australian philosopher and animal-rights activist Peter Singer relates the following story. Through an oversight, the American public learned in 1973 that the United States Air Force was looking for several hundred beagle puppies, 'with vocal cords tied to prevent normal barking,' to test the effects of poison gases and other similar noxious agents. This inadvertent leak to the public, Singer tells us, engendered more mail for the United States Department of Defense than any other single event, even surpassing the mail on the bombings of North Vietnam and Cambodia.[61]

With the failure of secrecy and privacy to maintain separate category boundaries, people sometimes simply refuse to think about the discrepancies. I did this, for example, when I entered a pet store and was faced with life in such a variety of forms, yet all reduced to commodities ('and I did not spend much time engaged in this sort of thinking'). But sometimes, for some people, such boundary failures constitute the most profound failure of coherence, of meaning, of order. In the next chapter we look at the efforts of such people to regain or refashion coherence in the relations between humans and animals. We explore the metaphors they seek to live by in trying to change prevailing human–animal relations in Western society: their efforts to reorder the natural world.

Chapter Five

Reordering the Natural World: The Civic Domain and the Invention of History

It is in human nature to make history.
Joel Kovel (1981)

... the body, the locus of pain and the voice, the locus of power.
Elaine Scarry (1985)

ORDER AND ACTIVISM

In a newspaper interview animal-rights activist Ingrid Newkirk, of the Washington-based organization People for the Ethical Treatment of Animals (PETA), remarked that as members of Western society, '[t]he two halves of our brains are not connected.' We wonder at the beauty and integrity of wildlife, she noted, we love our pets, and yet we raise animals for food, slaughter them, and experiment on them under often horrific conditions – sometimes the very same species that we love and admire. Causing untold unnecessary suffering, she concluded, we ourselves suffer from 'ethical epilepsy.'[1]

We have seen that the prevailing order in human–animal relations in the urban West must be continually bolstered through a variety of mechanisms. The aim of these mechanisms is to obscure contradictory practices by ensuring the strict separation of domestic and factory domains (a division already inherent in the structure of advanced capitalist culture), fostering learned ignorance in its several guises, and supporting privacy, secrecy, and other compromise mechanisms such as the distortion, muting, or removal of voice. Yet, despite these efforts at maintaining order, any notion of genuine coherence in human–

animal relations dissolves even on superficial examination. To elaborate on Newkirk's diagnostic analogy, the interspecies order the West has manufactured and lives by is unsound – infirm, fitful, precarious, estranged. *Dis-order* – category confusion – is only a thin cognitive-ideological boundary away. And from time to time, as in the accidental leakage of the U.S. Army's search for muted beagle puppies to experiment on, that thin membrane is breached.

For some people such a breach constitutes a decisive rupture, a turning point. The spell of learned ignorance is broken, and the suddenly clear contradictions between categories are so flagrant they threaten chaos. When people find that they can no longer rely on their doxic systems to keep meaning intact, when they can no longer use these systems to determine what is real and what is not, what is right and what is not, the confusion is too momentous to ignore. These individuals, often to their own surprise, turn to the public domain to raise newfound voices in protest. They become social activists.

Animal-Rights Activism

'The most important thing that we have to accomplish,' said Canadian environmental activist Paul Watson in a 1987 speech at a public meeting of the Toronto-based group Action Volunteers for Animals, or AVA, 'is to work towards rights ordained under law for nonhumans.'[2] The main goal of animal-rights activists is to secure rights for animals in the legal system and to see them practised routinely. The idea of protecting animals under law has a history of close to two centuries in the West, with animal-welfare and antivivisection groups active and vocal, and attended to with waxing or waning public interest, ever since. For the most part, the anti-cruelty movement rested on the presupposition that animals should be protected whenever their interests did not conflict with those of human beings. Avowed antivivisectionists were against the use of animals in experimentation under any conditions. In its modern guise animal-rights activism sees its aims as more far-reaching and radical than in the past: nothing less than the establishment of a new order of relations between humans and other animals.[3]

The cause of animal rights gained immense vigour in 1975 when Australian philosopher Peter Singer articulated many of the ethical dilemmas in contemporary human–animal relations in his book *Animal Liberation*. A passionate, cogently argued, data-laden but accessible work, it was immediately adopted internationally as the manifesto of the animal-rights movement. The gist of his and other investigations into existing human–animal relations is, in the words of British animal-welfare activist Judith Hampson, a call for 'a new moral agenda whereby animals are acknowledged as legitimate objects of moral concern, and accorded concomitant legal rights.' Whether the sphere of human ethical concern can, in practice, be expanded to accommodate nonhuman species remains an open question to observers and animal-rights activists alike: '[It] is a question,' says Hampson, 'for society as a whole to answer.'[4]

In the last two chapters I traced some ways of making real what has already been made up – in the domestic domain, the animal-as-human-kin; in the factory domain, the animal-as-artifact for human use. This chapter traces the more conscious construction of a new metaphor appropriate to the particular tasks these social activists have set for themselves: the restoration of being – sentience, subjectivity, the inviolacy of a valued life – to animal-artifacts and, ultimately, the restoration of order to the contradictory relations of humans with other animals and the rest of the natural world. This chapter also looks at how the animal-rights movement taps into 'the voice and other loci of power,' to paraphrase Scarry, in order to realize its project – how it makes up and makes real the metaphor *animal-as-citizen*.

CITIZENSHIP AND THE CIVIC DOMAIN

The ranks of animal-rights activists are filled with people who have been able neither to ignore nor to reconcile themselves to the categorical disjunction in human–animal relations traced in these pages. For such people, as noted above, the contradictions between human relations with animals as kin and their relations with animals as objects threaten everyday order with intolerable chaos. The failure in meaning, in rightness, inherent in treating animals as if they were artifacts is felt keenly and often, irreversibly in their personal lives. One activist described it this way: At the age of fourteen I became a vegetarian as a result of seeing a TV program about slaughtering chickens for Christmas, and I couldn't believe that they actually killed those things to eat them – I hadn't put the meat together with the living being. And once I realized that, I became a sort of *passive* activist, I suppose. It was on a very personal level, in that I refused to wear leather or anything – anything I knew was of animal origin I tried to avoid.' The response of individuals who go on to become activists is the decisive move from the personal sphere to the public domain, as my informant went on to illustrate: 'After several years I realized I wanted to be much more of an activist than I had been. Joined Action Volunteers for Animals. Became very involved, especially in the anti-fur movement. Studied literature, that sort of thing. Stood outside department stores and furriers' outlets in "skin-and-bones" every Saturday for about four years ... Now I can't turn it off. Once your eyes are opened you simply can't turn away.'

Bourdieu agrees that the move from the personal and private to the shared and public domain is a pivotal step: '"Private" experiences,' he says, 'undergo nothing less than a *change of state* when they recognize themselves in the *public objectivity* of an already constituted discourse, the objective sign of recognition of their right to be spoken and to be spoken publicly.'[5] To step knowingly (and there is no other way of entering this particular field of being) into the contemporary public domain of voice, rhetoric, politics, and power – into the civic domain – is to encounter and to engage in nothing less than a struggle over the culture itself.

The Civic Domain

Readers will be familiar by now with the next question, posed before in different ways, which must continue to be asked from both an anthropological and a practical perspective: What is there about a particular social-cultural-historical context that seems to call for one organizing metaphor over another? In other words, what is there about the various domains we have been investigating that summons up different meaningful models for the arrangement of human–animal relations in each? If, as in this discussion, we are examining the context as a nexus of relations between the mind at work and the world in which it works, then it is an artificial exercise to speak of the effect of cognitive practice on context without at the same time referring to its obverse. Thus, I have argued that the domestic domain in the urban West is a last, limited refuge for the legitimate expression of affiliation with other life forms, as long as these life forms are characterized as human kin; and that the factory domain has been structured like a great machine made up of coordinated metonymous parts, with no tolerance – no 'give' – within its precincts for anything that cannot be used as raw material; anything, breathing or not, that cannot be manipulated, altered, used, or sold.

What, in turn, can we say about the effects of the civic domain on the animal-rights activists' project? Given the ends of activists – to save animals from perceived needless pain, suffering, and death at the hands of humans – and given the means they have chosen to achieve these ends – a resolve to enter and engage in the political orbit – what would be an 'appropriate' metaphor for animal-rights activists to live by in this domain? To answer these questions, we need to examine the civic domain more closely.

As a life field, the civic domain as I define it is above all a political realm: it is that sphere of cultural life where people are continually negotiating relations of power in public. In Canada, the United States, and western Europe, as well as in other parts of the world, the form these negotiations take – the arrangements of power, authority, influence, and dissent – are ideologically rendered and formally structured as 'representative democracy.'[6] Such a structure holds dear among its central tenets notions of heterodoxy and concomitant rights to argument and free speech, citizenship and the rule of law, the free election of representatives, and the legitimacy of the few representing the many. Rule-bound opportunities to contest law, such as advocating and lobbying for 'rights,' however defined, and the gathering together of people into the alternative politics of social movements are now staples of this apparatus.[7]

The Realm of the Citizen as Person

The civic domain is the sphere in which the nodal political concept of 'citizenship' is enacted. It is a concept inextricably bound up with the principles and practices of an individualistic politics. A citizen is defined in individual terms and as a particular kind of person, that is, a 'person before the law,' a 'legal person,' or a 'person with juridical rights.'[8] Besides conferring legitimacy on the individual before the law, citizenship also makes the individual eligible to participate in the forms of political action, either directly or through representation. As we know, legal 'persons' need not necessarily be human beings: corporations and ships have also been designated persons in Western jurisprudence; and not all human beings are judicially considered persons. Battles continue to be fought to obtain 'personhood' for different categories of people, for, as Raymond Williams reminds us, '[t]here is some significant history in the various attempts to limit "the people" to certain qualified groups: freemen, owners of property, the wise, white men, men, and so on.'[9] To an important degree the lessons learned from this history – a history comprising often volatile episodes of the bestowal, contestation, divestment, and seizure of personhood – fuel the animal activists in their search for animal rights in law. History reveals what a fragile and arbitrary thing franchise is generally, and if it is so arbitrary, merely an invented condition, there is little reason to dismiss the idea of franchise for animals.

The Realm of Voice

The civic domain is also, and quintessentially, the domain of voice, of speech, and of the word; the primary venue in Western culture for the practice of articulate persuasion or opposition. Stemming from the ideals of free speech and of the validity of the few lending their culturally legitimized voice to represent the plight of the culturally voiceless many, the civic domain recognizes with Scarry that the voice is the locus of power. Thus, its principal instruments are instruments of language: oratory, rhetoric, debate, and the various media of communication. As Scarry argues, to be able to represent an issue *verbally* is crucial to the degree to which it will be represented *politically*.[10]

The Realm of Historicity

In certain respects today's civic domain is a keenly self-conscious domain with, some believe, a more finely tuned sense of history and possibility than in previous times. According to Touraine the modern era, particularly post–Second World War (and even more decidedly, we may add, the 'post-modern' era), is marked by an acute awareness of the invented nature of culture. The contemporary civic domain is the realm of *historicity*, as Touraine characterizes the self-invention of a society's history and culture. 'How,' he asks, 'is one to comprehend this work of society upon itself, this drama in which a history is being invented, the text of which has not been pre-determined?' Touraine provides a powerful analysis of contemporary social and cultural change as changed meaning. Increasingly, relations of power in the civic domain are not limited to politics or economics – in other words, authority and wealth simply changing class hands – but encompass the very direction of culture, that is, the negotiation of meaning and the construction of a shared reality. To Marcus and Fischer, in fact, 'the contesting of the meaning of things or events is what centrally constitutes politics.'[11] At present, Touraine believes, the principal agents of history, and thus of the invention of culture, are *social movements*. He sees modern social movements as fundamental struggles that people engage in to gain control of the cultural direction of a society through control of its meaning systems. The outcome of this struggle of competing definitions of reality will determine who will thenceforth, by imposing their own definitions and interpretations on events, create the cultural and thus also the historical direction of that society.[12]

Social Movements

Committed to changing Western society's mind and its manners vis-à-vis its traditional relations with nonhuman beings, animal-rights activists are acutely aware that they are involved in a complex process of culture change and the production of their own history. They also know that the radical change in human–animal relations they seek can only come about by engaging the entire society in the issue, and that to do this means to engage in the alternative politics of social movements.

Social movements are very much a part of the civic domain, springing up within the established social system itself. Anthropologists Luther Gerlach and Virginia Hine have defined a movement as 'a group of people who are organized for, ideologically motivated by, and committed to a purpose which implements some form of personal or social change, who are actively engaged in the recruitment of others, and whose influence is spreading in opposition to the established order within which it originated.'[13] According to the set of criteria suggested by Gerlach and Hine, animal-rights activism clearly constitutes a social movement: 1. The animal-rights movement comprises many heterogeneous, egalitarian, non-bureaucratized groups coming together into issue-based coalitions when needed. 2. Recruitment takes place through networks of personal relations. 3. Participants feel a deep personal commitment often amounting to a sense of changed identity. 4. A clearly articulated ideology states values and goals, provides a conceptual framework for motivating, directing, and interpreting practice, and unifying the otherwise autonomous groups, and defines the opposition. 5. Participants are, or perceive themselves to be, the targets of opposition from segments of the established order from which the movement has arisen.

Students of movements such as Touraine and Gerlach and Hine characterize them as *primary mechanisms* of social change in the civic domain. Both a cause and an effect of change, '[m]ovements are like tracer elements,' suggest Gerlach and Hine, 'coursing through a social system, illuminating its deficiencies and weaknesses. They serve to identify the points at which radical social change must, and will, take place.'[14]

Social movements have traditionally attracted people who perceive themselves to be relatively powerless in the midst of the formal machinery of the civic domain, or those who are looking for a more effective means to work on behalf of the powerless. Many people have come to view such movements as the *only* means of genuine political activity in the modern world, the one authentically democratic process in the civic domain, the one truly influential public forum in which ordinary people can participate.[15] Animal-rights activists, for example, see themselves not as experts but as part of society at large, that part which has decided – as ordinary citizens aware at some level of the inventedness of institutions – to engage in a participatory democratic process to change the status quo.

Social movements, Touraine declares, 'are not a marginal rejection of order, they are the central forces fighting one against the other to control the production of society ... [T]hey are an outward sign of the production of society by itself.' Modern movements are fundamental struggles between groups with competing definitions of reality to gain control of a culture's meaning-production, most particularly through its categories of thought. Competing with the established order for the legitimacy of their particular vision of the world, social movements derive much of their power, Bourdieu believes, from their capacity to 'objectify unformulated experiences, to make them public – a step on the road to officialization and legitimation.'[16] To be perceived and to perceive themselves as part of a larger movement rather than as fragmented and isolated fringe groups affords animal-rights activists an opportunity to press forward a powerful indigenous critique that, uncomfortable and threatening as it may be for the established order, is nonetheless less likely to be disregarded.

The ultimate hope of people who participate in social movements is to create a new doxa, or 'second nature'; in other words, to reorder the world so that it feels 'natural' to people to behave in certain new and desired ways. Social movements try to change people's worlds by changing their practice, to change practice by changing minds. Social theorist Ralf Dahrendorf has suggested that 'history proceeds by changing the subject rather than by progressing from one stage to the next.' Whether they are clearly aware of what they are doing or not, activists try to change the subject by changing the metaphors we live by. Within these movements, at least at the level of practical consciousness, it is well understood that, as Lakoff and Johnson put it, 'whether in national politics or in everyday interaction, people in power get to impose their metaphors.'[17] Indeed, *social movements are a major means by which a society's cultural models, the metaphors we live by, are renegotiated and redefined.*

Emphasizing that movements are engaged in a 'battle against social reproduction,'[18] Touraine captures a significant stimulus to the animal-rights movement. Animal-rights activists are engaged in a struggle to wrest cultural meaning and the future direction of society primarily from those established in and controlling the factory domain. Seeking to create a society that enlarges the sphere of ethical concern to include nonhuman animals, their most pressing aim is to disrupt and eliminate society's production of the organizing metaphor 'animals are artifacts.' Desiring above all to transmute animal-artifacts back into animal-beings, animal-rights activists need a metaphor to live by that will stand up to their radical agenda, one that will 'change the subject,' but not so completely as to cut off the discourse. For this purpose, the animal-rights movement has turned to 'citizenship' as a metaphor to live by.

MAKING UP THE CITIZENSHIP METAPHOR

As noted earlier, in the doxic and orthodoxic worlds of family and factory, metaphoric cognitive practice serves to reproduce or to manufacture – to make and keep 'real' – an interspecies relation that was 'made up' long ago. In the contemporary world of the animal-rights movement, the activists' project entails the double process of making up *and* making real a different interspecies relation. The task is to put into words, and especially into practice, a compelling new organizing metaphor, one that the society as a whole would wish to live by. Choosing the 'right' metaphor to suit the task is pivotal because the right metaphor both implies and sets the ground for the 'right relation' between humans and other animals. The act of choosing – whether rationally or, perhaps more often, intuitively – is central to the whole enterprise of social movements: activists must select metaphors that can, in Nietzsche's words, 'enter history.'

Exemplified by the British animal-rights movement's campaign to 'put animals into politics,'[19] the citizenship metaphor, while not directly named as such, has been adopted by animal activists the world over – with no evidence of debate or dissension – as the 'right' metaphor to suit the task. A Canadian activist put it this way: 'We recognized there was a very strong animal love sentiment in Canada, but not an animal *rights* movement. We needed a very vocal, *political* voice for the animals.' What, then, makes the citizenship metaphor seem so right for the movement's aims?

The more the chosen metaphor can imply sentience, subjectivity, and selfhood, the more useful it is for the project of battling against the social reproduction of animal-artifacts and of reinstating animals as living beings. By refocusing attention on certain features other animals share with human beings, with particular attention to those animals caught in the machinery of the factory domain, the citizenship metaphor, at least in imagination, serves to remove the animal from the realm of inert and valueless thing and to place it in the realm of culture and human concerns. By definition, citizenship accords 'personhood' to a being, thereby cancelling out its 'thingness.' When an animal is revitalized, perceived once again as an individual, a subject, and a sentient being, it becomes more difficult thereafter to use it blindly as a mere object in a class of objects, as a fully automated 'factory,' or as an instrument.[20]

Kinship to Citizenship: Metaphoric Entailment

The animal-as-citizen metaphor was not invented out of whole cloth; it takes much of its power from the fact that it is an extension of another deeply embedded metaphor we live by. We have observed that the primary metaphor organizing human–animal relations in the domestic domain, animal-as-human-kin, is a specific case of the more general animal-as-human-being. The emergence of the animal as citizen is really the unfolding of another *entailment* of this more general metaphor. Philosopher Mark Johnson explains a metaphoric entailment in the following terms. In any metaphorical projection, only part of the structure of the source-domain is typically projected onto the target-domain; this is the 'used portion' of the metaphor. One may extend a metaphor by drawing on the unused portions. This renders the new metaphor comprehensible and at least partially assimilable since some of the old meaning is enfolded into the new. Different entailments permit us to concentrate on some aspects and to mask others that appear to be irrelevant or even contradictory to the purpose under consideration in the particular instance.[21]

With each entailment of animal-as-human-being, different discourses and practices are considered suitable. In the domestic domain where we treat animals as young, dependent family members, the parts of the concept 'human being' that are highlighted include some that we investigated earlier: individuality and subjectivity, socialization, the place in the family, the need to care and be cared for, communication, nurturance, and so on. In the move from the domestic to the civic domain some aspects of an animal's 'humanness' that have been emphasized to accord with its potential for citizenship include the 'unacceptability' of its current status as the victim of other humans and of human practices, its voicelessness and lack of representation, its lost subjectivity, its right to 'rights,' and the legitimacy of lobbying and advocating on its behalf through the medium of social movements. (Activist Ingrid Newkirk has remarked, 'If you look back through history, the similarities between the anti-slavery movement and what is essentially *this* anti-slavery movement are absolutely stunning.')[22] Many entailments in the kinship and citizenship metaphors – for instance, the animal as being, as subject, and as valued – overlap, thus reinforcing the coherence between metaphors. With respect to metaphors people live by, coherence is not registered merely in language or thought; it is a complex network of metaphoric entailments that extends to action and emotion as well. It is this entangled network of coherences that makes the animal-as-citizen metaphor so markedly powerful and compelling.

Habitus

Another key reason for the exigency of citizenship as an organizing metaphor is the embeddedness of this idea in contemporary Western habitus. The citizenship concept is a deeply significant part of Western habitus, learned early, and emotionally highly salient both as an ideal and as a way of ordering the world. It is a concept that people are periodically called upon, and are sometimes willing, to die for. It is also part of the habitus of *all* members of this society, even those who daily render animals into artifacts. The idea of citizenship is in the realm of the thinkable, not to say valued, even to the movement's avowed opponents, since it is part of their habitus as well. It might almost seem 'inevitable,' then, in the doxic sense of tradition-made-nature, at the very least to consider this concept as an appropriate metaphor for changing human–animal relations. Thus, because 'citizenship' is so deeply embedded in Western habitus, the entire society has been preconditioned to perceive it as at least a conceivable – if not quite a legitimate or motivating – metaphor to live by.

Once actually appropriated as a metaphor to organize cultural practices, this familiar and valued mode of ordering the world is applied metaphorically to a completely new sphere, the realm of interspecies relations. In this latter realm, the citizenship metaphor is meant to act as a guide for a new, reordered set of relations between humankind and other species. But it is a set of relations that, still in the process of being made up, cannot yet be said to be part of the habitus of Western culture. This is to say that the animal-as-citizen metaphor is not yet, as Clifford Geertz might put it, a 'model-of' interspecies behaviour; it is still a 'model-for.'[23] But, unlike many metaphors, the source-domain of this metaphor rests securely in the habitus of the people; much of its potency thus stems from its immanence in the contemporary ethos of the entire population.

Since an organizing metaphor is not just a way of viewing the world but also a template for action, the true test of a metaphor-to-live-by-in-the-making is whether the society can function successfully in terms of it. Is it functional in practice? Does it change practice?

REORDERING THE NATURAL WORLD:
THE INVENTION OF HISTORY

In 1987 I accompanied a coalition of animal-rights activists on a protest march to the site of a commercial laboratory that had allegedly been conducting toxicity tests on rabbits and other animals. Among the tests being disputed were the Draize Test, which uses the delicate eye membranes of living rabbits to research the irritancy levels of various commercial substances, and the LD-50 Test ('LD' signifying 'lethal dose'), which calculates the dosage at which any substance will kill 50 per cent of the animal sample being subjected to it. The demonstrators hoisted posters and placards on the street, displaying blown-up photographs of animals in test situations. Some showed rows of rabbits immobilized in restraints, with ulcerated eyes oozing pus. Others displayed rabbits and other animals in too-small cages with gaping wounds, festering abscesses, and necrotic tissue sloughing from various parts of their bodies. My field notes barely convey my revulsion: 'Dreadful pictures of mutilated animals,' I wrote. 'Something especially awful about the eyes.'[24]

An episode of 'street theatre' followed the arrival of television cameras and other media. In this performance activists in costume enacted the capture and immobilization of rabbits in stocks, the administration of toxic substances by researchers in lab coats, and the subsequent 'liberation' of the animals by masked intruders in black balaclavas. The performance was, unexpectedly, affecting. The audience of protesters, media people, and onlookers remarked later how eerily 'animal-like,' yet how recognizable, were the cries of the performers impersonating the animals.

As this protest march illustrates, one of the most important entry points for reordering the human–animal world is through the shared experience of *pain*. This is perhaps surprising because, while there is nothing more radically real to an individual than intense pain, there is nothing less readily describable to another. 'Physical pain does not simply resist language but actively destroys it, bringing about an immediate reversion to a state anterior to language, to the sounds and cries a human being makes before language is heard,' writes Scarry.[25] As the activists demonstrated in their street theatre, it is precisely this wordless quality that forces us to acknowledge that in intense pain, human and other animal cries *sound alike*. The sounds an animal in torment makes, especially another mammal, are so completely familiar, so close to self-sounds, so utterly evocative of the personal experience of suffering, that only the consistently reinforced overlay of the artifact metaphor through performances of denial or cutting the vocal cords entirely can mute them sufficiently for people to continue to manipulate animals as things.[26] Thus, if nowhere else, it is in pain beyond the bounds of language that the common experience of human beings and other animals must at last be conceded. It is through the shared vehicle of pain that the reordering process can begin to take place.[27]

Disordering

'Words *wreak havoc*,' says Sartre, 'when they find a name for what had up to then been lived namelessly.'[28] In uncovering and publicizing the pain of animals in the factory domain, moving the reality of pain from private cry to public outcry, animal-rights activists sow revulsion and confusion, introducing havoc and disorder into the lives and consciousness of 'just plain folks.' *This disordering is deliberate.* If, as Touraine suggests, social movements must gain control of a culture's meaning systems and its meaning-production to achieve their ends, they must somehow disrupt and discredit the prevailing cultural currencies. The introduction of disorder is a way of rendering permeable hitherto encapsulated givens and loosening the boundaries of established practices, an important step in the task of reordering the natural world. The creation and management of disorder are among the most critical yet most often overlooked aspects of culture change. Disorder announces that patience with the old order has run out, that there is a need for change, and that henceforward the rhetoric of change will be allied to practice. Apprehension over activism stems precisely from the fear of disorder – fear of the radical, the unpredictable, the 'unsocialized,' the loosing of the 'wild' beyond the pale of culture. Among the many ways to create disorder, the following are three rather dramatic ones garnered from my field research: the demolition of order, its subversion, and rituals of disorder.

The Demolition of Order

Activists I interviewed alluded to instances of 'direct action' that had taken place or were being planned. This worldwide initiative ranged from interference with seal hunts, wolf kills, and traplines in Canada, through sabotage of foxhunts in Great Britain, and, farther afield, to disruption of the kangaroo hunt in Australia and of drift-net fishing operations in the North Pacific. Other 'direct actions' included the vandalism of research laboratories, meat-packing plants, and fast-food outlets. An example cited was a 'Meat Is Murder!' graffito spray-painted in enormous black letters on the outside wall of a Toronto fried-chicken franchise. Virtually all the activists I interviewed were adamant that their aims and tactics did not and should not include hurting other people.

Among the heroes of the animal-rights movement is Paul Watson, a Canadian environmental activist who directed the demolition of an Icelandic whale-processing plant and the sinking of illegally operating whaling vessels in 1986. Here is one newspaper account Watson gave of those exploits: 'Trashing Iceland's whaling facilities was easy ... All it took were sledgehammers and monkey wrenches ... We destroyed everything – six diesel engines, computer panels, flaying knives and equipment ... log books. The sea valves were opened, the engine rooms flooded; and the two ships are on the bottom now.' Pointing out that a cardinal rule of his Sea Shepherd Society was never to risk injuring anyone and that a third ship with sleeping watchmen on board had been cut loose to drift safely in the harbour, Watson said the damage done did not bother him: 'There seems to be a lot of respect for private property, but there doesn't seem to be much for the lives of the whales.'[29] On another occasion he discussed a plan to interfere with drift-net fishing operations in the North Pacific off the coast of Alaska, which in addition to the intended catch kills millions of marine birds, mammals, and other fauna caught 'incidentally' in these miles-long 'curtains of death.' 'Each of those nets is worth about a million dollars. We intend to destroy them, hoping to provoke a confrontation with the Japanese, the Taiwanese, and the Koreans which will blow this issue into a proportion where world governments would be forced to act upon it.'[30] While this plan of destruction is presented as part of a larger and well-reasoned strategy, one detects in Watson and in members of his audience more than a trace of zest in the act of destruction itself. Touraine proposes that 'in every social struggle there is also present an element of protest against society, an aggressiveness towards people and property, a longing – as a student we worked with in Amiens expressed it – to "bust up the works." '[31]

The Subversion of Order

Some animal-rights activists practise yet another form of sowing disorder and confusion into the doxic universe of human–animal relations. This is the more careful and deliberate conceptual dismantling of the animal-as-artifact metaphor through systematically undermining beliefs about the 'good' that animal 'goods' are thought to render to humans. For example, some critics of medical research grounded in animal models base their major arguments not on the rights of animals nor on their distress, but on the uselessness and potential harm to humankind of relying on animal models, highlighting the thalidomide tragedy and other research disasters. Animal research, critics assert, actually delays advances in human medicine because it wastes resources gathering data that cannot be applied to humans. One prominent American critic of traditional medical research, Dr Robert Mendelson, interviewed on a Canadian radio broadcast in 1987, insisted that the real question is, 'Why should the research be done in the first place if it's not good? If it gives you misleading results? If your baby is more likely to be damaged as a result of trying to extrapolate from research studies [on animals] than to be helped?' Vicki Miller, a noted Canadian animal-rights activist based in Toronto, called the medical research industry 'the disease agencies that prey on the fear of the public, their fear of death and disease.'[32]

Vegetarian activists often take a similar tack. In 1990 singer k.d. lang, raised in the heart of Canadian cattle country, launched a public-relations campaign with the slogan 'Meat Stinks.' Others furnish detailed evidence that animals raised for food under intensive farming conditions are in reality 'walking drugstores,' as social critic Mike Schwab termed them. In a public speech he claimed that

> because of factory farming, because of the crowded conditions, the unhealthy conditions, they're using more antibiotics today. Things like penicillin, streptomycin, tetracycline, neomycin, and the list goes on. Over five hundred chemicals and medicines are used in animals. And if that doesn't seem like much, one half of the production in North America of all the drugs goes into animals. That's including everything in the hospitals, everything on your drugstore shelf. One half of that is going into the production of meat for the table ... And the reason for that is because these animals become very diseased.[33]

Together these arguments against the use of animals rest on the subversion of tacit understandings – that animal research and animal husbandry are beneficial for humankind. They are thus *arguments of disorder*, for they systematically unravel the fundamental argument on which the animal-as-artifact-for-human-use metaphor is based.[34]

Rituals of Disorder
Animal-rights activists are acutely aware that while disorder is necessary, it must be managed. Sometimes this disorder is managed through what might be called 'rituals of disorder.' Bourdieu claims that '[r]itual practice ... always aims to facilitate passages and/or to authorize encounters between opposed orders.'[35] Like all ritual, rituals of disorder give shape, structure, and significance to changing conditions and thus, paradoxically, minimize chaos.

At a meeting I attended of Action Volunteers for Animals, ARK II, and other groups planning the demonstration described earlier, the discussion revealed just how seasoned in the arts of ritual management these activists were. In planning the street-theatre episode, group members focused on the symbolism of black balaclavas, which, they said, had become associated in the public mind with the Animal Liberation Front, a radical group that engages in self-styled 'lab terrorism.' Do the balaclavas have an unnecessarily oppressive connotation? asked some members. After a lengthy and sometimes heated debate, the final decision was that black balaclavas, having come to symbolize disorder, made the statement the coalition wanted; it was this message of the balaclavas, carefully stage-managed through the ritual of street theatre, they sought to convey.[36]

Civil disobedience is a recognized ritual of disorder used by social movements at least since Mohandas Gandhi's time. It depends for its effect on creating a disturbance by disrupting the routines of the people whose attention it seeks. One activist ruefully described the lengths to which her group had to go to create an event out of what threatened to become a non-event. Dressed in animal costumes, the activists descended on a hotel where an association of scientists who specialized in training and research with laboratory animals was meeting. Although the protesters attempted to disrupt the convention by sitting in on meetings in their costumes, blocking doorways with their bodies, and singing protest songs, the ploy did not seem to be working. 'It was quite amusing really, because they [the hotel staff] didn't want to arrest us,' said my respondent. 'They just wanted to leave us. So eventually we had one of our own members go to the phone, pretending to be a hotel employee, and crying that we were "really messing up their day," and would they please get us out of here.' (According to my informant, some of the research scientists who were climbing over the protesters' bodies to leave the building managed covertly to 'get in a few really good kicks.')

Rituals of disorder thus communicate an interruption in meaning systems. Since the ultimate aim of the movement is to appropriate the means of meaning production and substitute metaphors of their own invention, the introduction of disorder and the ritual shake-up of the old meaning systems signal the beginning of reordering.

Reordering

Animal-rights activists are engaged in reordering the natural world – that is, human–animal relations – mainly through promoting and enacting aspects of the citizenship metaphor. Citizenship being above all the recognition of an entity as a person under law, many of the movement's activities centre on creating persons. This includes re-vitalizing animal-artifacts, returning their voices, and linking the struggle for animal rights to similar struggles in human history. Another crucial aspect of the struggle of some of these activists is the conscious reshaping of their own habitus and embodying in their everyday practice a changed relation to other animals.

Creating the Person

Animal-rights activists are never far from a profound awareness that their project entails the re-creation of living beings from animal-artifacts. To prepare animals (in the human mind) for citizenship and personhood, and thus to qualify them for rights under law, it is necessary first to rescue them perceptually from their categorization as things and reinstate them as sensate and sentient beings. They need to be revived and re-innervated, endowed with flesh and nerves and feelings, to be considered doxically as 'experiencing subjects of a life,' as philosopher Tom Regan puts it. And this, as we saw before, is most actively pursued by portraying, in image and in sound, their pain. Through the imagery and theatre of public demonstrations, videotapes smuggled from factory-domain settings, photographs and graphic reports distributed in newsletters and magazines, vivid rhetoric and impassioned oratory – through 'the voice and the eye'[37] – activists engage in an unceasing campaign to remind us of the creatureliness these animals share with human beings.

Compassion and shrewdness in equal measure fuelled the campaign strategies I was able to study. Never far from the participants' consciousness was a calculation of the potential impact a particular action would be likely to have on public hearts and minds. For example, lengthy debate at one meeting focused on the plight of animals transported to slaughterhouses. Animals ready for the meat-packing plant are often loaded onto vehicles and transported long distances, sometimes for days on end, without food or water. A number die en route. Once herded into the slaughterhouses they are still not fed or watered, even though they may wait for several days before being butchered. The participants at this meeting discussed the ethics of going to slaughterhouses to feed and water animals destined for imminent death, astutely gauging all the while the impact of portraying such a hopeless task in the media. Said one person: 'I think activists, dedicated people, quietly going in to slaughterhouses and feeding animals, I think that has more of an impact. If we feed and water an animal, and show that it has a need for food and water just like you and me, it seems to me that people reading about that in the paper, they would be turned off meat.'

To further prepare the human mind for animals-as-citizens, another useful tactic is to minimize their species-character and to stress their subjectivity and individuality, for the citizenship concept is based on recognition of and value for the individual. The 'Debbie Campaign,' founded on the potency of renaming, is a good example of how the animal-artifact may be shattered and the animal-as-person recreated. In 1984 Canadian activists heard that a baboon, known as specimen number B43, was being subjected to painful experiments in a scientific laboratory at the University of Western Ontario. They understood the baboon to be part of a cholesterol experiment that kept it confined to a restraining chair, it was said, for weeks on end. Animal militants broke into the lab and took pictures, and activist Vicki Miller led a hunger strike to free the baboon.[38] In the activists' renaming the animal 'Debbie,' a number of things were accomplished. Debbie became a subject rather than a specimen; her individuality and uniqueness, including her unique suffering, were emphasized over her species-character; and, bearing a personal name shared by humans, she was more readily gathered into the sphere of human culture and human care.

Returning the Voice

The right to free speech and the right to speak out on behalf of others are both basic to the traditional machinery of Western representative democracy. It is not a great leap, therefore, to consider it logical to speak out on behalf of animals. 'Who else will speak out for them?' ask animal-rights activists.

They speak out in two critical ways. First, by scaling the walls (sometimes literally) of the factory domain's orthodoxy, they return the anguished voice to muted animals by revealing and publicizing the sounds and sights of creatures being mutilated routinely in the course of human enterprise. To do so they rely unapologetically on impassioned oratory, on appeals to emotion, on a rhetoric and an iconography of suffering. '[A]nd thus,' as Scarry notes with reference to human suffering, 'there come to be avenues by which this most radically private of experiences [pain] begins to enter the realm of public discourse.'[39]

Second, and equally important, animal-rights activists provide a 'reasoned' voice to describe and oppose the condition and fate of animals-as-artifacts. In this mode activists rely primarily on logical argumentation, both philosophic and scientistic, and on the marshalling of mountains of diverse, and usually highly accurate, data. Among the most sought-after spokespersons within the animal-rights movement are people with a legitimate 'expert' or 'scientific' persona, for such people confer legitimacy on 'the cause' not only for the general public but also for those who are part of the movement itself. Having been raised in the Cartesian West, activists must count within their own habitus a deep if not always conscious susceptibility to respect 'observable fact.' It is quite likely that in the eyes of its highly educated following the animal-rights movement gained as much of its popularity and impetus from the reams of 'hard data' and lucidly argued opinion as it did from the appeals to sympathy and compassion. This 'desire for data' accounts in part for the extraordinary success of Peter Singer's book *Animal Liberation* – providing as it did such an extravagance of carefully documented information – in rallying many more people to the animal-rights movement in the 1970s than had ever participated before. The desire for scientific legitimacy also partly explains the jubilation activists felt when renowned primatologist Jane Goodall finally turned her attention to the plight of apes in research laboratories and unreservedly pronounced her opposition to their incarceration and treatment. 'She is going to be a scientific leader,' one of my activist respondents exulted. 'People who have been doing research are now going to be saying, "Well, if Jane Goodall says it ain't right, I'm not going to do it either!"'

In lending its voice to uncover contemporary conditions in the animal estate, the animal-rights movement has made masterful use of the communications media. Activists know, to paraphrase Scarry, that the ability to represent an issue *in the media* is crucial to the degree to which it will be politically represented. They would agree with Bourdieu when he says that 'any language that can command attention is an "authorized language."'[40] Most of the movement's tactics have the media in mind, especially television. The media are always contacted in advance of a public event such as a protest march, media kits are carefully prepared, and the protesters are primed in minute detail on their various roles. As if choreographed, experienced marchers seem to know immediately how to position themselves physically, massed together or spread out, as the video or photo 'opportunity' demands. Messages are succinct, tailored to a thirty-to-sixty-second time slot. The content is graphic, frequently simplified, and highly visible. Activists also dress for audience and occasion – suit and tie for him, pearls and fashionable shoes for her when representing the movement to establishment institutions; running shoes and jogging suits when 'just plain folks' are demonstrating out of a frustration born of 'plain human decency'; combat fatigues and other warlike insignia when a more militant message is seen to be needed. For giving voice to the animal condition, animal-rights activists are consummate manipulators of what is, in effect, their most familiar medium, that is, the everyday media of Western urban popular culture.

Creating History

'Physical pain,' Scarry has written, 'has no voice, but when it at last finds a voice, it begins to tell a story.'[41] Animal-rights activists have found yet another way to give voice to animals and allow animals to tell their story, and that is by enfolding them into human history. They do this through knitting together the struggles for animal rights with those waged for human rights. Discourse in the movement is regularly punctuated by linkages with human struggles for personhood and franchise – the anti-slavery movement, the civil-rights movement, the women's movement. We are reminded again and again that the noble pens that wrote so eloquently against slavery and the oppression of women in the eighteenth and nineteenth centuries spoke and wrote equally forcefully against cruelty to animals. We are told, for example, that the Toronto Humane Society, founded more than a century ago, was established to counter cruelty to all beings, with no distinctions being made at that time between humans, especially children, and animals.[42] The heroes that grace the movement's rhetoric are activists of the past with a moral sense capacious enough to house humans and animals equally. Animal-rights orators seek to create a history that centres not on animals as resources for human use but on the being-relationship between humans and other species. They tell a story in which animals figure not as species but as individuals, as persons. In this way, activists join the past and thus also the future of humans and animals. In doing so they grant animals a history, a story, another avenue by which their most muted of experiences can enter the realm of public discourse.[43]

Re-Inscribing the Human Body Schema

Reordering the natural world requires not only the reinstatement of animals as the 'experiencing subjects of a life,' but also a profound change in human beings. As Gerlach and Hine point out, true social change involves some degree of personal transformation on the part of individuals. They maintain that 'a successful movement is the point of intersection between personal and social change.' Indeed, as Kovel comments, the record of humanity's self-transformation is what history is all about.[44]

As mentioned elsewhere, Bourdieu proposes that culture inscribes the body schema of each individual with the time, place, and objective conditions of his or her birth – enculturates it, in short, into its particular habitus. As a result, each successfully socialized agent possesses a 'socially informed body.'[45] We may surmise that in the course of culture change, a process of *re*-inscribing the body schema must go on, consisting of some means of reshaping the habitus. This implies that *becoming* is a critical aspect of animal-rights activism, as of all social movements.

People truly committed to a movement and a new metaphor do appear to try to change their own lives first, testing their ideas out in their own practices, on their own bodies. The new metaphor is not an intellectual exercise, no matter how articulate its proponents; it is above all a discipline of the body. Activists are involved in what Giddens calls the 'transformation of the body into an instrument of acting-in-the-world.'[46] Culture change is the inculcation through practice (in both senses of the word) of altered tendencies to engage in and interpret the world. However, since, as Scarry notes, 'what is "remembered" in the body is well remembered,'[47] this revised practice is probably never totally successful in the sense of being 'second nature.' Residues of 'well-remembered' original embodied tendencies are probably always retained, and so activists find that they must continuously, consciously, self-consciously rededicate themselves to the discipline of a new practice. Some, of course, finding the regimen too stern, remove themselves. But without a commitment to a changed practice, there is no real culture change.

The activist's journey of becoming, of re-inscribing the body schema, is thus a lifelong discipline of re-educating the body and reshaping the original enculturated habits of habitus. Perhaps nothing illustrates this conjuncture of flesh and politics so poignantly or so intimately as the decision of some activists, as a gesture of conscience, as an act of protest, to become vegetarian. Here is what one woman, who does not consider herself to be an activist yet, said:

> I became a vegetarian about six or seven years ago. I suddenly thought –
> you see, if I thought that a cow was living on a farm and being raised to be
> eaten, that was always fine with me. But then I didn't realize *how* they were
> being killed and *how* they were being fed ... And then I was interested in
> going to see one of these animal rights movies. It was on factory farming.
> And it threw me for a loop ... What I saw about the factory farming was *hor-*

rendous ... And I don't say I'm right and they're wrong, but now I have my choice I won't eat meat. I won't take what they're giving. Let other people do it, but now that I have a choice, me personally, I won't eat meat or chicken, or eggs that are from hens that are kept in those little boxes.

I have a long way to go yet. I'm still thinking a lot about animals, and how far in my life I want it to go. I've started to go off cosmetics now, because I know they're using animals. Cosmetics! And – detergents! I mean, it's too much. I don't know how to stop it [the exploitation].

This attitude was common among the animal-rights activists I spoke to. In his book *Beast and Man* Roy Willis comments: 'Food taboos remind us how potentially dangerous an activity eating is. It involves the assimilation into the body of external matter. Now the human body is itself ... an elemental "natural symbol" for society.'[48] Human beings are what they eat and what they don't eat, and what they do-and-do-not-eat contains a world of meaning. Another activist said:

That's the most personal commitment you can make, to become a vege-tarian or a vegan. That is the most personal commitment you can make because instantly it impacts on your family life. It impacts on your social activities. You lose friends: 'What do you mean, you don't want to come to the steak house with me?' It means you're putting yourself on the line. So it is probably the last step that people take. If you're committed from your absolute *gut-level* [she went on, unaware of her pun], then none of it is an effort, none of it at all.

That 'what is remembered in the body is well remembered' is illus-trated by the innocent exhortation another activist gave to her audi-ence: 'The most important thing that an individual can do to help animals,' she began, 'is to try to stop eating meat. And it's difficult. Especially for someone who has been raised to eat normal things.' The audience laughed uproariously at her choice of words, for in them they recognized their shared habitus.

The discipline of vegetarianism-as-protest is an ultimate discipline, and not one that every activist chooses. It does indeed mean, as one person put it, putting your *self* on the line. For many who take this route, refraining from eating meat is the embodiment of the animal-rights movement's most important aim, that of changed relations between humans and other beings. For them, the choice to become vegetarian is literally 'meaning made body.'[49]

CITIZENSHIP, BIOPHILIA, AND THE LIMITS OF METAPHOR

Biophilia in the Public Domain

The animal-rights movement is a response to the rift in meaning that people perceive when the contradictory practices in human–animal relations are revealed. In the course of working to heal this rift, the movement has succeeded to some extent in introducing biophilia – the human sense of care and affiliation with other animals – into the realm of public life. 'Suddenly you realize,' one activist commented, 'that the Buddhist belief in *ahimsa*, or reverence for all life, extends to every single portion of your life.' Through their own practices, activists have rallied a small public ready and willing to express their biophilic impulses in the civic domain. The notion of care for animals has begun to widen out from the effusive intimate expression of love within the confines of the family to a more impersonal, impartial public expression of care, voiced in the call for an expansion of the sphere of human ethical concern to include other species. In either guise, the practice remains one of caring for other living beings.

Activists have opted for care in the public domain in a particular guise: care wrapped up and delivered in the flag of citizenship. In other words, they have opted to care for animals *in their guise of honorary humans*. As in the domestic domain, biophilia may be acknowledged and expressed in the public sphere, but first it appears to be necessary to represent the animal as a 'humanized' being, a 'person.' In urban Western culture at least, the intimate connection with other life forms seems to be limited to revealing itself in the form of caring for an animal as human kin or as co-civilian, not as recognizing and caring for a creature that is different, an other. Once again, as in the domestic domain, animals are humanized, and human beings, their animal being muted as ever, are not altered in any fundamental way.

Is this the world that animal-rights activists have sought?

Limits to the Citizenship Metaphor

The choice of citizenship as a key organizing metaphor in reordering the natural world reminds us once again that 'nature' is an emic concept, developed from a native point of view: a cultural system constructed out of the needs of human beings in particular times and places, out of their interpretations of the objective conditions they find themselves in, and out of the constraints of habitus – what they can perceive and conceive as possible in a particular moment of located history. In fashioning their new order, activists have been limited by Western culture itself, which, like all culture, as Ortner reminds us, constrains people most profoundly by the ways in which it controls our definitions of the world and limits our conceptual tools. As Kovel has noted with respect to the West's contemporary relations with nature: '[W]e are part of nature but split from it so that it dwells, transformed, within us, while our own works are projected into and transform it.'[50] In trying to heal the contradiction in human relations with animals, this opposition between biophilia in the domestic domain and the zest for invention, manipulation, and profit in the factory domain, animal-rights activists have had a limited source of metaphors to choose from. '[W]hat sorts of alternatives,' Ortner wonders, 'are people being dis-abled from seeing?'[51]

Ortner goes on to note that '[c]hange is largely a by-product, an unintended consequence of action, however rational action may have been ... To say that society and history are products of human action is true, but only in a certain ironic sense. They are rarely the products the actors themselves set out to make.'[52] What are the consequences of having chosen the citizenship metaphor for reordering the natural world? Animal-rights activists routinely allude to a vision of human–animal relations based on a biocentred world-view. However, in its desire to effect real culture change and its understanding of what might best realize this desire, the animal-rights movement chose to promote rights for animals in the realm of human culture. In doing so, the movement has unintentionally minimized the animalness of animals, the otherness of animals. In adopting this strategy, has the animal-rights movement also, incidentally (and inadvertently), moved Western culture further away from a deeper knowledge and perhaps a more sound basis for human being-in-the-world and human–animal relations – away from the liberation of its totemic imagination? That is, away from the 'gut-level' acceptance of the human as an animal among other animal beings?

The next section examines the constraints that Western culture puts on imagination, experience, and the invention of its history, speculating on what might be needed to further the reordering of relations between human and other animal beings, and suggesting ways the discipline of anthropology can play a major role in this reordering.

PART THREE

Naming the Other in Western Culture

Ototeman – He is a relative of mine.
Claude Lévi-Strauss (1963)

Chapter Six

Missing Metaphors

It is time ... to look to the very roots of motivation and understand why, in what circumstances and on which occasions, we cherish and protect life.

Edward O. Wilson (1984)

REFORM OR REVOLUTION?

The animal-rights movement has declared its agenda to be a radical one: nothing less than a basic reordering of human–animal relations. All animal-rights activists urge that Western society acknowledge its biophilic sentiments. Most advocate a path of bio- or ecocentrism, supporting the adoption of practices based on a view of human life as one with all other animals in the biosphere. And yet the primary metaphors Westerners have appropriated for their relations with other animals, including the citizenship metaphor chosen by the animal-rights movement itself, continue to place humanity in a dominant role. These organizing metaphors persist in fostering the assimilation of other creatures into human cultural life. Whether humans live by a metaphor that encourages the control and manipulation of other animals, or one that recognizes an affiliation with animals as (human) kin or as (human) citizens, the world-view remains at bottom the same: it is practice thoroughly informed by a very particular humanist perspective. It is, according to ecologist David Ehrenfeld, humanism as religion, or in philosopher Luc Ferry's terms, 'metaphysical humanism.'[1] It is a humanism in which human beings remain steadfastly the measure of all things in the cosmos, the centre of all concerns. While animals are nudged ever more decidedly into the human domain, the human side of the equation – consideration of human beings as but one unprivileged animal species among the rest – has not really been touched at all.

The humanist response is a far cry from activists' professed desire for that more revolutionary cultural transmutation – for a biocentric world in which all living organisms, including human beings, are 'plain citizens of the planet.'[2] The animal-rights movement's most consistent response has turned out to be a reformist one after all. Why should this be so? Why has the animal-rights movement failed to take the revolutionary leap?

Humanism as Sanctuary

While it is true that most animal-rights activists harbour the biocentric vision as an ultimate goal, for most of them the primary project is to save animals. Theirs is above all a rescue mission. In practice, therefore, the movement's ethical agenda does not readily permit the unfolding of the sort of long revolution that profound cultural change must allow for.[3] We saw how, in its desire to make changes *now* for animals caught in the winches of the factory domain, the movement had to select a metaphor to live by that would be immediately meaningful to at least some of the general population and provide acceptable guidelines for an alternative practice. If it would accomplish its most important task, the saving of animal lives, the chosen metaphor had to be available to enter history without delay. It had, therefore, to be ready-to-hand, embedded in the embodied culture or habitus of society. We saw that the central humanist notion of citizenship fit the bill nicely. Seen in the light of the familiar definition of politics as the art of the possible, the choice of citizenship as a metaphor to live by was what we might call an instance of an expedient politics of cognition or, more specifically, a politics of metaphor-in-practice.

There is another critical although perhaps less evident point to consider. Now more than ever the factory domain's animal-artifact model has taken on new and more powerful forms whose consequences are at present only dimly conceivable. Most significant of these are the new biotechnologies and associated legislation that minimize barriers to transgenic research. As pointed out in chapter 4, one may now readily tinker with the genetic make-up of animals – one may make them up or invent them – and patent the resulting organisms. *Homo sapiens* is the only animal that has remained, up until now, and now with increasing instability, legally inviolate.[4] Thus, until the present, all of nature except for human beings has been considered, with relatively little opposition, patentable – raw material to be processed and marketed. This being the case, the more automatically an animal could be thought of and treated as a human being, the safer it has been from such interference. Thus, paradoxically, sometimes *flight into the human cultural realm* has been the only means to ensure nonhuman creaturely life a modicum of safety in Western culture. The persona of the quasi-human may have been the only refuge available for animals from the ultimate manipulation of being 'made-into.' From this perspective, the inclusion of animals in the human sphere in the guise of metaphoric humanism is not only an expression of biophilia; it is also an embrace of sanctuary. It is ironic that the Western cultural realm itself should offer the only 'safe house' for animals from Western culture's own propensity to categorize and treat others as artifacts.

Humanism as Prison

How important is it whether a society chooses to cast its 'new' relations between humans and animals (and thus humans and nature) in terms of animals-as-citizens-of-human-culture or in terms of humans-as-citizens-of-the-biotic-community? Even if one wished to opt in the long run for the latter metaphor but chose the former out of a more immediate desire to find sanctuary for animals in intolerable conditions, what difference would that make? Is there a price to be paid for seeking immediate public responsiveness over the long, the deep revolution? Is Evernden right when he asserts that 'the price paid for public attention [is] the ability to speak of what matters'?[5]

Evernden is not alone in this assessment. Langdon Winner also believes something important is lost. He suggests that relying on accepted paradigms while neglecting to introduce less familiar but perhaps more important concepts and values onto the cultural agenda is a dangerous practice. Because a familiar, accepted master value may attract a wide consensus, he notes, 'it is sometimes used as a conceptual Trojan horse by those who have more challenging political agendas they hope to smuggle in. But victories won in this way are in other respects great losses. For they affirm in our words and in our methodologies that there are certain humane ends that no longer dare be spoken in public. Lingering in that stuffy Trojan horse too long, even soldiers of virtue eventually suffocate.'[6]

Relying on humanism as a tactical move to introduce less readily acceptable ideas, therefore, may be a mistake. We need different ideas, as Williams says, because we desperately need different relationships. Old ideas, too-familiar ideas, may seriously hinder the development of new relationships. Metaphysical humanism persisting as the touchstone of contemporary Western practice creates an insurmountable obstacle to a revolutionary reordering of human relations with the natural world. It tends to mute our biophilic tendencies. It tends to stifle any remaining sense of the animal nature of human beings that we mostly urban beings might have. And it tends to obscure our apprehension of the continuities and interconnectedness among all species. Yet these are all central preconditions to embarking on the long revolution toward a biocentred world-view. The greatest danger may therefore be, not that an idea or a value dare not be spoken in public, but that it no longer *can* be – when its language is forgotten and its imagery obscured. ('If you did away with all the animals in the city you would be missing something, but you'd be hard-pressed to say what it was.') Confined within the Trojan horse of humanism, the deeper voices of our totemic imagination become muted, and are in danger of losing breath and spirit altogether.

NATURE AS A WESTERN CULTURAL SYSTEM:
MISSING METAPHORS

The Legacy of the 'People without Natural History'

A number of writers have traced the ways in which a current of non-manipulative attachment to animals and the natural world, an acknowledged biophilia, has run beneath the surface of Western culture throughout its known history.[7] At times deeply submerged, at times closer to consciousness, the sense of common cause with the rest of the natural world has never disappeared entirely. Naturalists, poets, and philosophers in the English-speaking world such as Gilbert White, Wordsworth, Thoreau, and of course Darwin articulated these sentiments in the eighteenth and nineteenth centuries and found widely enthusiastic audiences newly awakening to an appreciation of nature's myriad manifestations separate from human concerns. But a folk tradition of human–animal relations existed also, among populations we might call, borrowing from Eric Wolf,[8] the 'people without natural history': people whose interactions with other life forms were seldom recorded, and then usually only inadvertently. It is only by interpreting this historical palimpsest that we can discern somewhat the (to us, extraordinary) extent to which 'human society' really meant, in early modern Europe and America, 'human–animal' society.

Throughout the millennia and well into the modern period, to a degree largely incomprehensible by our current standards, humans and animals shared in each others' society. For, as historian Keith Thomas depicts so vividly for England, humans and animals actually lived in closer proximity than the regnant ideologies implied. They were often housed in the same accommodations or in adjoining quarters. Far more numerous in the early modern period in proportion to the human population than today, all kinds of animals – cattle, pigs, horses, sheep, poultry, dogs and cats, kept to work or to be eaten or as pets – were to be found everywhere in rural and urban areas alike. One could come upon animals in the most unlikely places in the cities, roaming the streets unattended, perhaps, or even within town houses, where they were often kept and bred. Ordinances to stop people from milking cows or keeping pigs in the streets failed to work. For centuries, wandering pigs were a notorious hazard to urban existence. London poulterers kept thousands of live birds in their cellars and attics, while one Jacobean starchmaker was known to have had two hundred pigs in his backyard. In 1842 a contemporary found that chickens were still being reared in town bedrooms, and that dogs and even horses lived inside the town houses. Thus, even in the city, people had intimate acquaintance with all manner of importunate nonhuman life.[9]

People 'without natural history' seem to have behaved in most circumstances as if none of the grand metaphors of the modern age – neither the inalterable stasis of God's Great Chain of Being, that great ordering principle of nature since medieval times that in theory discouraged tampering with Nature's organisms, nor the Cartesian depiction of animal and plant life as inert, reactive, clockwork mechanisms – made any great difference to their actual relations with other animals and the natural world. On the one hand, ever intrigued by nature's plasticity, individuals engaged unselfconsciously in developing new breeds of plants and animals, thus altering organic being at will. On the other, habitual and complex social interchanges between humans and animals belied any notion of animals as mere automata. Animals were known individually, many were named, and people matter-of-factly trained them to work and perform tricks without compunction about the creatures' supposedly limited ability to understand. As Thomas points out, if everyone thought that animals were mere automata they would never have been considered to be trainable, but 'their owners, unlike Cartesian intellectuals, never thought them incapable of understanding.'[10] Interspecies participation provided instance after instance of the reserves of discrimination, inventiveness, sociality, and curiosity displayed by all creatures: 'Farm labourers knew that animals could be taught to perform many complicated operations. Shepherds had never doubted the sagacity of their sheepdogs. Horse-trainers had always regarded it as axiomatic that their charges had memory, imagination and judgment. The bee, thought an agricultural writer in 1616, had "a kind of wisdom coming near unto the understanding of man."'[11] To this we may add Margaret Cavendish, Duchess of Newcastle's observation in the mid-seventeenth century: 'Man may have one way of knowledge ... and other creatures another way, and yet other creatures' manner or way may be [as] intelligible and instructive to each other as Man's.'[12]

During this period of European history, there appears to have been little difference made between the treatment of humans and other animals. To those people who actually had to maintain domestic animals on a daily basis for their own livelihood, the entrenched dependence of each species upon the other was likely to have smacked less of mastery than of mutual obligation, if not outright indenture.[13] Cruelty toward most animals, as toward other human beings outside the habitual circle of moral concern, was unremarkable: the baiting of bulls, bears, and dogs, sport hunting, cockfighting, and children routinely tormenting animals were part of the unconsidered activities of everyday life. Little difference, similarly, was made between human and nonhuman in the use of 'pet' names, epithets we still largely use without much thought today. Thomas comments that such names, interchangeable between animals and (most often juvenile and female) human beings, were common intercourse stretching all the way from the distant horizons of Western history: 'kid' and 'cub' for young offspring and 'runt' for weakly offspring, 'colt' for an apprentice, 'duck' and 'hen' as a husband's affectionate appellations for his wife and 'cow,' 'shrew,' and 'vixen' for the less affectionate moments, 'crone' (originally an old ewe that has lost her teeth) for an aged female, and so on.[14] But what was different between then and now, Thomas argues, was the weight of meaning carried by the very proximity of these animals in everyday life then compared with their relative or absolute absence now. In an earlier era, that very cheek-by-jowl intimacy would have served to underline the pulsating immediacy of the relation suggested by the epithet, whereas for today's speakers such names are used far more figuratively. To us they evoke highly anthropomorphized, story-book-like figures rather than the flesh-and-blood, odoriferous, toothy, webbed, clawed, kicking, clacking, snorting, intent, stubborn, sometimes dangerous living beings our ancestors shared their lives, lofts, and labours with. This interchange of terms for humans and animals in the early modern period was an indication for Thomas that men and beasts inhabited the same moral as well as physical universe. 'It is therefore perfectly true,' he writes, 'that, as one late-seventeenth-century observer contemptuously put it, "farmers and poor people" made "very little difference between themselves and their beasts." They went out with them in the fields in the morning, toiled with them all day and returned home with them in the evening.'[15]

Thus, in a not-so-distant historical past, in a past we call modern, in fact, we can make out a closer, more interactive everyday practice between human and nonhuman species – although certainly not always a completely benign one – than any ideology would have us believe, and much evidence for more permeable boundaries between the species than we would recognize today. Ordinary people were content with an everyday, practical logic that included the rest of life as a matter of course. They went on interacting with the animal world in much the same way as they had through millennia past. The 'people without natural history' continued to reproduce practices, both cruel and benign, true, but always with the living world, never with insensate machines with built-in adventitious noises that did not really communicate pain, pleasure, contentment, or rage. Rather, as historian Gerald Carson notes, they insisted on building bridges to other animals through sympathy.[16]

Even in contemporary urban North America, as we have seen in earlier chapters, the muted underground stream of biophilia has never stopped flowing, even beneath the sturdy pavement of an anthropocentric humanism informed by advanced capitalism and post-industrial technology. As we have noted, it has just taken on different guises. The importance of this observation cannot be overestimated: despite much loud protestation to the contrary, *the pull of biophilia and the totemic imagination are not entirely alien, neither to our culture nor to our time.* However, the shared, cultural *expression* of these sensibilities has been severely attenuated. The acknowledged experiencing and valuing of affiliation with other living beings, and the sense of human being as animal being, have long been submerged in the pursuit of the artifact metaphor – in getting and spending all of nature as a resource. What we have lost are appropriate shared metaphors through which to live the biophilic and totemic experiences. Indeed, a contemporary naturalist felt compelled to make up the awkward word 'biophilia' to reclaim some of these experiences. And, to paraphrase Kovel, totemism is no longer named at all in the languages of our Western history.[17] Is it not time now, as Touraine suggests, to 'rediscover the spring hidden beneath the cement, the word beneath the silence'?[18] Is it not time, as Edward Wilson urges, to look to the very roots of human motivation and understand why, under what circumstances, and on which occasions, instead of dominating and exploiting, we cherish and protect life?

Deep Ecology and the Long Revolution

A growing critique of humanism as a prison of thought that paralyses the development of new and more appropriate practice has recently emerged in several Western countries. There is an expanding realization that we need a new philosophy of nature. This move toward a new philosophy is in large measure a reaction to the 'ecology-as-resource-management' approach – a response to environmental crisis that seeks to push through reforms in the existing human-centred system while leaving its basic rules and assumptions unquestioned and unchanged. It is against this form of 'shallow' or reformist environmentalism, decried by an increasing number of cultural critics, that deep ecology positions itself.[19] Thus, at one important level deep ecology is a sustained critique of mainstream environmentalism, the reformist stance most in evidence today in the policies and projects of established institutions, primarily universities, governments, and international agencies such as the United Nations.[20] Reactive, short-term, technocratic, and, above all, managerial in its approach to the earth, reformist environmentalism never touches the question closest to the hearts of deep ecologists: whether the world is ours to manage in the first place.

At another level deep ecology seeks to develop universal philosophical principles regarding the relations between humans and nature. For Arne Naess, the Norwegian philosopher most closely associated with deep ecology as a philosophical and moral position, the aim is not to develop a formal or systematic 'eco-logic,' but to apply general philosophical principles to ecology. The aim is to keep asking ever-deeper questions (hence the name), questions about ultimate ends and ultimate values. Deep ecologists, writes Evernden, 'attempt to attend to the root assumptions that lead to environmental destruction rather than simply to the technical symptoms of that malaise.' As Winner points out, they are searching for a radically new ethical, aesthetic, and metaphysical grasp of the human relationship to nature.[21] As philosophy, deep ecology asserts that we must abjure humanist solutions and try for a more profound redefinition of the relations between humans and the rest of nature – indeed, a redefinition of the sort animal-rights activists had hoped for. For deep ecology takes the biocentric perspective in which nature is conceived as a complex and inextricably connected and interdependent network of phenomena, including yet not privileging human beings. Nature exists in its own right, for itself (even though, as writer David Cayley comments, 'our whole culture denies nature an independent existence').[22] Recognition of the inherent value of all life, human and nonhuman, but particularly the latter, is of central concern.

To many of its proponents, deep ecology means more than critique and more than philosophy: it means cultural revolution. It means fundamental changes not only in our perceptions, ideas, and moral stances, but, most important, in our practices. Committed to deep ecology as a social movement, these people are working toward a change in relations between humans and the rest of the natural world so complete that it will result in changed meaning. Their radical goal is a fundamental cultural shift: to dislodge humanity from the centre of the universe, from the metaphysical centre of its own concern. As bioregionalists, organic farmers, lobbyists, alternative politicians, or ordinary people committed to a new vision of human culture, these social activists have opted for the long revolution.

Deep ecology has many critics. To most mainstream environmentalists deep ecology is sheer utopianism: impractical at best, at worst immoral and misanthropic in its call for the transcendence of humanism.[23] Criticisms from more sympathetic quarters are concerned about the lack of sophistication of deep ecology's analysis. Social ecologists and eco-feminists have criticized deep ecologists for the latter's highly selective attention to history and context, the neglect of ethnographic data, and the relative lack of attention to the social and cultural patterns in the West that have resulted in the current ecological crisis. They have been concerned above all about deep ecologists' failure to address issues of power. To social ecologists and eco-feminists, questions such as, who does, or does not, make the environmental decisions in a society; who benefits; and which class, or group, or nation of human beings is adversely affected along with the physical environment – these are the vital questions to probe. Absent from the writings of deep ecologists, they claim, are discussions of class, race, gender, non-Western culture, or colonialism. Even more glaringly and troublingly absent, for eco-feminism in particular, is a critical analysis of the patriarchal values still so firmly embedded in most environmental dialogue, deep or shallow. To eco-feminists, the very concept 'anthropocentrism' falsely lumps men and women together and denies the conflation thereby of anthropocentrism with androcentrism. They believe that females have a very different, more connected relationship to the natural world, one that cannot be subsumed under this term. Deep ecologists respond that their critique is an attempt to go beyond intra-human power politics and to focus instead upon the problems of speciesism and anthropocentrism as general human-centredness. Against the more general charge of misanthropy, they claim that their aim is not the overthrow of human beings but of this same human-centredness. Their ultimate concern, they insist, is about the damage human beings *as a species* have done to the natural world.[24]

To my mind it is a mistake to pit these different forms of biocentric ecology against one another too rigidly. Social ecology, eco-feminism, and deep ecology should all be seen as variants of radical environmentalism. All are part of a necessary cultural conversation. All three foster an ecological sensibility, although self-identified deep ecologists make the strongest distinction between bio- or ecocentrism and metaphysical humanism, or anthropocentrism. All of these orientations ought to be seen as different voices of a broad green social movement engaged, from different perspectives, in a critique of Western culture and its nature-habitus. Deep ecology may be thought of as one aspect of this broader movement, one trying to articulate a new human-nature vision in clear, acceptable, yet transformative terms. The dialogue and action of all these different voices together may eventually constitute movement on the long road to some as-yet-unknown form of general ecological consciousness and practice.

Much as deep ecologists desire to take the revolutionary leap, however, they are having trouble articulating the sort of alternative biocentric vision that a broad range of ordinary people can embrace. Deep ecologists are having trouble finding meaningful metaphors for people to live by, metaphors that would resonate with contemporary Western habitus. We still have no recognized Western practice, and no metaphor to guide practice, that truly captures a biocentric sensibility. We have none that acknowledges the radical otherness of other life forms, that is, their inherent value outside the human ethical domain. We have none that acknowledges the animal nature of humans. We no longer have access to an animal imagination: we have little enough imagination of the animal nature of other animals, and none at all of human beings as animals. In short, we have no organizing metaphors for human–nature relations that are more totemic than anthropomorphic, through which humans could be seen to be related to animals and other biota on their terms, not on human terms. Hampered by centuries of metaphysical humanist and economistic thought and language, whatever elusive ecological and biophilic wisdom has remained to us has lost its names, and Western culture no longer knows how to visualize its desire to join as plain citizens in the world of living things.[25]

Whether the words and the names for biophilia and the totemic imagination were lost by self-muting for reasons of political expediency, or were overwhelmed by the prevailing master values of humanism, economism, and 'technological exuberance,'[26] centuries of privileging this kind of thought and language over a language of connectedness with the biosphere have led to the extreme difficulty we now face in Western society in framing a new human–nature relationship. 'It's not that nature refuses to communicate with us,' says feminist ecologist Dolores LaChapelle, 'but that we no longer have a way to communicate with it.'[27] An experience may be felt individually and privately, but if its shared name is lost, has it not been lost to culture, and to history? And is it irrevocably barred from entering history and culture once again? Once a society begins to lose shared language about a shared experience – a cultural loss – might it be in danger of losing the experience altogether? In this connection, Edward Wilson quotes T.S. Eliot: '[U]nless we have those few men who combine an exceptional sensibility with an exceptional power over words, our own ability, not merely to express, but even to feel any but the crudest emotions, will degenerate.'[28]

How can we call up the biocentric imagination? What shall we call it? This, I suspect, is the fundamental problem facing the deep ecology project. Their primary task might be characterized as a *search for missing metaphors* capable of resonating with the spirit of Western culture and of naming the deeper visions. Finding the 'right' metaphors might, just possibly, allow deep ecologists to mobilize the popular allegiance necessary for the long revolution. But until those metaphors are found, or invented, the current poverty of our metaphors leaves the West with a distorted cultural conception, a lingering conception – still very much in keeping with the now-outmoded modern project – of nature as a *simple system*.

Nature as a Simple System

The nature of order is fundamental to this inquiry, most particularly the question of nature as it is humanly ordered; that is, as cultural system. I introduced this exploration with the idea that while human beings everywhere are able, or need, to sense some orderliness beyond human language or even comprehension, to the degree that we can grasp and communicate about order and system, these meta-concepts are not universal but culturally constructed. Nature is conceived as a cultural system because we, its natives, imagine it, and perhaps only then experience it, to be so. And once nature is defined as a particular cultural system, as we saw in previous chapters, a society and its citizens must devote great effort to ensuring the continuance and coherence of that order. Thus, whatever systematicity we discern in nature, it is we who ensure its perpetuation, through the metaphors we adopt to guide our practices, and through our continued loyalty to engaging in the practices themselves; that is, to living out the metaphors.

Earlier anthropologists, including and perhaps most notably symbolic anthropologists such as Clifford Geertz, have left us with an underlying assumption (or perhaps more accurately, an *aspiration*) that a cultural system can actually be known in some significant, if partial, way. Practice theory, in taking symbolic anthropologists' aspirations a step further by acknowledging and attempting to account explicitly for more complex ideas of cultural, social, and cognitive systematicity, came up with concepts of systems that were less tidy, more fluid, more contingent, and more implicated with time, human agency, and power. But simpler or more involved, these cultural systems are still presumed to be ultimately knowable.

Evernden observes that nature is a hypothesis that every society needs. The purpose of this hypothesis is to preserve a sense of the ultimate 'knowability' of the physical world. But given the limits of human comprehension, the very need for a knowable order necessitates a certain blindness to glaring contradictions. The logic of cultural systems thus stems not only from the human need to order and to understand our world, but also from the need to resolve, remove, or ignore contradiction. How can we, however precariously, satisfy two basic but seemingly incompatible motivations in one system of nature: the capitalist economic imperative to preserve the stance of 'alienation from nature' in whatever way possible in order to commodify every thing and every relationship more easily and thus ensure sustained market growth, and the desire to nurture biophilic, life-enhancing interspecies relations? The answer is that our Western cultural system of nature depends on its missing metaphors: that is, *nature as we understand it depends on these metaphors remaining missing.* At the very least, they need to be securely compartmentalized.

The simplicity of our understanding of nature is thus primarily achieved through muting to achieve a sense of coherence and order, and through the resultant poverty of our system's metaphors. We lack metaphors to understand other creatures or ourselves as creatures. Despite the wealth of knowledge we have from centuries of field naturalism and countless movies and television shows on the subject, there is a stubborn sparseness of language or other shared means to popularly reflect an acknowledgment of the complexity and intricacy of the lives of other animals and plants, as individuals and as communities. We still find it fanciful to attribute individual histories – biography – to real animals' lives.

Further, we have little language to reflect the variety of needs, interests, and vital concerns of humanity as animals: our needs to survive and reproduce, to nest, to produce, to exercise our own *funkionslust,*[29] to relate and cooperate, to forage and to kill in order to eat. There are also too few metaphors in Western culture to do justice to the breadth of human experiencing of sociality, spirit, symbiosis, and the essential mystery of the other – all of which, for all we know, are emergent aspects of our organic, creaturely being, or of life itself, rather than some other, equally mysterious, peculiarly 'human essence.' We suffer a poverty of expression for anything not bought or sold, not made or unmade, not lost or won. The crucial metaphors that are missing are those that relate to biophilia, the totemic relationship, and the sense of oneness with the biosphere: in a word, we are missing metaphors of *being.*

Being and making, biophilia and world-alteration, integration and self-assertion[30] are both deeply present in the human condition, and deeply inform our relations with the rest of the natural world. In this we share with the rest of life, for in the most straightforward sense possible life may be said to consist entirely of being and making. The simple system we live, however, demands that Western society make a choice between these two elemental (and, in the final analysis, inseparable) conditions. And in this cultural system, making is simply more valued than being. In ordering the natural world, the West vastly privileges making – human dominance, manipulation, technique, and the transformation of nature – over being – the reception of bioconnectedness, and the recognition of arrival.

In counterpoint to this tendency Ehrenfeld presents us with the observance of the Jewish Sabbath. Practising the injunctions of the Sabbath, he believes, serves to make people more humble with respect to the earth. On this day people may create nothing and may destroy nothing, and must celebrate the world as it is, in all its fullness of life. For this one day in the week humanity is enjoined to *leave the world alone*. Indeed, observing the Sabbath acts as a weekly reminder that it *can* safely be left alone.[31] On the Sabbath, humanity refrains from doing and celebrates being.

However, for most of us the Sabbath or a similar 'day of rest' no longer elicits such a non-practice, if it ever did. Instead, the far more common non-practice, our failure to name whatever experiences of being we do at times apprehend, such as totemic or biophilic impulses, perpetuates the dominance and privileging of metaphors of 'making' over all others. This omission ensures that we no longer attend seriously to any 'confounding' emotional experiences of biophilia or creatureliness we may personally have; and it ensures that we will ignore the turn these experiences might urge toward biocentrism. Will the absence of metaphor lead inevitably to the absence of thought? And are we, through absence of thought, in ultimate danger of losing experience?

What is needed? We need to create a balance. We need to cultivate an understanding of 'being' negatively, as refraining from doing. And at the same time we need to give voice to a more positive sense of being, one that would include the totemic sense of human as animal or creaturely being – a sense that has become muted almost to inaudibility in every experience – so that it too can enter Western culture, enter history, and re-enter experience.

What more is needed? As Touraine warns, 'Historic analysis must ceaselessly guard ... against the temptation to reduce events to a system.'[32] Since human beings are inherently ordering animals, however, in creating that order we need at the very least to be able to tolerate, in our everyday lives – indeed, in our very habitus – more complex systems.

Deep Order: Nature as a Complex System

Students of the history of Western ideas such as Lovejoy, Williams, and Evernden have pointed out that giving one name, nature, to a multiplicity of phenomena and processes leaves us with the illusion that in naming nature we understand its 'essence.' We labour under the illusion that nature is, if not simple, at least a graspable and controllable entity. The effect of this illusory unity is to erase any trace of the human mind in making up the idea of nature that constitutes our contemporary world. Nature becomes doxa – tradition made (in this case, literally) nature. In fact, only the word 'nature' is simple. The effect of gathering many complex phenomena and ideas into one idea is to obscure the ceaseless dynamism and infinite diversity of the activities, processes, relationships, and things that make up the natural world. To give it unity, even a complex unity, is to reduce it and distort it. Ultimately, this reductionism feeds humanity's ignorance of what our actual relations with nature may be. Our cultural critics make a plea for a far more complex understanding of natural systems, and, as a hoped-for result, more complex, or multiplex, relationships between humans and the rest of the natural world.[33]

The capacity of Westerners to conceive of multiplexity in the natural world has grown in recent years in a number of scientific fields. Modern physics stands as a prime example of tolerance for and curiosity about disorder. With the refinement of dynamical systems theory and the ability to express some of its key concepts mathematically – concepts such as 'chaos,' 'emergence,' 'far-from-equilibrium stability,' and 'self-organizing systems' – some physical scientists and biologists have been stimulated to think very differently about the natural world. Living systems are increasingly being thought of as 'open,' irreducibly enmeshed, and operating far from equilibrium, where emergence and creativity can take place without collapsing the system as a whole. We are beginning to get a glimpse of spectacular universes of deeper order at the core of disorder itself. According to Fritjof Capra, complexity theory as 'a theory of living systems consistent with the philosophical framework of a deep ecology, including an appropriate mathematical language and implying a nonmechanistic, post-Cartesian understanding of life, is now emerging.'[34]

If we can speak of an 'essential' quality to this kind of post-modern scientific thinking, it would be 'relational.' Nets and networks, interlacings, webs, contexts, communities, symbioses, nodes, and rhizomes are some of the terms and metaphors now being tried out to express the new emphasis on the primacy of process, interconnection, and multiple loci of eventfulness and participation over discrete 'things,' polarities, and hierarchical ordering in the physical world. Along with exhibiting defining characteristics of indeterminacy, multiplex interactions, decentralized decision making, and irreducibility, complex systems are said to do away with ideas of foundations, building blocks, edifices, and apices. In this world, no part is any more fundamental than any others. The hierarchical construction model of knowledge has been deconstructed in favour of a sort of 'ball of energy-strings' model, with (so the mathematical equations apparently tell us) inner nodes of entanglement called 'strange attractors,' where 'things tend to happen.'[35]

It is easy to see the rise of ecology as a discipline, as well as practice theory as a promising approach in the social sciences, as part and parcel of this same general orientation toward trying to understand organized complexity. Yet, other than the thought-experiments of physical scientists like Capra and Ilya Prigogine linking complexity theory to human relations and human–nature relations, in anthropology complexity theory has as yet, apart from the unclassifiable work of Bateson, seldom been applied in any seriously sustained way to cultural analysis.[36] These analyses are just beginning to be tackled elsewhere in a variety of ways. For example, historians of science such as Donna Haraway and Bruno Latour, as well as a current re-reading of nineteenth-century naturalist and writer Henry David Thoreau, have led us to detect weaknesses in the hitherto impermeable nature-culture 'barrier.' We will explore their separate attempts to describe or theorize a multiplex nature–culture relation in the next chapter.

Yet, while this sort of multiplex thinking is taking place in certain as yet marginal scientific enclaves, our everyday understandings, our everyday speech, and the everyday metaphors we live by work to keep our cultural system of nature simple. A great deal of energy is expended in maintaining a semblance of closure through the maintenance and reproduction of various traditions. Through socialization into a particular habitus, through routinization, muting, and living out given metaphors, we try, if not to entirely close, at least to contain our cultural systems in forms we can continue to recognize and value. But cultural systems, like all natural systems, are perhaps more accurately thought of as far-from-equilibrium, open systems, as systems closer to the 'edge of chaos' than its natives would wish to think. In our post-modern period of quasi-institutionalized disordering (one way, inci-dentally, that we have managed to maintain a livable order while per-mitting ourselves to imagine otherwise), it is time for our popular ideas of nature and of human–natural relations to be disturbed as well. Perhaps a greater tolerance for complexity, ambiguity, disorder, and chaos in our customary thinking about cultural systems will lead, as it has in physics and biology, to the discernment of deeper order, and an appreciation for a more fluid and unpredictable systematicity in nature and humanity's place in it.

Nature can become a more complex cultural system, more reflective of that small part of its infinite variety that human beings can appre-hend, when we dare to name more of our experience of it, more of its missing metaphors. Existentialist philosopher Martin Buber suggests that in the I–Thou relationship, the quintessential being-relation, '[t]here is nothing that I must not see in order to see, and there is no knowledge that I must forget.'[37] In this understanding of a more com-plex nature and human–nature relation, none of its aspects – making, being, humankind, other animals – is privileged above the others, none masked or muted in the service of coherence. Naming missing meta-phors would introduce a renewed cultural discourse that, in turn, could lead to a shared acknowledgment of biophilia, biocentrism, and totemic sensibility as *cultural values*.

The task, then, is to struggle against the tendency to adopt a simplis-tic, unitary view of nature, and to learn to live within a more complex and dynamic paradigm. Our contemporary challenge is to *complicate* our everyday understanding and our experience of nature through naming *more* of what we experience, even when – especially when – these experiences are contradictory, and to tolerate the resulting per-plexities and contradictions as 'truer' than our previous, more homo-geneous views. In seeking (or rather, creating) order, can we come to tolerate a consciousness of order that is less orderly than has heretofore been admissible? Can we live with a conception and an experience of order that are more complex and more elaborated, that can tolerate greater uncertainty? Will we be able to stand the clangour of hetero-doxy, the confusion of paradox, the threat of incipient disorder, the verge of meaninglessness that might herald a deeper order?[38] And can we do so without slipping into cynicism, resentment, apathy, rage, or – as the post-modern moment has tended to handle it – unbridled irony? Perhaps the most important factor in living within nature as a more complex cultural system will be the capacity of human nature and Western culture to tolerate such ambiguity and uncertainty well; indeed, not only to tolerate it but to develop the negative capability to thrive on it. In order to do so, we would need to learn to build more ambiguity, more seeming chaos into our very perceptions, expectations, and representations of systems, and to invest these with value rather than resignation. The engagement with complexity would have to become part of our Western habitus.

However, in a culture still firmly based on science, technology, and classical economics, where all things are assumed to be ultimately quantifiable and 'therefore explicable,' where ambiguity is often experienced as uncomfortable, 'unnatural,' unresolved, and temporary, where the detritus of deconstructionism is feeling more and more like hazardous waste, where (it must be said) even the science of complexity aims to corral this very complexity through the mathematical encoding of nature's chaotic 'rules,'[39] this will not be an easy task. Despite the condition of post-modernity we have been living through, the West still has great difficulty in anticipating, acknowledging, articulating, and living with ambiguity. Thus, when it must be done at all, refraining from closure is at best undertaken as a sullen exercise, perceived as the necessary result of a bankrupt system, rather than seen to with anticipation as part of some infinite indeterminate unfolding. Refraining from closure is not really a part of everyday Western habitus.

Of equal import to this discussion is the deep-seated Western conception of order as moral responsibility. The different perspectives on cosmic order held by Western philosophies and the New Guinean Iatmul, discussed in an earlier chapter, serve to highlight the West's perhaps peculiar sense of order. We saw that while the Iatmul granted to mythic humankind a modest (although culturally celebrated) role in removing disordering elements and otherwise leaving the cosmos to organize itself, Western world-views – certainly as these are reflected in our institutions – are based on the active interventions of an ordering Being. With God less directly interested in humankind and our world since the Renaissance, this obligation to impose order and so keep the world intact became central to the practice of humanism.

Western humanism has at its core a deep distrust in the universe's ability to take care of itself, and a concomitant obstinate ('dogged'? 'mulish'? 'pigheaded'? 'bullheaded'?)[40] trust in humankind (and in humankind only) as able to save the universe from chaos. If a moral activism is at the heart of Western humanism, how can we expect the idea that our world is inherently self-organizing to gain practical currency? If imposing order is so central and so deeply rooted in the Western ethos, then how are we to nurture, in our more complicated sense of nature, the important choice to *refrain* from imposing order? How are we to foster the turn toward restraint? While conceptions such as 'nature's economy', 'nature's wisdom,' and 'self-ordering nature' have become fashionable in certain circles, still, they appear to omit humankind from their moral, let alone their practical, implications. To embrace a trust in other than humankind to keep us 'safe from chaos' may demand an immense breadth of vision we are not used to cultivating. An embodied sensibility of restraint remains alien to the deepest reaches of Western habitus. Equally to the point, removing human responsibility leaves the world completely (and frighteningly) unpredictable, and we have no culturally legitimate recourse to, say, trickster figures to help contain or explain the inevitable surprises.

Raymond Williams has commented that 'what a society needs, before all ... is as many as possible conscious individuals'.[41] In this context, that means to me as many people as possible who can, with some equanimity, simultaneously register contradictory perceptions, entertain inconsistent thoughts, accommodate dissident values, acknowledge discordant emotions – who can, in short, name, praise, and even, at times, live conflicting experiences. To echo Buber, there is nothing that conscious individuals must not see in order to see, and there is no knowledge that they must forget. They would have the capacity to remain perpetually struck by wonder at nature's infinite variety.

The ability to tolerate and integrate more ambiguity, disorder, and restraint into conceptions of order and systematicity would constitute a great change in Western habitus. It would mean enlarging the capacity for our categories of meaning to hold some contradiction, heterodoxy, and irresolution. It would also mean accepting that nature as a cultural system is an artifact; and artifacts, as Edward Wilson noted, are incomparably poorer than the world they imitate. We need to understand all of our systemic thinking as metaphorical thinking, as mere approximations to actual experience. Our increased capacity to tolerate ambiguity might lead to the final realization and acceptance that as human beings our understanding of order is forever limited, forcing us as a society to acknowledge and live with this limitation. 'The truth is,' says Wilson, 'that we never conquered the world, never understood it; we only think we have control.'[42] The truth is closer to Friedrich Engels's vision: 'If man, by dint of his knowledge and inventive genius, has subdued the forces of nature, the latter avenge themselves upon him, by subjecting him, insofar as he employs them, to a veritable despotism independent of all social organization.'[43] If we were to espouse nature as a complex system, this attitude would demand that we perceive and honour the natural world as infinitely complex, 'uncanny and unpredictable,' as Evernden phrases it,[44] and ultimately beyond human control or complete comprehension – as Other.

THE OTHER

What do we mean by the 'Other'? In much of contemporary anthropology the other is the term used to connote a condescending and subtly pejorative stance toward those who do not control the established institutions that define reality by those who do.[45] (These are the very definitions of reality that, as noted in the last chapter, Touraine considers to be so crucial to the invention of culture and history.) It is with this meaning of the other in mind that John Berger could write that animals are always, to human beings, the observed, the fact that they can observe us having lost its significance.

There is another sense to the term 'other,' however, and it is this one that I want to explore here. This alternative position, a way of thinking that stems from viewing nature as a complex system, presumes that others – other humans or nonhuman beings – are in the last analysis mysterious and unknowable. When defined as ultimately unfathomable, others cannot so easily be treated as if they were lesser beings or mere objects, nor can they be so readily subsumed under the human dominance hierarchy. Once perceived to be beyond complete human understanding, other beings, human or nonhuman, can only emerge as Other – that is, as other subjects and, most particularly, as subjects apart from and unrelated to human (or to one individual or group's) need or desire. This is not to say that we cannot mutually understand something about one another, person to person, species to species, for it appears in practice that we can, but simply that we cannot presume to ever *completely* know, or be known. It is from this stance that philosopher Tom Regan called for the valuing of nonhuman lives: precisely because they are other, because they are the experiencing subjects of a life, with inherent value outside and beyond the human cultural or ethical domain.

Animal Being as Other

We saw in previous chapters that while other societies may view members of various animal species as subjects, that is, as other in the sense I am pursuing here, Western anthropologists have had difficulty translating into 'meaningful' ethnography the many instances of interspecies social relations they were able to record and describe so vividly. With significant language missing from Western culture for expressing the sense of intimate sociality between humans and other animals as revealed, for example, in Evans-Pritchard's descriptions of the Nuer and their cattle and Fernandez's of the Asturians of Spain and theirs (as mentioned in chapter 2) and in Rappaport's ethnography on the Maring of New Guinea and their relationships with their pigs (recorded in chapter 3), and without that sense of animal imagination suggested by reports of totemic observance in many other cultures, anthropology has been unable, on the whole, to do justice to the totemic sensibility and biophilic experience in human lives. More often, as we saw, Western anthropologists have sought in the records of these relations between humans and other animals some other, less direct, more abstract, more materialist, or more symbolic message than the natives themselves have attributed to them; above all, some message pertaining solely or primarily to the human group.

Yet my own fieldwork experiences left little room to doubt that even in urban Western society, people simply value relating with living beings other than human beings. In the domestic domain animals are subjects and not mere utilities or toys. In the factory domain the perennial threat of animals' subjectivity breaking through to their handlers' consciousness and disrupting the smooth functioning of factory life means that special efforts are needed to counteract this eventuality, and so performances of denial are an important part of practice in that arena. In the civic domain ordinary people in the animal-rights movement expend a great deal of time and energy in ensuring the transfer of human–animal relations, as social and political relations, from the realm of custom to that of contract: fighting, in other words, to ensure the personhood and subjectivity of animals under law. As the last chapter concluded, the animal-rights movement is a public, political expression of that widely held but mostly private and largely unnamed experience in Western culture that Edward Wilson has called biophilia. And deep ecology is all about living as if every living being had its own integrity and value. All are manifestations in Western society of some level of recognition, whether disguised, or muted, or clear, of the animal as other.

Human Being as Other

For another shading to the term, let us look at humankind as other. We human beings are intermittently aware of our otherness, as often enough expressed in the desire to find a place in the order of things. In *The Great Chain of Being* Arthur Lovejoy documented the history of Western irresolution with regard to humanity's place in the natural order: Are humans closer to angels, or closer to beasts?[46] Indeed, we might ask where God, the Final Subject, would place humans in the Great Chain of Being. Where might other animals, in observing human beings, place us? What is humankind as viewed from the outside, as other?

Here once again we confront the great dilemma of Western humanism in the Ecological Age, the very problem the deep ecology movement must contend with. The threat of environmental catastrophe demands that humankind remove itself from the centre of its own concern in order to restore order – that is, nature. But humanism's very essence, its definition, stems from Man's place and agency at the centre of that order. Is it possible for human beings to truly remove ourselves from our centre of concern, and think of ourselves merely as subjects among other subjects? Here is Edward Wilson once more, this time watching insects:

In a twist my mind came free and I was aware of the hard workings of the natural world beyond the periphery of ordinary attention, where passions lose their meaning and history is in another dimension, without people, and great events pass without record or judgment. I was a transient of no consequence in this familiar yet deeply alien world that I have come to love. The uncounted products of evolution were gathered there for purposes having nothing to do with me; their long Cenozoic history was enciphered into a genetic code I could not understand. The effect was strangely calming.[47]

It is possible that, even for ordinary people who are not naturalists, one of the key attractions of wild places and wild beings is the experience, however fleeting, of a world beyond the human, where the human being is of no consequence. Savouring the memory of an all-too-brief but blessed emptying of ego, perhaps we carry away from such encounters a fresher intimation of humanity's place in nature: as just one kind out of an infinity of accidental creatures. It is in such moments, and in their remembrance, that certain famous words by the poet Rainer Maria Rilke become transparent and ring clear, perhaps even prophetically so. Rilke speaks of a 'love that consists in this: that two solitudes protect and border and greet each other.'[48]

If totemism is no longer named in the languages of our history, how can we follow Touraine's advice and rediscover the stream flowing in its hidden bed beneath the city's cement, the words that will populate the silence of forgotten relations? This is surely a task for the long revolution. And the long revolution, we must hope, *will* find purchase wherever it can, even amidst the esoteric dialogues of scholars. As a pertinent experiment, let us return one final time to the discipline of anthropology, to trace out for it some of the possibilities that Rilke named in his advice to the young poet, calling it love.

Chapter Seven

Anthropology as Natural History

We are not the only unique species.
Mary Midgley (1989)

Must it remain inevitable that the spirits flee the islands when the anthropologists arrive? Are we in the West forever barred from discerning relations and kinships apparent to people in other societies through their different ways of knowing? The underlying question, for me, is whether it is possible for Western civilization to overcome this ideology of unbridgeable separation between body and soul we seem to live by. If the passage from nature to culture has been anthropology's central problem up until now, given our current recognition of environmental crisis and our consequent urgent need to understand human relation to habitat, I submit that anthropology's central problem from now on and well into this century will be to track humanity's passage *through culture back to nature.* Can we, in the process, reclaim a more complex, biophilic imagination and regain a more multivocal, totemic voice for ourselves? This undertaking will be, I believe, anthropology's primary contribution to the West's long revolution toward a biocentric world-view. Along the way, this task may permit us, too, to distinguish, name, and pay respect to some of the spirits other peoples have encountered and come to know as kin.

As environmentalism sought to move toward a more probing 'deep ecology,' one dedicated to asking 'deeper questions,' so too a 'deeper anthropology'[1] is called for in this century, an anthropology devoted to rethreading webs of connection between humanity and the rest of life. *By returning to its roots in natural history,* this renewed discipline may yet help us along the long, albeit too-long-postponed, revolution toward dislodging humankind as the only meaningful centre of the universe.

Let us explore how likely it is that anthropology would, or could, take on such a task.[2]

ANTHROPOLOGY'S ROOTS IN NATURAL HISTORY

Anthropology's first question was, 'What kind of animal is the human animal?' Let us review the career of this question briefly. Western societies had long pursued separate and particular interests in many aspects of human life, from archaeology, philology, and folklore to anatomy and physiognomy, each with its own distinct intellectual history. Gradually converging under one 'study of Man' in the eighteenth century, anthropological thought occupied itself with studying humanity as both an organic and a cultural being, a being with body as well as soul. Linnaeus had by then 'confirmed' the animal nature of our species by placing human beings among the primates in his ordering of the natural world, thereby granting human beings biological kinship with the rest of nature. After nineteenth-century Darwinian evolutionary theory had provided the West with a plan of the order of nature emphasizing this relation, Darwin's *The Descent of Man* (1871) and *The Expression of the Emotions in Humans and Animals* (1872) then furnished further (and surprisingly little-contested) means to think of humans as continuous with other animals not only in anatomic but also in behavioural and emotional terms.[3] In this atmosphere anthropology sought to build a naturalistic study of human beings as 'one or more physical species in the animal world,' and by the last decades of the nineteenth century ethnographic method depended on data collected by natural scientists calling themselves 'anthropologists.' Field expeditions undertaken at this time under British direction, such as the Torres Straits Expedition of 1898 led by A.C. Haddon, consisted largely of such personnel. They saw their project's mission as retrieving data not only on the folklore and customs of the native peoples they wished to study but also on their physical properties and habitats. Historian George Stocking surmises that it was Haddon who imported the term 'fieldwork' into anthropology from his earlier natural-history days. Early anthropologists, such as Haddon, William Rivers, Charles Seligman, and in the United States Boas and others, seem to have perceived their vocation in far more ethological terms than ethnographers would perhaps admit to today. As Stocking remarks, for people trained as nat-

uralists the holistic study of human beings would not seem such a difficult undertaking because 'for a field naturalist ... the behavior, cries,
and physical characteristics of animals were all part of a single observational syndrome.' Thus, in these early years of the discipline the
emphasis was on Man the creature as well as the culture-bearer, and on
anthropology as a form of natural history.[4]

This emphasis on anthropology as natural history gained even more
prominence as fieldwork, defined as on-site information collected
by the scientists themselves, took hold as the methodology of choice.
Natural history had always been defined principally by its method:
collecting data concerning the organisms of interest in their native habitats. For the great Western natural historians of the eighteenth and
nineteenth centuries such as Gilbert White, Alexander von Humboldt,
Alfred Russel Wallace, Henry David Thoreau, and Darwin, personally
conducted fieldwork constituted the very heart of their wide-ranging
observations and underpinned the originality of their theories. In the
latter decades of the nineteenth century fieldwork undertaken by aca-
demically trained scholars became the rage in all the natural sciences:
astrophysicists, geologists, and oceanographers as well as anthropologists roamed the world (particularly those parts of it made safe
for them by concurrent colonial expansion) in search of personally
collected or eyewitness data. Anthropology itself was placed among
the natural histories in the early years of the British Association for the
Advancement of Science, around the mid-nineteenth century.[5]

But the convergence of humankind as organic being and as cultural
being, and the coincident characterization of anthropology as natural
history, was fragile. As early as the 1860s, rifts between what would
soon become physical anthropology and ethnology were already visible. Exacerbated by often vehemently opposed views on race, eugen-
ics, and slavery, the bitter struggle between biological determinists and
ethnologists, the former ardent about Galtonian genetics and utopian
dreams of the purification of the human race, the latter increasingly
appalled by the implications of this racist orientation, eventually led
some ethnologists, particularly Americans, toward a staunch and at
times extreme determinism of their own: the conviction that culture
was completely divorced from biology or evolution, that humanity
had leapt beyond the boundaries of nature, and that human life was
moulded solely by cultural factors.[6]

The discipline had already begun its move toward a more decidedly
social and cultural slant, focusing on the study of civilization and most

especially its 'primitive' shadow, with Edward B. Tylor's 1870 publication of *Primitive Culture*. In time, the findings of ethnographic fieldwork itself were of great influence in promoting this shift, for in the field no one-to-one association between belief or behaviour and habitat, no universal pattern of adaptation to environment, could be pinned down. The astonishing diversity and hitherto unimagined complexity of human cultures, no matter what the environment, could not be gainsaid.

A further impetus to the shift toward a more specialized, sociocultural anthropology was the discovery of the utility of cultural differences as political tools. As it turned out, ethnological speculation proved useful for employment in the revival of political and cultural nationalisms in Europe in the mid-nineteenth century, as it was in the contestation for aboriginal territories in North America. And throughout the rest of the already colonized world, it served its masters well in dealing with the routine exigencies of imperial administration.[7] Without a doubt the effort to distinguish humanity from the rest of the animal kingdom as a supremely cultural being was also an attempt to shore up a crumbling certainty about human distinctiveness in the face of the Darwinian assault.

Over time, then, anthropology's first – and to my mind currently most important – question changed emphasis. While the first decade of the twentieth century was the period in which the discipline most consistently sought to establish a holistic practice, by the end of the second decade it began to fragment along its historical faultlines, and the new discipline's balance shifted decisively from 'what kind of *animal* is the *human* animal?' to the *human* side of the equation. Quite soon, the organic aspects of the study of humanity became the sole purview of physical anthropology, and social and cultural anthropological theory was left to flourish unencumbered by the clay feet of our species' creaturely constitution. Anthropology changed course from natural history to social science. Gradually, the *Ur*-notion of culture as a superorganic efflorescence of human being became the major preoccupation of cultural anthropologists.

Of most consequence in these developments, I believe, is the fact that the two subdisciplines of physical anthropology and ethnology, at such serious odds since their formal beginnings, seem never to have overcome their rift and soon ceased to have much to converse about, each going its separate way. As I suggested in chapter 2, in the subsequent history of anthropology, and especially in the future shaping of its basic assumptions about nature, the resultant absence of dialogue concerning humanity's animal subjectivity, our culturing creatureliness (how difficult to find appropriate words!), proved to mark a critical juncture. And at the beginning of the twenty-first century, mainstream anthropology has changed little in the ways it orders humanity vis-à-vis the natural world. The disciplinary split between human subjectivity and organic being is still mostly taken for granted, in practice if not always in discourse. Ironically, as it turns out, Linnaeus's leap, and that of the nineteenth-century naturalists and early anthropologists, was more prescient than they could know, for modern biology and genetics have borne out beyond anyone's imaginings the closeness of the biological ties between humans and other animals. And yet anthropology has maintained, in its practice, a split that reverts to a much earlier era. This fateful turn in anthropology's nature-habitus during its formative years, dividing human nature and human culture into non-communing subdisciplines, was thus a fork in the road of the discipline's history that I believe we need to revisit seriously in our present day if anthropology is to have relevance for the future.

ANTHROPOLOGY AS NATURAL HISTORY

What do I mean by 'anthropology as natural history'? I do not intend, in these pages, to outline a programmatic guide to a new, or to a renewed old, science, but I *am* encouraging a shift in the customary and largely unexamined humanist frame of reference practised in anthropology today. I am suggesting that we recall and explicitly recognize anthropology as the study of the natural history of the human species in all its complexity and variety. I am advocating, in this brief sketch, not that anthropology become a branch of natural history, but that we never forget that *it is already a full expression* of it.

To keep this small adjustment in mind we need to remember our biological reality, the round of life – procreation, birth, and death – we share with one another and with all other organisms. We eat other beings in order to live, and, without reverting to a vulgar Marxism, sociobiology, or utilitarianism, it is critical to re-emphasize that much of the activity that we call culture has its source and inspiration in this basic fact. Human beings are inescapably biological beings, and the reorientation of anthropology as natural history would entail recognizing and investigating our human nature and its links with the rest of nature *as these are complexly expressed in social and cultural practices.* For we cannot doubt that this biology matters – to making society, to making culture, to altering our environments, to ordering the cosmos – although in ways we mostly do not yet understand. For good and ill, with all our attributes, we are a species that belongs in the order of nature; we are neither tourists nor aberrations.[8] This kind of recognition might permit us to reopen the necessary dialogue concerning humans as a particular species of culture-making animal subject.

Furthermore, like all other species, we are a species of animal in constant, inextricable relationship with ecosystems. Anthropology already studies the human species in habitat: ecology and economy, originally the studies of household knowledge and household management, are literally the subjects of ethnography, the stuff of local, situated wisdoms. We cannot really extricate habitus from habitat, although right now we know so little about how these interact. Bearing all this in mind, we can anticipate that anthropology as natural history would be open to the study of connections between human beings and the nonhuman environment that cannot be reduced to utility only. Anthropology as natural history would include the study of human biophilic tendencies as part of this connection with habitat.

Concurrently with the discipline's recent focus on time and space, anthropology as natural history would be able to deepen and enliven that discussion with the understanding that nature also has a local history, one that interacts with human history, as historians of ecology have begun to show us.[9] As well, as poet Gary Snyder puts it, 'nature happens, culture happens, *somewhere.*' Thus, not only are human life and culture historically impacted and multiply situated, 'multilocal'; so is nature, as we variously understand it. Furthermore, not only is human life 'situated' in sociopolitical snarls of power and ideology, as it is most common to analyse 'situated knowledges' these days, it is also situated *in habitats*, habitats with agency and effects of which we know nothing at present.[10] Anthropology as natural history should encourage richer conceptions of enquiry into the interconnectedness between habitat and habitus, paying closer attention to the interactive nature of human culture *in situ.* (The habitats of human beings, like those of migratory birds, could constitute 'travelling sites' as well as stationary ones.)

A basic question of ethnography has always been, What do people tell us about their habitats that informs their understandings of the world? In anthropology as natural history, practitioners would 'listen more closely to the material,' as feminist critics of science in particular have proposed.[11] Ethnographers would attend to these habitats with new interest, respecting them as agents, in some manner, in the lives of these societies. They would also listen more carefully to what their informants tell them about these habitats and the nature of this agency. They would, above all, take their informants' information more seriously as *theory*, not only as data: as theory crucial for anthropology's basic tasks. By this I mean that anthropologists, taking to heart Johannes Fabian's sober observation concerning classical anthropology – that the native informants' ethnographic presence is almost invariably coupled with their theoretical absence – would receive native theories about their world as situated theories, as valid, albeit partial, insights into the cosmos, nature, and human nature.

When the Koyukon, for instance, observe that the Canada goose, their customary prey, restrains itself when it could harm a human being, or when they express their belief that the whole country, connected together somehow under the ground, knows when bad things are being done to it, ethnographers would pay attention to these statements as legitimate theories developed from generations, sometimes hundreds of years, of recursive observation, verification, and intense peer review in the field. These theories deserve to be considered of equal, and perhaps at times more insightful, merit than those currently in vogue in Western science. Although the Koyukon undoubtedly present their views in terms quite different from those of the ethnographer or Western science in general (or, stated otherwise, although the ethnographer undoubtedly presents his/her views in terms quite different from those of the Koyukon), when the views of members of the host society and those of the ethnographer – each taken as partial, local, and situated knowledge – are placed together *in dialogue*, they could tell us something meaningful, and perhaps unanticipated, about human life.[12]

Finally (for this merest sketch), anthropology as natural history would commit to developing a knowledge base (possibly, eventually, acting as a basis for an ethic) beyond intra-human affairs, and including nonhuman nature: a biocentric world-view. In previous chapters I described some of the ways in which contemporary Canadian metropolitans attempted to express biophilic and biocentric inclinations, although the available language seemed inadequate to express them. A commitment to biocentrism (or, at the very least, to researching biocentrism as a serious alternative world-view) would mean a commitment to a humanism not defined, in our usual zero-sum arithmetic, *against* the other. It would commit to a biocentrism that includes human beings and the best of humanism – its compassion, its reception of interiority and subjectivity, its valuing of reflection and responsibility – while managing not to reduce either human or other living beings in the process. In a biocentric anthropology the humanist position would have to be renamed to reflect the possibility that other natural beings might also value and at times practise some, say, fishy, or bovinistic, or alfalfalike form of this same generosity toward one's own.

Why Now?

In the last chapter I suggested that the principal difficulty of deep ecology and the green movement generally had to do with finding compelling biocentric metaphors to live by. The West, in general, needs to get beyond the confining language of polarity we are currently stuck with. In this newly reconnected, ecological world, we need to find new metaphors, or perhaps retrieve old ones, to live by. Now, since the basic work of anthropologists consists of uncovering the metaphors other peoples live by, might it not appropriately fall to Western anthropology to reclaim the missing metaphors of its own culture? Its role might include disclosing experiences whose names have been lost to its natives, dredging up for shared scrutiny and reflection the muted metaphors of natural being that we in the West still cling to, as we saw in previous chapters, but live by only in disguised forms.

There is no doubt that we need more appropriate metaphors to carry us through to a more benign, respectful relationship with our habitats. We need new metaphors now because we desperately need new relationships now. It is vital that we complicate our Western ideas of what human beings are: our nature, culture, self, and relation to others. We also need ways to think in more complicated terms about our customary ways of knowing, about language and its relation to communication, for example, and about the divisions of knowledge production (and consumption) we have come to treat as fixed and inevitable. It is time for social scientists and humanists generally to correct the widespread failure to address habitat and non-utilitarian interspecies relations in human culture and society, as it is time for biologists and other natural and physical scientists to take more account of human society, and their own sitedness in particular societies, in their work. It is also time for an ecology of human behaviour that transcends the patent mistakes of sociobiology, one that places human nature in the web of all nature without thereby minimizing humanity *or* the rest of life. For anthropology as natural history, pulling together the dynamic interactions between nature and culture, society (habitus) and habitat, into one field of study, will be, I believe, unavoidable as well as enriching.

It will be important to study humanity in all its habitats, including Western habitats, and particularly in urban habitats. We need to do this not only because not to do so is to perpetuate the cultural colonialism anthropology has tried so hard to reveal and to shed, but also, and especially, because the Western city is such an influential ideological machine, shaping habitat and habitus globally. To paraphrase a famous adage awkwardly: not knowing ourselves, we are condemned to repeat ourselves elsewhere.

Most fundamentally, we need a critical reformulation of what counts as knowledge today. We need these new ideas and new ways of thinking because we urgently need to create new relationships between humans and environment. It is time not only to accept, but to extend, Bateson's contention that 'the whole of our thinking about what we are and what other people [and beings] are has got to be restructured.'[13] Turning this assertion into a practice will not be easy. It would require that anthropology, and thus Western society, examine afresh its formulation of basic categories of being and of knowing. Differently put, we would need to return to anthropology's original, radically simple question: What kind of animal *is* the human animal, today?

Of central significance in reframing anthropology as natural history is the obligation to re-examine the nature-culture divide. In my investigation of anthropology's nature-habitus in chapter 2, the conservative character of the discipline was evident in its protection of the entrenched distinction between nature and culture. I suggested that anthropology's unaltered position on this issue continues to legitimize the 'Great Divide' for the rest of Western society. Without some attempt to bridge this divide, however, or better, to collapse it altogether, the quest to create a more useful anthropology and a more ecologically farsighted, relational culture, can only fail. And yet, as we saw with regard to the animal-rights movement, when adequate language to encompass the more complicated ideas and relationships people seek to develop is missing, the task before them is not merely to invent felicitous verbal tropes, but, far more difficult, to invent metaphors that a significant proportion of the population would consider acceptable to live by. We need to find practical poetry that would link somehow with the world not only as desired but as understood, and that would be not too alien in practice from the habitus of this age. In the absence of such new conventions, it is not surprising that the path in search of the right metaphors to live by is littered with awkward neologisms and word implosions, convoluted problematizations and explications, and poetry that remains poetic but not programmatic, so to speak. Recognizing that all this litter is unavoidable residue from the bricolage of culture making, let us indulge in a little bricolage ourselves.

COLLAPSING THE NATURE-CULTURE DIVIDE

If since the beginning of humanism the West has asked, What are human beings as separate from the rest of creation? now it is crucial to ask, What are humans as beings continuous with the whole? Adopting Henry David Thoreau's project, which he set down in *Walden* about a century and a half ago, the charge for anthropology in the twenty-first century is to ground Western (and human) consciousness, and thus culture, in nature.[14]

Exploration of the West's peculiar nature-culture divide, its impermeable boundedness between human and animal, matter and spirit, self and other, is at last being accepted more generally as a serious form of inquiry. Not only in the chaos and complexity theories of mathematics and the physical sciences, but also at various sites in Western cultural criticism – as in some forms of anthropological reflexivity, deep ecology, and environmental historicism – we see people beginning to be engaged in projects aiming to complicate our conventional ways of understanding, and seeking to precipitate out some possible new ways of conceptualizing the world and of expressing emergent structures of feeling. We also see entire disciplines converging in projects directed toward collapsing the nature-culture divide and finding new metaphors for a post-modern, post-'well-ordered' world to live by. This is most evident perhaps in the various sociologies of science, as exemplified by Bruno Latour, and in feminist critiques of science, of which Haraway is probably the best-known exemplar today.[15]

In this task it is appropriate, if perhaps somewhat surprising, to (re-) turn to Thoreau. For this undertaking is not new; it is one with which he would have been very familiar. Throughout his career, it would be fair to say, Thoreau sought metaphors to live by that would transcend the nature-culture divide while keeping his feet firmly on the ground,

indeed, embedded in the earth. In *Seeing New Worlds* (1995), literary
critic Laura Dassow Walls achieves a convincing rereading of Thoreau,
particularly his later journals, in this vein. She illuminates this original,
this maverick, not as a lonely voice of nineteenth-century American
Romanticism and Emersonian transcendentalism – a common rendering of Thoreau's career – but, far more radically, as a harbinger of what
we are groping for in the twenty-first century.[16] For their part,
Haraway and Latour, each in their own way, are also attempting to theorize a multiplex nature-culture relation. In detecting and probing
instabilities in the hitherto stubbornly impenetrable nature-culture
barrier, both have come up with concepts that attempt to dissolve the
barrier altogether: concepts such as 'hybrids' and 'cyborgs' – entities
that give conceptual solidity to Alexander Wilson's assertion that
humans and nature construct one another. Together with Thoreau's
insights, primarily as interpreted by Dassow Walls, I rely on Haraway
and Latour to trace out some possibilities for a responsible, creative
nature-culture collapse.

Chaos

Dassow Walls presents the progress of Thoreau's life work as the
unfolding of an ever-greater understanding of and tolerance for 'chaos,'
which – evident especially in his later journals – prefigures complexity
thinking in its most current sense. From early on in his career Thoreau
had tried to capture in his writing his growing perception of nature as
complex and dynamic process. He wanted to ground his own consciousness in nature's rhythms, to capture nature's insights – its sea-
sons, its cycles, its 'furred life,' its processes of growth and decay. In this
he manifested a totemic yearning: a search, through personal experience unbound by convention, for connection with the rest of life.
Through language, Thoreau tried to take his readers beyond culture
and in a sense beyond language itself, to direct encounter. 'Where is the
literature,' he asked, 'which gives expression to Nature?' 'He would be
a poet who could impress the winds and streams into his service, to
speak for him; who nailed words to their primitive senses, as farmers
drive down stakes in the spring, which the frost has heaved; who
derived his words as often as he used them, – transplanted them to his
page with earth adhering to their roots.'[17]

Yet Thoreau intuited that we can never completely understand the
wild, observing, as we do, from a 'compromised and cultivated land-

scape.' But that landscape too was 'part and parcel,' as he put it, of nature. It was not necessary to remove humanity from the natural world. Influenced by German naturalist Alexander von Humboldt, he came to believe that culture and nature, the civil and the wild, were reciprocal forces in this ever-fluid, ever-emergent system. The Concord woods in his time were already the product of centuries, at least, of human intervention, yet to Thoreau they were no less natural. He became progressively at ease with the 'generative equation,' the creative and emergent properties of habitats and beings in connection with one another, with minimally ordered patterns that were acutely sensitive to highly complex processes, and even with apparent disconnection. Thoreau had discovered chaos: 'a new insight into the imbrication of all order with disorder, disorder with the emergence of order, the *self*-organizing power of a chaotic nature quite apart from human desire or even presence.'[18]

Thoreau saw human knowledge as an active although not necessary agent in this chaotic, emergent view of life. Such knowledge could change people and could change nature: 'Do not thoughts and men's lives enrich the earth and change the aspect of things as much as a new growth of wood?' Nor did he see himself, as an individual, on the sidelines: he was an active participant in all this self-organization. He was a poet-naturalist who, in his chosen activities of observing and writing, could 'translate the unspoken natural world into words,' thus helping to bring the world into a new state of organization by making comprehensible to others the insights he had gained both from the wild and from the compromised locales of Walden Pond and Concord's environs. He was clearing a path for nature to enter human culture and habitus.[19]

These latter places especially, the kinds of locations Thoreau called a 'middle earth,' implicated as they were both in human cultivation and nature's successions, became increasingly important in his thinking. At Walden, in preventing the weeds from encroaching on his bean field, Thoreau showed what hard, unrelenting work was involved in keeping nature and culture separate, what a sustained effort it was to keep the boundaries clear. As a surveyor who created legal boundaries, he knew well that long after the surveyor's lines had faded and the land, cleared for settlement and settled, had been abandoned, unattended nature would take over once again, interacting with the traces of human habitation to create yet another succession, another regeneration.

This equivocal position between the civil and the wild, the 'middle earth,' became for Thoreau an authentic place from which to observe and participate in the world. It meant living on the frontier, as a 'borderer' between civil and wild, understanding that a border meant not a division (although it can mean, as Dassow Walls points out, a difference), but a relation. Thoreau sought a vantage point from which people would be able to discern the civil and the wild as allies, not antagonists, linked by the individual who understands himself both as a member of society and as part of nature. Thoreau had come to understand that we are all hybrids and live in a hybrid world. To live on the frontier, much as Walden itself was a frontier, meant acknowledging that hybridity, welcoming it, truly living it.[20]

Hybridity and Mediation

'Hybrids' is the word Bruno Latour might use for Thoreau's compromised places, because, like everything else, Latour believes, they are composed of the material world, the social world, and that of language all entangled. The world, says Latour, is real, collective, and discursive all together, and one cannot separate these aspects out into categories.[21] For Latour 'the modern world' means a world artificially separated into categories of nature, power, and discourse. To be modern in Latour's sense means to live and recreate an Enlightenment culture based on clear distinctions, on what he calls 'The Modern Constitution': a culture committed to polarizing the world into simple oppositional categories, into forms of self and other, while at the same time muting and refusing acknowledgment, let alone agency, to the mixed-up, unclassifiable world of nature, society, and language in which people live in real life. This separation (the effects of which we saw played out in human–animal relations in previous chapters), is the essence of the modern. We try hard to purify our concepts, separating them out from one another with such dedication that the real world, the world of mixed categories or hybrids, fills up the centre, that is, our lived lives, while we cannot think or speak about them because we have emptied out those more complex categories that would have allowed us to name some form of hybridity. We are, in other words, missing the metaphors with which to name and engage this complex centre, this busy, well-trafficked terrain revealed only by the collapse of the nature-culture divide.

In this instance, Bruno Latour's and Donna Haraway's concerns and orientations are in essential agreement. For Haraway, what will 'count as nature and as matters of fact' gets to be constituted through nodes of humans, nonhumans, and material, semiotic, and social technologies. Bifurcated categories, she says, 'are reifications of multifaceted, heterogeneous, interdigitating practices and their relatively stable sedimentation, all of which get assigned to separate domains for mainly ideological reasons.' Latour's notion of hybrids, too, is reminiscent of Haraway's conception of 'cyborgs': 'the offspring of implosions of subjects and objects and of the natural and artificial.' Haraway, however, takes the idea somewhat further in emphasizing the importance of tracing the relations among human beings, other organisms, and machines as they unfold in specific times, places, and conditions: What is going on in the world here and now, or then and there, to spawn these particular cyborgs?[22]

In Latour's language Thoreau the poet-naturalist would be a *mediator* between the two polarities the West has set up in order to be modern, and indeed this is how Dassow Walls characterizes him. From his equivocal position as a borderer in a middle earth, he is able to describe more fully the hybridity of what he actually experiences: events and entities that partake of the natural, the social, and the discursive all at once. Thoroughly non-modern, Thoreau could allow paradoxes to be and yet would acknowledge them as such. He was able to 'stand to one side and articulate the marvelous and disturbing hybrid phenomena that were modernism's burgeoning progeny, born of the marriage of human and natural: the farm boy building a waterwheel in a meadow rill; fish and lilies stocking an artificial pond in a cemetery; forests made by squirrels, acorns, and axes; a villager borrowing an axe and building a cabin on the shores of a glacial lake on the edge of town.'[23] As in Martin Buber's characterization of the I–Thou relationship, in which there is nothing a person must not see in order to see, no knowledge that he or she must forget, for Thoreau the only real kind of knowing came to be a relational kind. Always aware that he was the observed as much as the observer (perhaps more so) on his famous 'walks' and not some 'undercover agent' skulking around, observing invisibly from behind tree trunks and boulders, he felt himself a fully participating part of the habitat, a being fully cognized by other beings. 'Man must realize that the gaze does not belong to him alone: nature *looks back.*' The very opposite of relational knowing, of I and Thou, to Thoreau, was 'the sterile inbreeding of man interacting only with man.' And so he attempted to give equal voice to all the phenomena he experienced.[24]

Leaving either/or behind, Thoreau developed comfort with paradox, with both/and, with hybrids and with mediation. The nature he
participated in and wrote about became 'increasingly decentered, dis-
junctive, open-ended, multiply created by agents ranging from grass
and acorns to pines, squirrels, and loons, mountain rocks to meadow
rills, Concord farmers and German scientists to Harvard libraries and
the Walden woods, surveyor and engineer to author, to reader.' Thoreau cracked open the dichotomies we are so comfortable with even
today, and then imploded them in a startlingly familiar post-modern
way by putting all these seemingly unrelated elements together, 'a rich
compost of pairings and disruptions,' in one collage. But there is this
great difference between Thoreau's collage and the post-modern pas-
tiche: for in Thoreau there is no trace of irony, no aesthetic shrug, but a
passionate plea for people to see differently, more inclusively. It is not
what you look at, but how you look and whether you see.[25] It is as
though Thoreau were observing the underside of Latour's Modern
Constitution. Acting as a mediator in his non-modern way by describing what he saw both above (the categorizations people tried to live
by) and below (the world as complexly metamorphic and continually
emergent), he tried – through the acute multi-sensuousness and multilocality of his participant-observation, and through the use of appropriate, and multivocal, language – to make sense of the whole.
To know nature, he understood, one had to bend one's entire consciousness to its knowledge. And even then, as he cautioned, '[t]he
highest that we can attain to is not Knowledge, but Sympathy with
Intelligence ... It is in the light up of the mist by the sun. Man cannot
know in any higher sense than this, any more than he can look serenely
and with impunity in the face of the sun.'[26]

Situated Knowledges

'Man is but the place where I stand,' Thoreau wrote, and in yet another
memorable series of observations he prefigured a concept finding
immense resonance today for our present-day needs. He spoke of
'sited knowledge': 'Nature and human life are as various as our several
constitutions. Who shall say what prospect life offers to another?' Here
was a profound understanding that all knowledge is embedded in
habitus. This kind of awareness came, he believed, from the sudden
revelation that nature looks back at you. Realizing that there were
other minds ('not all Mind, but a *fox* mind') and other concerns than

those of human beings, Thoreau perceived the meagreness of one point of view, one form of knowledge. In particular, he grasped the importance of acknowledging this reality and of bearing witness to it. Allowing all the contradictions to be, but recognizing them, listening attentively to each voice: this was the essence of sited knowledge.[27]

The conception of situated knowledges is currently elaborated most fully by Haraway. In a manner close in spirit to Geertz's 'local knowledge' as well as Thoreau's anticipatory vision, Haraway brings us back to a sobering acceptance that our grasp of the overall is forever limited, partly by our peculiarly human, species-specific perceptual/conceptual apparatus and physical capacities for agency and activity in the world, but also by our largely culturally shaped habitus, informed and constrained by the particular metaphors we live by. Precisely because of these limitations, Haraway argues, we have a responsibility to be aware of the limitations of our particular standpoints. Most critically, she emphasizes the necessity to *converse* with others, by which she means not seeking a dominant or majority point of view, nor even consensus where that is forced, but rather fostering the expression of all voices (including those of nonhumans) and competing points of view. Only in this way can one reach something we can truly call 'objectivity,' for only in this way can the limits of each 'version of the truth' be spelled out as clearly as possible. Conversing is also a way to become comfortable with both/and, with paradox, with the absence of one true centre; for, of course, the centre disappears when there are but shifting points of view. 'Could a greater miracle take place than for us to look through each other's eyes for an instant?' asks Thoreau.[28]

Awareness of the sitedness of knowledge emerges not only from the sudden revelation that nature looks back, but also from confrontation with otherness of which we cannot be a part. There are things we can never really know, or participate in, such as the nocturnal world that comes awake as human beings sleep: 'The recent tracks of the fox or otter, in the yard, remind us that each hour of the night is crowded with events, and the primeval nature is still working and making tracks in the snow.' And there are other things we can never know because their otherness is so radical, and so unexpected, that we are at a complete loss even to conceive their existence: they make no sense. Such an experience was Thoreau's on his infamous climb of Mount Ktaadn, where he encountered nature unmediated – unimaginedly real, utterly inaccessible – and the way to further knowledge barred: 'Why came Ye here before your time.'[29]

A final paradox: As Thoreau was discovering this creative chaos in nature by actually entering into the landscape and encountering the physical world on foot, ardently empirical, radically participatory, all senses alert, seeking a non-reductive form of knowledge obtainable only through intimate contact with other beings, Harvard University and the American Association for the Advancement of Science were busy demoting field naturalism to amateur status in favour of laboratory work as 'real science'; and 'real science' was developing apace as the search for the spare, predictable laws of a stable universe. Thoreau's later writings and journals, leaning ever more toward a decentred vision, were interpreted as the exhausted jottings of a failed, sick, intellectually bankrupt natural historian rather than the herald of another way of knowing, the sort of knowing we need today in collapsing the nature-culture divide. As Dassow Walls remarks, the insights Thoreau experienced in isolation in his lifetime we are experiencing more than a century later as a culture.[30]

REORDERING ANTHROPOLOGY

To move to anthropology as natural history, it would not be enough simply to name anthropology *as if* it were natural history; that is, as a mere figurative metaphor. It would have to be practised – lived – as natural history. Collapsing the Great Divide would force a fundamental reformulation of the nature of modern anthropology itself. In the process of reordering its ways of knowing, anthropology as natural history would shift its ontological foundation from the side of God and the angels toward animal being, and its epistemological base from an entrenched dualistic cast of thought toward a more context-informed, flexible shape-shifting. And in a subtle but significant shift in its encounter with the other, anthropology would extend the spirit of profound civility it has achieved toward human others to nonhuman others.

New Grounds for Self and Other

Of the new ways of thinking called for, the most important is undoubtedly a reconsideration of self and other. The great metaphors that still shape the nature-habitus of our age, the spatial metaphor of the Great Chain of Being and the temporal metaphor of the evolutionary tree, have underlined our basic connection with other animals; but they have also helped us to maintain our distance from them. Human beings invariably end up closer to the top of the chain or the tree than other beings. As Fabian showed with respect to non-Western human communities at the margins of the Western metropolis, distancing in both space and time has resulted in primitivizing other people, rendering them 'lesser' than Westerners. So it is with animals banished to lower links and marginal branches: they become, by virtue of their allocation to a particular place on a metaphorical tree of knowledge, lesser than humans. Such distancing, to further borrow Fabian's argument, makes it difficult for us to perceive other animals as fellow travellers in life's unfolding.[31] They remain inexorably the (disparaged) other.

Reluctance to acknowledge human–animal continuities still lurks deep in the West's ways of knowing. We find it even among people like ecologists, conservationists, and animal-rights activists whose interest in and concern for other animals is unquestioned. When other animals are accorded significance, that curious reversal in value noted in earlier chapters almost invariably occurs: now it is the human being that is deemed lesser. Whether positive value settles on one or the other, it appears impossible to remove the distinction in value itself. For, based as it is on these metaphors of separation in space and time we live by, it recreates the perception of a decisive split between (human) self and (every) other, Latour's Modern Constitution.

It is salutary, in this context, for us to view the human species in the position of the simplified other. As discussed in chapter 1, in some versions of sociobiology human beings have had a taste of the reductionism usually applied so unquestioningly to other animals. While sociobiology made an important attempt to link humankind to the rest of nature, this thought-experiment in biology drastically diminished the multivocality of interests and motivations – and, egregiously, the varied cultural ways of knowing – that inhere in human life. The gross oversimplification of human beings that has ensued merely underscores the reductionism to which all of nature is continually subject in any science based on a narrow and unrelenting positivism. When simplifying habits of mind take over, the results are nothing short of insulting. If human beings, unsceptically, are imagined so reductively by their own kind, what can we be doing to the integrity of other animals? For the brief time of its ascendency, sociobiology did try to stress continuity among all species, including our own. If in the end the sociobiology experiment failed to create a new, more inclusive branch of biological science, this view of life – reminding us that humanity is but one of innumerable species – did afford us, for a time, a humbling image of humanity as other.

As we study human interrelationships with other natural beings, assumptions will have to shift radically. Instead of habitually hypothesizing in other beings less or none of what we consider valuable in ourselves – interiority, history, language, complex social relations, invention, economy, ecological impulse, and above all, agency – it would be more productive to leave open the possibility of analogous, or perhaps even homologous, motivations in the entire continuum of life. For it is never really a question of, once and for all, 'self' or 'other,' 'nature' or 'culture,' 'animal' or human,' but of each perspective – and sometimes both (or several) together – as appropriate. There is, of course, no nature without culture, or vice versa: they make sense only in relation. So too with the rest: self-and-other, humans-and-other-animals. It is the pair, the triad, the group, the I and Thou, the hybridity, if you will – in short, the conjunction – that approaches the unitary apprehension we sometimes sense but so rarely can name. How can we turn this wisdom into knowledge, into ways of knowing? Can we begin to study human–animal, human–natural interactions in terms of situated, multilocal, and multivocal dialogues? Or, as Thoreau would have it, in terms of relational knowing?

A reconsideration of self and other along these lines would perhaps begin by redistributing the capacity for agency and sociality. In this mode, Haraway describes the work of field primatologists for whom the animals are co-producers of the scientific knowledge they record: '[T]he animals resist, enable, disrupt, engage, constrain, and display. They act and signify,' she says. Not only collaborators in scientific research, humans and animals are increasingly viewed by these primatologists as socially interactive. 'All that is unhuman,' Haraway remarks further, ' is not un-kind, outside kinship, outside the orders of signification, excluded from trading in signs and wonders.' In this view, then, to study human–animal relations would partake of explorations in that quintessential anthropological domain, kinship.[32]

Rethinking self and other calls for questioning the yes-or-no, on-or-off habits of polar thinking we have gotten used to under the Modern Constitution. Can we not cultivate the cognitive ability to move from self to a dissolution of self in, or an integration of self with, a particular context, and back again as the situation demands? Learning to develop contextual reasoning, to move back and forth with agility and without apology among possibilities, will be essential. It will be necessary to gain more comfort with ideas of continuum and continuity, and with the habit of probing *the intelligence that we find resonating between two extremes*, much as Latour suggests in mediating between the upper and lower halves of the Modern Constitution. We will need to learn to think in terms not only of hybridity but also of *shape-shifting*, the capacity to hold onto and make use of more than one way of thinking simultaneously. Biocentrism, to take a germane example, does not mean negating either self or humanity in favour of the rest of nature: it means integrating humanity and humanism with the whole of life. The task of anthropology as natural history is to negate neither humanity nor other beings but to clear a conceptual space to allow engagement in a renewed, more inclusive, hybrid human–nature dialogue.

A renewed dialogue between humankind and the rest of nature would recognize human similarities with and differences from other life forms, conceived as different, not as opposite, perspectives on the whole. Biophilia, to take another relevant instance, is basically the acceptance of difference, the love of and intense interest in the other, while the totemic imagination accepts the likenesses between human and other beings, and acknowledges and respects their relation. Our biophilia, in reminding us of our true links with other beings, may actually reawaken totemic sensibilities. Above all, the recognition of biophilia and the search for totemic relation could foster that indispensable attitude of solidarity with the rest of nature so necessary for embarking on the long revolution. For this is what biocentrism, *in practice*, is about: the act of recognition in which solitudes (selves, individuals, differences) that border, protect, and greet one another also take up a common cause.

It is here that the totemic imagination could come into its own. In little over a century, totemism moved from being studied, first, as someone else's cultural institution, then, as a chimeric product of the human mind's oppositional tendencies, to, at last and perhaps fullcircle, what I am suggesting we think of as the cultural expression of a (possibly universal) experience of interspecies relation. In an urban post-industrial context the totemic imagination connotes not some mysterious psychic phlogiston but, more prosaically, an everyday but authentic sense of connection with the rest of nature, one that recognizes in human lives the emotional and ritual linkages with all of life the concept has always implied. The totemic imagination encompasses culture and society as part of nature and nature as, deeply, part of society. The anthropology of the twenty-first century will be, at its best, an anthropology of such relation and connection; and twenty-first-century totemism, should we be prepared to acknowledge it, will be both an emotional recognition and a cultural celebration of that relation.

Creating Permeable Boundaries of Discourse

Language and Communication
In our pride, we have made a major error. Because humans use verbal language, we have reduced the rest of nature to silence. Much of my argument can be viewed as a plea to listen more carefully to the rest of the natural world. We have found out even in studying the human animal that, while verbal language is clearly important, it does not explain everything. Nor does participant observation rely only on what people say they do. In truth, verbal communication is used less than is commonly realized, since anthropologists can usually understand the language of the host community only imperfectly, if at all, and often miss the references, metaphors, ironies, and so on, that carry a lot of the intended meaning. Indeed, every language misses important nuances of lived experience available to speakers of other languages.[33] In any case, much of human communication and reflection is non-verbal. Similarly, since humans clearly do not rely on verbal language as the primary mode of communication with other animals, natural history-derived anthropological techniques are readily transferable to the study of human–animal interactions. By allowing the researcher to bypass verbal discourse, ethnographic methods open up the possibility of observing human relations with others without having to rely on a managed or authorized version of events, on ideology more generally understood, or on the spoken word at all. To my mind, any theoretical perspective that, like practice theory, strives to capture purposeful, cognitively implicated activity not easily articulated in language – that allows us to write ethnographies of those aspects of any society that are 'without history' – has great potential in the investigation of human relations with the rest of the natural world.[34]

Perhaps more radically, a post-humanistic, biocentred position would require a move from dependence on the linguistic to define our humanity to a more serious investigation of additional forms of human knowing, such as haptic, olfactory, pheromonal, and aural. We need to move away from the notion that verbal language completely sets apart and somehow elevates humanity. In the scheme of things, verbal language is just one evolutionarily newer way to communicate, but do we know whether it is necessarily a better way? We might think of it as a technology; and like all technologies we discover or invent, it is still so new to us in the historical sense that we are still enamoured with it, tinkering with it and seeing what we can make it do. Perhaps we are still so taken with this new technology that we have privileged it above other, deeper ways of knowing, perceiving, and judging, means we have and use that we may rely on more profoundly if less knowingly. Thoreau understood this as well. The true scientist, he suggested, would take in the natural world with senses more acute and fine-tuned than that of ordinary people: 'in spirit he is a poet, perhaps *the* poet of the natural world.'[35]

Disciplines and Dialogue
In describing hybrids Latour shows that we cannot in reality separate out the things we are interested in from the metaphors chosen to express their existence and activities or from the disciplines organized to study them. The real world, the ordinary world people live in, always and only consists of these mixed-up hybrids of 'life, labour, and language,' as Foucault had put it. What appears natural is humanly and discursively contaminated; what appears to be humanly created is constructed through language and materials; what appears to be pure language is agreed to by the collective and takes the poetry that gives it is meaning – its metaphors – from nature. Nonetheless, Latour says, we still try to make these separations, to 'purify' our ideas and critiques about nature, society, and language. One of the ways we do this is by segregating the disciplines we have assigned to study their various aspects. In the modern constitution we have separated out the investigation of nature, society, and discourse without permitting them a place in which to fraternize, exchange notes. As a result, we tend not to refer to other disciplines for insights into the whole. To mount a critique of nature (or of language, or of society), we may not borrow insights from other disciplines or discourses. Not only the hole in the ozone layer or Pasteur's bacteria (Latour's examples), but also human–animal relations in the city are purified by adherence to the metaphors we have chosen to live by. These metaphors mute their hybridity, their impure creation, and also their proper observation and study.

In reordering anthropology as natural history we would have to find ways to loosen the boundaries between the situated knowledges of scholarly disciplines. One logical first step in this process would require a closer dialogue between physical and cultural anthropology. In a renewed anthropology, both subdisciplines would be engaged in the joint project of seeking to understand human being simultaneously as animal being and as subject. The next logical step would be to make connections between anthropology as a whole and the other life sciences in the project of grounding human nature in all of nature. The need for sustained conversation among disciplines would suggest in turn, no doubt, the adoption of at least some common metaphors to live by. Indeed, with anthropology practised as natural history, as the study of a form of 'wildlife' (in its broadest sense: including the wild, the tamed, the domesticated, the feral forms we may take at different times in our lives), the boundaries between ethnology and ethology might begin to blur, with each enterprise opening up the knowledge, methods, and metaphors of the other for reflection and reconception. Anthropology might eventually consider it crucial to be able to record the contributions of both humans and other animals in the interspecies relation. And this has already begun. Anthropologist Elizabeth Atwood Lawrence, you will remember, had named as an explicit personal goal the expansion of ethnography to include as much as possible the input of the animals themselves in human–animal associations. The primatologists studied by Haraway are also developing this more complex and more respectful form of field naturalism. In this endeavour, practitioners would need to learn to understand, insofar as is possible, the semiotic and analogic systems of communication of other animals – their sign and metaphor systems. But since, as Bateson reminds us, in terms of relationship we share with other mammals a reliance on our comprehension of non-verbal communication, human beings may learn to understand, with attention and effort, the messages of many other animals almost as readily as we can those of other human beings.

Anthropology's Contribution to Natural History

In being reformulated for the twenty-first century, can anthropology move forward from social science to natural history without putting aside the field's accumulated wisdom? And in the process, can it contribute to the understanding of the other natural sciences? I believe it can, for what would be involved is a shift more in perspective than in actual practice. For instance, it has already been pointed out that anthropology is the only Western discipline to have studied human–animal and human–natural relations in such consistent breadth and depth. It is thus already part of the discipline's nature-habitus to observe and document the human–nature connection. Virtually its entire canon can be read as a description of the varieties of human–nature interaction and relation peoples have displayed and do display worldwide. Adding the findings of archaeologists and primatologists extends the canvas to ancient humanity and other primates as well. This fertile mass of ethnographic material is ripe for a rereading with the shifted sensibility suggested in these pages. What is new in this rereading is a far broader and more inclusive conception of kinship and genealogy than the field has hitherto embraced.

Hybridity
For new data anthropology depends largely on ethnographic field-work – itself, as we saw, a direct descendent of natural history. The face-to-face encounters of ethnographic method retain the non-reductive values of natural history. Everything may – should – be observed. Anthropologists are preconditioned by training to observe keenly and describe not only intra-human but also human–natural interactions in context, while bracketing off their own world-views as much as humanly possible. For Latour, in addition to other knowledge thus gained, these are promising methods for doing away with the Modern Constitution. He notes that anthropology is the only discipline that has successfully described nature-culture mixes as a matter of course. An anthropologist usually brings together in a single report, with no apparent anxiety, incidents of language, nature, and society all interwoven: equally represented are a group's myths, political economy, religion, and history, their genealogies, literature, ethnosciences, and law, their rituals, technologies, and syntax. In a word, anthropologists deal routinely in hybrids. 'In works produced by anthropologists abroad, you will not find a single trait that is not simultaneously real, social and narrated.'[36] It is his hope that anthropologists turn these revealing methods to a dismantling of the Modern Constitution at home, showing at last that we have never been modern even in the West.

Situated Knowledges
One of the great strengths of anthropology has always been its intimate involvement with the local: with life as lived in persons and in places,

and with knowledge as expressed and practised there, by them, at that time. A respect for sited or situated knowledge is basic to its orientation and is supremely compatible with its alliance with natural history. How global issues affect people at the local level, always an important part of this understanding, is crucial in today's world and has potential as one of anthropology's more general contributions to knowledge. Haraway makes the point about the work of conservationists, for example, that it needs to grasp 'the complex global and local politics of participating in reconstructing the meanings and social relations of "nature" within a decolonizing world'[37] – all issues of long-standing concern among anthropologists.

Further, in developing the possibilities inherent in participant observation, anthropologists have refined the art of attending not only to the behaviour of the observed but also to the *observing self's* sensations, emotions, associations, and imaginative flights in encountering the other, as data. In thus blending, to some extent, observer and observed, the discipline continues to develop the use of the self as an instrument to understand the other. Making use of the multivocality within the self, practising an interior sort of shape-shifting, and understanding better than ever the critical importance of situated knowledges – these constitute another of the great strengths of anthropology's methods, methods that can be developed further in conjunction with other disciplines.

Chaos and Self-Organization

'Do not thoughts and men's lives,' Thoreau wrote, 'enrich the earth and change the aspect of things as much as a new growth of wood?' If one allows that human knowledge is an unprecipitable part of the whole of nature rather than being mere observation and commentary on the passing throng, then human knowledge has wider agency than is usually assumed. So too with the knowledge gleaned from the practice of anthropology. What anthropologists have to say is an integral part of the self-organizing of the natural world. In this view, what an anthropologist – or any researcher – says, does, contrary to some popular opinion, matter. There is responsibility in this. In situating itself locally, as the natural history of one of innumerable species living in interaction with the rest of the world, anthropology could help to recreate a radically new Western (or post-Western) sensibility.

Relational Knowing

By acting as an antidote to too much theorizing, the fieldwork encounter permits the unfolding of surprise. Corollary to Wilson's observation that artifacts are incomparably poorer than the life they imitate, the life-to-life encounters of fieldwork are incomparably richer than any imaginings that will have preceded them. Among the surprises in store may be the discovery of hitherto unsuspected continuities between human and nonhuman behaviour, or unexpected traditions of interspecies communication previously obscured by the Western tendency to limit its understanding of communication to the forms of human utterance. Perhaps, with the assistance of other peoples, we may even be privileged one day to recognize when we have encountered a 'fox mind.'

Shape-Shifting

A last word on this subject concerns its practitioners. Anthropologists routinely 'live' more complicated cultural 'systems' than most people are ordinarily called upon to do. Living out their professional lives in the field as outsiders (whether abroad or at home) and thus regularly subjected to humbling experiences as other, constantly registering complex impressions as self-in-encounter-with-the-other, anthropologists can be said to practise cognitive shape-shifting as a matter of course. Familiar with living and naming conflicting experiences as a routine part of their working life, they learn to tolerate extreme ambiguity. Accepting inconsistent thoughts, discrepant emotions, and antagonistic values as an everyday part of field research keeps alive the necessity to refrain from premature closure on understanding. A stint in the field serves to defamiliarize life at home, reminding scholars of the ultimate unknowability of even the most 'well-known' systems. These shape-shifting abilities, in which observer and observed keep changing places, boundaries are continually dissolving, and perceptions and emotions reveal themselves with a sometimes bewildering multivocality, these flexible skills and multiple perspectives so necessary for embracing nature as a complex system and humanity as integral to it, are already a part of the anthropologist's cognitive and emotional practice.

Anthropology as natural history is one means for the West to formulate a less-scientistic science, rejecting not science itself, as a carefully elaborated cultural expression of humanity's enduring desire to understand the universe, but a narrowly rationalistic, simplistic, exclusionary mode of knowing the world that was more suitable to other times, to eras presumably overburdened with the confusion of too much miracle. Now, because too much of what is apprehended is left out of what is named, there is talk of the need for a 're-enchantment' of science, for the breath of *anima* into nature, and of nature into humanity. Ethnographic fieldwork, basically the preserved and embellished techniques of natural history, will have a major, *grounding* role (in the Thoreauvian, evidentiary sense) in this quest.

CONCLUSION

What I am suggesting here under the term 'anthropology as natural history' is thus not a new, but a renewed, discipline. In its deeper, more contextualized form, anthropology would remember with Midgley that we are not the *only* unique species. Having revisited and profoundly recast its old nature-culture debate, such an anthropology would rest its practice on a belief in and value of human being as a form of animal being, and culture as a particular, although not unique, way of being in nature. The wealth of observations on human–natural relations the discipline has accumulated would be regarded as core rather than accessory data, treasured substance rather than mere adventitious local colour. Most significantly, as I have been saying all along, this renewed discipline would remember that it has always been a natural history of the human species.

Anthropology as natural history would, of course, not be free of contestation. There are pitfalls, and not merely theoretical ones, in a biocentric anthropology as natural history. An obvious argument against this position would be the concern that anthropology as natural history biologizes and thereby essentializes human life, reverting to an unwelcome biological determinism. But this concern, as I have attempted to show earlier, is based on a serious misconstrual of biology as unnecessarily simplified. In this misrendering, nonhuman beings are conceived essentially as a collection of anatomical parts and physiological functions. Only in human beings does this collection of parts and functions, slightly differently arranged, somehow manifest the emergent properties of which we are so proud. Far from 'biologizing' anthropology in a reductive way, I believe that anthropology as natural history, in alliance with other natural sciences, would suggest a different, less deterministic, way of perceiving both humans and other beings. We know so little about what 'life' itself is about. Perhaps many of the things we think of as peculiarly human may inhere in, or emerge from, the physical processes of life itself, things like communication, culture, consciousness, relation, love, sorrow, and so on. Our own complexity is an animal complexity; we will have to accord to the rest of life the possibility, or the probability, of complexity at least equal to, if different from, our own. Situated as we are in time, place, tradition, and the limits of our imaginations, we need to accept that we will never grasp the entirety of nature. But we can learn to hear more beings, and to listen better.

Another objection might be, Oh no, here's yet another unnecessary reordering gambit: a 'new anthropology' for every anthropologist. I have great sympathy with this objection. Yet, we do need to formulate new ideas, hoping that some will take, because periodically we need to make these new relationships. Today it seems as though we have little choice but to ally ourselves cognitively and experientially – in habitus – with, not against, the rest of life and environment. Perhaps more people are concerned about how the world is perceived today than may be apparent on the surface. Perhaps anthropology as natural history will seem to many people to be a valuable, apt metaphor to live by, at least for the near future.

Far more difficult to counteract would be objections stemming from the implications of this position for the existing political economy. Who gains from the way things are now? Who gains from the perpetuation of casting nature and human nature at odds with each other? Global corporate capitalism depends on the Modern Constitution, on the separation of human beings, who are or can be made to be consumers, from the rest of the world, seen as resources for eventual consumption. When the Modern Constitution breaks down from time to time, revealing (as we saw with respect to human–animal relations) how, for example, language can spill blood, some people turn into quite effective political animals, an awkward shape-shift at best for the regnant political economy. A more generally biocentric ethos or understanding of the world would precipitate a Constitutional paralysis, or rather (it is to be hoped), a Constitutional Chaos. In this instance we would need to invoke once again Jeremy Bentham's idea of 'deep play':[38] the stakes are so high that it is foolish to engage in this sort of activity at all. Yet, not to play, not to attempt to grasp and restrain the free hand of the market in the service of the entire planetary body, would likely mean that there would no longer be any game to play at all.

As scientific animals and as a society, can we move entrenched ways of thinking and boundaries of knowing from the nature-culture dichotomy to a notion of relational knowing, to interspecies relationship? And can we learn to include our own animal selves and our own cultural societies in a community of natural communities?

Perhaps the most difficult shift to achieve in practice will be to attend to human being as animal being and to culture as a way of being in nature. It will be most difficult, perhaps, if that human being is from the West (perhaps even oneself) and that habitat is the city. The anthropology perspective advocated here requires the examination of nature as complexly embodied and expressed in the structures of feeling and unconsidered practices, as well as the institutions and rituals, that individual and group (human) animal life displays in all its permutant variety. In anthropology as natural history, this interplay between the needs and proclivities of human animals in interaction with habitat and their expression – anthropology's perennial subject matter – would be explicitly investigated as such: it would be understood as the self-study of one of the innumerable species resident on this planet. In studying others (and in being studied ourselves, we ought, like Thoreau, to begin to presume), anthropologists as natural historians would have uppermost in their minds the field's original question, and would add to that the world's currently most pressing question, What is the human animal's relation with the entire biosphere? While the discipline would continue to be practised as it has in the past, as a form of self-reflective natural history, the deeper form of the discipline would legitimately – and necessarily – join with the rest of natural history in common interest, common wonder, and, at last, common cause.

Do we see the development of any broader inclination, either in anthropology or in Western society itself, to seriously define culture as part of nature? Is there any more general sign of such a radical shift, in either our ways of knowing or in our values, from a cultural to a natural perspective, from humanism to a post-humanistic commitment to biosphere as the proper definition of community? We have looked at a number of starts in this direction, emerging from a variety of sources and couched in different metaphors, which nonetheless converge on a common search: for new metaphors to live by; for a new or renewed language and practice through which to express our human experiences of relation with the rest of the natural world.

I leave the last words of this essay to Clifford Geertz (along with a last bit of mischief to the Trickster). Geertz usually speaks from a steadfastly human-centred orbit. Nonetheless, let us perform the following experiment through the medium of his eloquent voice. Let us remove from the following passage a mere word – the one word 'human.' With that merest elision, that minor muting, his voice comes closest to expressing the awakening world-view of some natives of urban Western culture – some animal-rights activists, deep ecologists, maverick anthropologists and other scholars, and ordinary people who shared their worlds with me for a brief time in my fieldwork or in their writings. Perhaps this altered perspective will, one day soon, claim all of anthropology, and the rest of the West, as well:

> To see others as sharing a nature with ourselves is the merest decency. But it is from the far more difficult achievement of seeing ourselves amongst others, as a local example of the forms ... life has locally taken, a case among cases, a world among worlds, that the largeness of mind, without which objectivity is self-congratulation and tolerance a sham, comes.[39]

'Midsummer Night's Dream' (1967, concrete, chromed steel) by Wessel
Couzijn (b. 1912), High Park, Toronto (photo Alex Capon; courtesy Alex
Capon, June Ardiel)

A Dream in a City Park

Shall I not have intelligence with the earth? Am I not partly leaves and vegetable mould myself?

Henry David Thoreau, *Walden*

It is summer in Toronto's High Park. Looking for a place to spread your blanket, you notice a choice spot ahead. Approaching, you see a couple stretched full-length on the ground, embracing. At least, that's what you think it is at first: a couple lying together, as many have done and will do over the years in the twilight summer grass, perhaps listening to an outdoor production of a Shakespeare play, catching words sailing upwind. When you come closer, the figures get bigger, and change character.

It is a sculpture made of rough, pebbly concrete and steel bands, less clearly defined up close than it had appeared from afar. From here, it appears as if you have come upon beings of vaguely but discernibly human shape, partially joined; or perhaps it's a being incompletely cleft. Some life form just now, as you approach, growing and taking form from the earth, or just now returning to it. Shape-shifting material. Dangerous dirt.

Poised between other and self, eternity and history, within listening distance of a poet's durable metaphors, artist Wessel Couzijn's *Midsummer Night's Dream* encompasses all we can truly know about humanity's place in the order of nature.

Notes

Introduction: Nature and the City

1 Grady 1995, Mays 1994. Grady tells us that there is actually more 'nature' in Toronto now than in the past: 'A city attracts wildlife to it that otherwise wouldn't be found within hundreds of kilometres of the place' (8). He says further: 'We have altered our environment to suit ourselves, and we have found to our amazement and sometimes consternation that this new world also suits a few uninvited species' (9).

2 Leach 1964, Levinson 1972, Shepard 1978.

3 Williams 1983, Tuan 1984, Serpell 1988: 50.

4 Merchant 1982.

5 See Cobb 1977 on the flowering of the ecological imagination in Western childhood.

6 E.O. Wilson 1984.

7 See chapter 6 for an elaboration of these points.

8 Williams 1972.

9 See, for example, the United Nations 1987 Report of the World Commission on Environment and Development, *Our Common Future*, popularly called the 'Brundtland Report.'

10 It is intriguing to remember that several interests are represented in the presence of this remarkable installation in Metropolitan Toronto. While the artist imagined and created *The Pasture*, a major corporate enterprise commissioned, bought, and continues to maintain it, and those responsible for urban design and the choice of public art in the city have approved its public display. Thus, whether specifically intended or not, the itch to deep parts of our collective urban Western consciousness that *The Pasture* provokes is a gift not only of art but of commerce and a faceless public bureaucracy as well.

11 Williams 1977, 1985. Reference will be made to Raymond Williams's useful concept of the 'long revolution' at different places in the text. While at one level, the poetic, the notion of a 'long revolution' is completely graspable, Williams himself admits to great difficulty in delineating his subject logically, through reasoned argument. For this all-embracing cultural/social/economic/political phenomenon, characterized by an unlikely convergence and interlacing of ideas and practices, is really experienced only in structures of feeling, appreciated only as gestalt, and revealed only in hindsight, through history.

Chapter 1: Nature as a Cultural System

1 Bateson 1972: xxiv–xxv. On order, see also Bateson 1980.

According to *Webster's New Collegiate Dictionary* (1980), the word 'order' comes from the Latin *ordiri*, meaning the arrangement of the threads at the start of weaving. Perhaps this accounts for the prevalence of the weaving metaphor in the anthropological literature, with its constant couturier(e) allusions to 'warp,' 'weft,' 'threads,' 'fabric,' 'designs,' 'patterns,' 'tapestry,' 'seamless wholes,' 'shreds,' and 'patches.'

2 Richard Rorty (1979) says that we seem to have an internal need to tell a coherent causal story about our interactions with the world. It may be that human beings are not the exception in this, for it seems as if all living things have a need and a bent for order. See Thompson, *On Growth and Form*, 1961.

Who knows whether or not other forms of life apart from the human endow the world with meaning in some way, as humans do? Who knows whether this 'endowing with meaning' is not something that is an inherent, emergent property of all life? According to complexity theory, hand in hand with entropy in the universe goes constant structuring, ordering, and organizing at every scale. Complexity theory speaks of 'the story of order: a kind of deep, inner creativity that is woven into the very fabric of nature' (Waldrop 1992: 102). See also chapter 6, as well as Casti 1995, Kellert 1994, and Capra 1996 on self-organizing systems.

3 Rorty 1979: 315. See also Fernandez 1986: 70, n.30: 'The fact seems to be that men have, at once, both a sense of the continuity of experience – about which we can neither speak nor whistle – and a need to reduce that ineffable continuity to order and discrete categories. We both search for dichotomies and seek to escape them.'

4 See Douglas 1966. Disorder is not 'no-order': it is a response shaped to the prevailing order. To understand the difficulties people have in experiencing no-order, we need merely recall the many lengthy and severe disciplines developed worldwide, such as Zen or psychoanalysis, to attempt to overcome

the profound human (perhaps organic?) urge to create order with whatever materials are available. The seemingly bizarre cognitive-emotional reorganization that occurs in people during episodes of acute psychosis similarly suggests a deeply embodied inclination toward, a basic need for, some sort of order.

5 Compare the brilliant move that complexity theory makes in its search for an algorithm for life at the edge of chaos (e.g., Waldrop 1992). If it can be shown that activity at the edge of life is most vital, most self-organizing, most imbued with the process of ordering, is it not more likely that people would find it less difficult to conceive of and play with notions of uncertainty, unpredictability, and emergence?

6 Knight 1981: 25.

7 Bourdieu 1977. Bourdieu's elaboration of practice theory, of which the concept of habitus is an integral part, is of tremendous use generally as a theoretical approach in anthropology. (See also Ortner 1984, Giddens 1984, and Lave 1988.) The practice approach seeks to comprehend the everyday, common-sense, often unverbalized levels of thought and action as principal loci for the expression of culturally modelled habitus. It is the study of microprocesses – of how ordinary people, as self-motivated but interacting agents, work out the course of their lives (subconsciously for the most part) within a context that offers both cultural illuminations and constraints. Psychologist Jean Lave's concept of 'just plain folks' captures the basic assumption that nowhere can one better observe the workings of a particular culture than in the unideologized, out-of-awareness micropractices of everyday life. Ordinary people – people going about their everyday, not their 'expert' business – are, in terms of practice theory, the supreme culture-bearers.

Anthropology is hugely enriched by the practice perspective, which, for the first time, systematically introduces non-discursive behaviour, individual agency and motivation, history, value and feeling, and social and political inequality into anthropological theory all at the same time. In its hospitality to complexity, practice theory accords well with the contradictions of post-modern sensibilities.

8 Bourdieu 1977: 86. In its elaboration of the idea of habitus, Bourdieu's social-cultural theory conforms well with Freud's psychological theory of human social development. As sociologist Dennis Wrong remarks, Freud's theory of human nature 'does justice both to the readiness for and the resistance to socialization of human beings born in a helpless undeveloped state requiring prolonged dependence on others' (1994: 158). To this insight Bourdieu adds the critical contributions of historical and cultural (and, by allusion, physical) contexts in the infant's and youngster's socialization.

9 Fernandez 1986.

10 Nietzsche, *Philosophenbuch* (1872), quoted in Cantor 1982: 72; emphasis Nietzsche's.

11 See, e.g., Ornstein 1973, Lévi-Strauss 1963 and 1966, and especially Nietzsche in Cantor 1982, on the primacy of metaphor as a cognitive modality. Indeed, it has often been suggested that metaphor as a cognitive mode may be older than and parallel to logical thought.

See Bateson 1972: 364ff. on metaphor in animal behaviour. In a delightful anecdote psychologist Roger Fouts recounts that he had observed Moja, a signing chimpanzee who was well acquainted with the word 'purse' and its function, putting a purse on her foot and walking around signing 'That's a shoe.' See Masson 1995: 217 and note p. 266.

12 Lakoff and Johnson 1980.

13 For the term 'common-sense knowledge' see Geertz 1983a; the term 'practical consciousness' is used by Giddens 1984.

14 Lakoff and Johnson 1980: 5 and passim. See also Lakoff 1993, Fernandez 1986: 6, and Nietzsche in Cantor 1982.

15 In his book *Keywords* (1983) Williams's cross-references highlight a web of symbiotic understandings that together make up the flavour of a cultural tradition. By tracing a cultural history of the West through the development of some of its most significant named symbols, he provides an illuminating perspective on how tightly woven the fabric of 'culture' can be. What Williams brings to us is a fabric not of logic but of *recurrence*. No matter where one begins in *Keywords*, everywhere one re-encounters the same central concepts in different guises exerting different pressures on other concepts, and these latter on still others, and so on, until a pattern emerges of a dense network of interconnected, or split-off-yet-still-echoing ideas, schemes, hopes, and values – what one might call, following psychoanalyst Joel Kovel's terminology (1981), a Western history of desire.

16 Williams 1983: 'Culture.' It is most interesting for this essay that the term 'culture' as we use it in anthropology is a metaphor taken from animal and plant husbandry, where it was used to mean 'the tending of natural growth.'

Williams also notes that the term culture is still historically active, which accounts in part for the plethora of often conflicting definitions still in use, and the consequent well-founded fear of the formidable task of definition. For the difficulties in definition, see Bohannan (1973) on what culture means in anthropology.

17 Williams 1972: 150. One means by which practice theorists tried to temper the neatness of functionalist and structuralist thinking and to introduce a

measure of unpredictability, asymmetry, and contradiction – messiness – into theorizing about social life was to retain, as much as possible, the active echoes of history in practice theory's concepts. See Ortner 1984.

18 See Evernden 1992.

19 Along with a vagueness of definition, the word 'nature,' in its tones of certainty, transparency, complacency with contradictory ideas and maxims, public accessibility, and a common presumption that everyone is an expert, partakes of many of the characteristics of 'common sense' adumbrated by Clifford Geertz in 'Common Sense as a Cultural System' (1983a). See also Johnson 1987 on 'system,' and especially Evernden 1992 on the social creation of nature in the West.

20 See, e.g., Willis 1974, Serpell 1986, and Rowan 1988.

21 Lovejoy 1964: 198–9.

22 See, e.g., Leiss 1974, Roszak 1989, Kovel 1981; and see chapter 4, below.

23 Fernandez 1986; and see also Berger 1980.

24 Lovejoy 1964, Glacken 1967, Williams 1972.

25 This is evident even, or especially, with the twentieth-century development of the sciences of complexity. These studies of apparent disorder – turbulence, chaos, unpredictability, non-equilibrium dynamical natural systems, the emergence of unsuspected phenomena from supposedly determinate sources – were previously avoided by most scientists other than physicists precisely because they disrupted all assumptions of an orderly cosmos. The current popularity of these sciences of disorder has a lot to do with their re-signification as the study of 'extremely complex information,' as N. Katharine Hayles (1991: 1) puts it, rather than as the absence of order. Equally important is the way in which nonlinear mathematical equations represent and 'tame' complexity theory, promising the discovery of ever-deeper order in the universe. See Hayles 1991, Kellert 1994.

26 Good examples are Shepard and McKinley 1969, Devall and Sessions 1985, Haraway 1989, and Evernden 1985, 1992.

27 But see chapter 2 for a change in Lévi-Strauss's conceptualization of this issue.

28 Glacken 1967. The paucity of appropriate language does not help. As environmental historian Alice Ingerson puts it, the disjunction between nature and culture 'is so deeply ingrained in our everyday language that anyone trying to work around that dichotomy sounds at best idiosyncratic and at worst mystical' (1993: 44). See Ingerson, 'Tracking and Testing the Nature-Culture Dichotomy,' in Crumley 1993: 43–66.

29 Haraway 1989: 54, her emphasis; and see also Berger 1980.

30 Haraway 1989: 249; and see bibliographic entries for Fossey, Goodall, and

Schaller in her book's list of sources, 432–72. In this same book, *Primate Visions*, Haraway does show how a younger generation of primatologists, many of them women, has succeeded in altering, somewhat, this distanced stance in the West; how Japanese and Indian primatologists start from another set of presumptions altogether than the 'nature-culture divide'; and how Western scientific ideas of 'objectivity' and 'what may count as nature for late-industrial people' (1989: 1) are changing.

31 See Ingold 1988, Bonner 1980, Masson 1995. The contrast of these contemporary, tenaciously reductionistic convictions with the dynamic visions of nineteenth-century naturalists Darwin, Alexander von Humboldt, and Henry David Thoreau on continuities and connections among all creatures combined with forces of indeterminacy, which foreshadow modern complexity theory, is quite amazing. See Desmond and Moore 1991 on Darwin, Dassow Walls 1995 on von Humboldt and Thoreau, and chapter 7, below.

32 See Fabian 1983 and 1991 on anthropology's role in perpetuating this perception, in part through the discursive conventions of ethnography.

33 The literature is voluminous. For excellent examples see Lévi-Strauss 1963 and 1966, Hallowell 1975, Lee and DeVore 1976, Willis 1974, Serpell 1986, and Rowan 1988. See also text, below.

34 Nelson 1993: 216.

35 Ibid.: 218.

36 Ibid.: 213.

37 Ibid.: 220.

38 Ibid.: 214.

39 Ibid.: 202.

40 Ibid.: 204.

41 Masson 1995: 130f.

42 Wilson 1980.

43 Ibid.

44 Among the most interesting critiques are those by Sahlins 1977, Rose, Lewontin, and Kamin 1984, Kitcher 1985, and Lewontin 1991. Most critics make a distinction between pop or vulgar and scientific sociobiology. They grant that, unlike pop sociobiologists, who rely on a simplistic presumption of genetic determinism, a 'one gene-to-one-behaviour' model, scientific sociobiologists make a more rigorous and comprehensive attempt to place social behaviour on sound evolutionary principles. Indeed, some sociobiologists do not subscribe to the idea that the theory of evolution offers direct insight into human nature at all, but are nevertheless interested in the evolution of behaviour in animals and in humans. Serious sociobiologists have been discredited for things they have not claimed, such as the reductive

gene-for-behaviour formula; in turn, they have charged their critics with positions the latter have never taken, for example, cultural determinism or the infinite malleability of human beings. Founding biologist Wilson himself has disavowed the extreme reductionism of pop sociobiologists, but he maintains emphasis on the importance of natural selection in moulding human behaviours for maximizing fitness, and sticks with the idea that environment has comparatively little to do with behaviour when balanced against the (to him fairly wide) limits set by genetic endowment. See Wilson in Kellert and Wilson 1993.

45 Anik Bay, personal communication.
46 Haraway 1989.
47 Evernden 1992: 24.
48 Ibid.: 96.
49 Haraway 1989.

Chapter 2: Anthropology and the Natural World

1 See, e.g., Lévi-Strauss 1963 and 1966, Geertz 1973a and b, Willis 1974, Douglas 1975, Blurton-Jones and Konner 1976, Berlin 1978, Fernandez 1986, and Kellert and Wilson 1993. Good examples of ecologically and economically oriented anthropology may be found in Rappaport 1968 and Wolf 1982.
2 See, e.g., Anderson 1986a and b, Rappaport 1968, and Rowan 1988. Serpell 1986 provides an interesting overview of human–animal interactions from the anthropological literature and other eyewitness sources.
3 Lévi-Strauss 1963: 13.
4 Only a few studies, and these recent ones, consider the interactions of human and other species, as social phenomena, to be worthy of curiosity and exploration in their own right. Notable among these are Anderson 1986a and b, Perin 1981, Lawrence 1984, Ingold's 1988 edited volume, and Noske 1989. Dutch anthropologist Barbara Noske's book *Humans and Other Animals* was one of the first in anthropology to trace the political implications of contemporary human ties with the animal world.
5 Willis 1974.
6 Ibid.: 15, 21.
7 Evans-Pritchard in Willis 1974: 13.
8 Marcus and Fischer 1986.
9 See note 4, above.
10 Fernandez 1986: 4.
11 Geertz 1973a: 418–19.
12 Ibid.: 419.

13 Ibid.: 448.
14 Lawrence 1984: 8–9, vii. As a veterinarian as well as an anthropologist, she is
    well equipped for this task. Similar undertakings would be possible in inter-
    disciplinary teams and through other innovative means of scholarly con-
    necting. Joint research in these areas is at present virtually non-existent. See
    below, chapter 7, for the need for more permeable disciplinary boundaries.
15 See Ingold 1994 (1988): xxiii for a critique of this stance.
16 Sahlins in Marcus and Fischer 1986: 143. This is apparently not a new
    insight. In the eighteenth century Jean-Jacques Rousseau commented: 'For
    the 300 or 400 years since the inhabitants of Europe have inundated the
    other parts of the world, and continuously published new collections of
    voyages and reports, I am convinced that we know no other men except the
    Europeans' (quoted in Diamond 1974: 101–2).
17 Two semi-exceptions that stand out in the anthropological literature are
    Sahlins 1976: 170–9 and Lévi-Strauss 1966. Sahlins presents a 'modest'
    (informal) but suggestive analysis of human–animal relationships in Amer-
    ica in which certain animals – dogs, horses – are characterized as subjects
    while others – pigs, cows – are objects, with important consequences pursu-
    ant to this classification for both human and beast. Lévi-Strauss speculates
    briefly on contemporary French society's relations with the beasts and birds
    in their environment. Neither of these authors lays any claim to presenting
    a thorough ethnographic account of human–animal relations in his respec-
    tive milieu.
        In his book *Toronto the Wild: Field Notes of an Urban Naturalist* (1995), writer
    Wayne Grady provides a welcome, if unusual, glimpse into the flora and
    fauna of an urban landscape and some vignettes of urban human–animal
    relationships. He also presents the city itself as part of the natural ecology.
18 It need not be underlined that animal *use* is a source of endless speculation,
    research, and commentary. I am focusing in this discussion on relations of
    intersubjectivity, not subjugation.
19 The field of semiotics, which studies all kinds of messages ('systems of
    signs') and their meanings, has been interested in this area of communica-
    tion to some extent. In particular, zoosemiotics, which in the writings of
    Thomas Sebeok and others is an attempt to combine the insights of ethol-
    ogy and semiotics, looks at non-verbal communication across the animal
    spectrum from humans to insects. Latterly, a broader form of biosemiotics
    has gained a great deal of currency. In this arena the field of study is all of
    nature and its signs, including the codes of DNA and of human linguistics.
        To date, mainstream anthropology has not, for the most part, borrowed
    from this field of research, largely for reasons that will be developed in the

discussion to follow. Gregory Bateson, long interested in animal and inter-species communication, cannot be classed among those scholars who greatly influenced mainstream anthropology, particularly not in this area. Anthropology has, on the contrary, maintained a strong distinction between linguistics as the study of human verbalization and the communications of other animals. (But see note 20 below.) For interesting discussions of biosemiotics see Sebeok 1972 and 1975, and, more recently, Hoffmeyer and Emmeche 1991.

20 This is not to forget the work of primatologists such as George Schaller, Jane Goodall, Birute Galdikas, Dian Fossey, Franz de Waal, and the generation succeeding them, who have indeed focused on how the primates they were studying communicated together. Nor can we dismiss the newer curiosity about 'whale music' and other forms of communication by animals considered 'intelligent' by human standards, but whose anatomies differ so substantially from ours that they preclude duplicating the primate language experiments. Nevertheless, it remains true that we have very little insight into the communication patterns of most other mammals, birds, reptiles, and insects, not to mention plants. Even the communicative dances of bees, made famous more than half a century ago by ethologist Karl Von Frisch, are far from fully understood today. Still, animal trainers, pastoralists, farmers, and some hunters have practised the craft of interspecies communication for many centuries. For primatologists, see Haraway 1989, and Hearne 1986 for an example of communication between animals and their human trainers. Masson 1995 reports on the importance of communication in the emotional life of animals.

21 Masson 1995: 229. Masson reminds us that the possession and use of spoken language by human beings has never prevented people, when they so desired, from considering unwanted human others as lice and rats and murdering them en masse.

22 See Stocking 1992, and chapter 7, below.

23 See Haraway 1989 on English-speaking primatologists; for Japanese primatology, see particularly 249ff.

24 See Haraway 1989 for an illuminating argument regarding the effects of the colonial mindset on primates, women, and physical anthropology.

25 Haraway 1989: 12.

26 See Fabian 1983, 1991 on 'primitive' as a temporal category in anthropology.

27 Evernden 1992: 56.

28 Kuper 1983: 57.

29 On the history of totemism in anthropology see Lévi-Strauss 1963, Leaf

1979, Evans-Pritchard 1981, Kuper 1983, Fernandez 1986, and Stocking 1992.

30 Certainly Lévi-Strauss's work on the structural aspects of totemism and myth has provided the field with stimulating new ways to think.

31 Lévi-Strauss 1963, Evans-Pritchard 1981.

32 Stocking 1992.

33 Jenness in Lévi-Strauss 1966: 37.

34 Kuklick 1991.

35 See Leaf 1979 and Stocking 1992.

36 Lévi-Strauss 1969: xxvii, xxix–xxx.

37 We must not forget, of course, that while the line we draw between nature and culture is meant to be an impenetrable one, it is neither static nor uncontested. In the West, on nature's side are grouped all things alive that are not human, or, like rocks and winds and tides, not made by human beings. In a more extreme but quite common variant (as several of my informants made clear), nature is everything not human that has not been interfered with by human beings, which thus excludes domesticated and tamed animals and plants, even though they are conceded to be alive. In a third, also quite common although much disputed variant, among human beings themselves females are sometimes assumed (by some females as much as by some males) to be closer to nature than are males. The jury is still out on this latter debate; however, the fact that there is a debate between two categories at all is what I find most intriguing in this context.

38 Desmond and Moore 1991, Gruber 1981.

39 Masson 1995: 99.

40 Fabian 1983 on sight versus sound. See also Ackerman 1990 for a more general discussion of the importance of all the senses for human understanding.

Chapter 3: Reproducing the Natural Order

1 E.O. Wilson 1984. While Wilson admitted that the 'hard' evidence for his assertion was lacking, he attributed this to the scientific neglect of this question rather than to any real absence of evidence: 'The biophilic tendency is nevertheless so clearly evinced in daily life and widely distributed as to deserve serious attention. It unfolds in the predictable fantasies and responses of individuals from early childhood onward. It cascades into repetitive patterns of culture across most or all societies, a consistency often noted in the literature of anthropology. These processes appear to be part of the programs of the brain. They are marked by the quickness and decisive-

ness with which we learn particular things about certain kinds of plants and animals. They are too consistent to be dismissed as the result of purely historical events working on a mental blank slate' (1984: 85).

Wilson's statement about the 'quickness and decisiveness with which we learn particular things' about the natural world is amply borne out in the work of ethnobiologists and some psychologists. For cross-cultural evidence for possibly 'universal' propensities for human beings to classify the natural world in similar ways see Berlin 1992 and Brown 1984. This does not, of course, imply that a biophilic tendency must necessarily follow.

The 'biophilia' idea proved so compelling to scholars – whether positively or negatively – that a collection called *The Biophilia Hypothesis* (Kellert and Wilson 1993) looked into it in some depth. While the range of scholarship was wide, from ecology and biology through eco-feminism to anthropology and psychology, no consensus could be reached either on a standard definition of 'biophilia' or on incontrovertible evidence for its 'nature' or 'nurture.' The concept itself, however, remains useful and certainly, in my own fieldwork experience, aptly descriptive. See also the work of Katcher and Beck (e.g., 1988), which strongly supports the presence of some positive relationship between particular animals and particular human beings; much of their evidence comes from physiological studies of animals and humans in interaction.

2 For Thomas on pets, see 1984: 112ff.
3 For example, White 1969. For speculation on the human–wolf association see Carson 1972 and Clutton-Brock 1981. Archaeologist Juliet Clutton-Brock presents contested but not disproved evidence from 125,000 years ago of some proto-partnership of wolves and humans on Palaeolithic sites, for wolf skulls seem to have been intentionally placed in the mouths of caves (1981: 11). For a description of the late Palaeolithic burial find in Israel, see Serpell 1986. With respect to Greeks, see Carson 1972, and for Romans, Toynbee 1973. Herscovici 1985 presents material on the ancient Hebrews, and Thomas 1984 and Oelschlaeger 1991 on early and medieval Christians.
4 Serpell 1986, 1988; Rowan 1988.
5 Serpell 1988: 42.
6 Serpell 1986: 48.
7 Serpell 1988: 45.
8 Rappaport 1968: 59. Rappaport surmises that this human handling, along with the constant availability of food, was critical in maintaining the pig as a domestic animal when it could so easily turn feral and forage in the forests. At some point, however, these pigs became part of the herd to be con-

sumed on ritual or emergency occasions. Rappaport does not reveal the steps by which a pet became a comestible in this society.

9 E.O. Wilson 1984: 81.

10 Sarton 1957. The documentary on pets was shown on TV Ontario, December 1986.

11 Carson 1972: 9.

12 See also Hickrod and Schmitt 1982, Fogle 1981.

13 Peter Fleming in Serpell 1986: 50.

14 Willis 1974: 96.

15 Lave 1988.

16 Ibid.: 123.

17 Serpell 1986; see also Katcher 1981.

18 Kovel 1981: 117. See also Poster 1980 and Schneider 1980. From another point of view, that of cultural geography, Alexander Wilson reminds us in *The Culture of Nature* that the home, and the symbolic clearing in which it stood, had long been thought of as a refuge from the world of alienated labour. See A. Wilson 1992: 97.

19 Schneider 1980: 40; emphasis mine.

20 Kovel 1981: 116.

21 Schneider 1980: 49.

22 The argument that pet keeping in the context of the home is an expression of biophilia merits further exploration; perhaps it may solve the puzzle of why the practice is spreading so rapidly in heavily industrialized and urbanized societies formerly indifferent (or with a different kind of relationship) to the creatures that are becoming companion animals. Ritvo (1987, 1988) insists that in Victorian England widespread pet keeping was a sign of increasing confidence in Britain's mastery over nature, and also of the benevolence of Empire, a power that controlled many of the world's peoples and much of its natural resources. This seems to me to be an insufficient answer, for pet keeping is not only a time-consuming and sometimes expensive occupation, demanding long-term commitment, it is also found worldwide among many peoples (including Canadians) far from the hub of empire or ideological positions of mastery over nature, as Serpell, Rowan, Rappaport, Willis, and many others have shown.

23 Ortner 1984: 154. Whereas anthropologists have tended in the past to focus largely on the roles of socialization, ritual, and public performance as mechanisms of cultural reproduction and maintenance, the practice approach turns to the reiterated practices of ordinary living.

24 Lave 1988.

25 Practice theory is largely preoccupied with the uneditorialized, the uncom-

mentaried, and the frequently unvoiced routines of everyday life, realms
that, although supremely cultural in their invention, are not always immediately accessible to either the native or the investigator in verbal discourse.
If, like practice theorists, we are attuned to collective ordering as more than
language, we can discern much else besides talk that goes on in the everyday unconsidered round of behaviours to resist disorder and cultural
entropy.

26 Ortner 1984: 154.
27 Bourdieu 1977: 164.
28 Ibid.: 15.
29 See, e.g., Hearne 1986.
30 Schneider 1980: 41.
31 For the significance of naming animals in Western society, it is illuminating
to compare the following works: Vicki Hearne's *Adam's Task: Calling Animals by Name* (1986) and Ursula K. LeGuin's 'She Unnames Them,' in *Buffalo Gals and Other Animal Presences* (1988). Together, these two works
provide profound if contrasting contemporary insights – via moral philosophy and literature respectively – into the systemic argument concerning
nature and human–animal relations that I am attempting to outline here
through the medium of anthropology.
32 Ralston-Purina Pamphlet # 23, n.d.
33 Hickrod and Schmitt 1982. For this reason, presumably, one usually does
not form as close a bond of affection with a neighbour's animal as one does
with one's own pet; the feature of routine interaction is missing.
34 See, e.g., John Livingston's *Rogue Primate* (1994). In his exploration of
domestication in human beings, Livingston discusses the consequences of
this human condition on the environment. He suggests that as an 'exotic'
species, that is, one not indigenous to a habitat but introduced, as is the case
with all domesticated species, or migrant there, human beings have overrun and taken over the planet's environments indiscriminately. We have
done so because we are not primevally rooted in the biotic relationships of
the habitats we find ourselves in, with their ancient checks and balances –
not 'wild,' in other words.
35 The concept of humans being at least as domesticated as their pet animals
is increasingly commonly acknowledged. Typical of this attitude is the
name of a pet-training and dog-walking service I came across, called
'Who's Leading Who?'
36 Giddens 1984: 4. Giddens is careful to distinguish between practical consciousness, which is knowledge that is usually out of the conscious awareness of the knowledgeable agent but can, through socialization and

learning, be described in discursive terms, and the unconscious, which he defines in the Freudian sense of knowledge that is, by definition, inaccessible to the agent's consciousness owing to a generally unbreachable barrier of repression.

37 Gregory Bateson highlights a human–animal connection that my own field data were too circumscribed to do: 'Mammals in general, and we among them, care extremely, not about episodes, but about the patterns of their relationships ... This is what mammals are about. They are concerned with patterns of relationship, with where they stand in love, hate, respect, dependency, trust, and similar abstractions, vis-à-vis somebody else' (1972: 470).

38 See Ortner 1984: 153.

39 Kovel 1981: 33.

40 Mays 1994: 320–2.

41 Along with our ignorance about certain sounds that dogs can hear, our relatively poor sense of smell (but see note 46 below), and our incapacity to echolocate like bats, we are learning that some birds 'see' magnetic fields, that fish can hear, that some undersea creatures detect electromagnetic fields with specialized sensors, that elephants hear sounds too low for us, and that birds' aural acuity can distinguish sounds temporally in ways we cannot even conceive (Masson 1995: 194ff.). Masson ventures a speculation that such animals may possess an aesthetic completely unimaginable to us, that they may possibly be appreciative of varieties of 'subsonic, infrared, or electromagnetic beauty' (198).

42 Kovel 1988: 148.

43 Bateson 1972: 375.

44 Some ethologists speculate, says Masson (1995: 21), and most pet owners would insist, that many animals are better at reading human body signals than humans are at reading those of animals.

45 To this list of offensive animal effluvia we might we add allergens, for many people find that they are allergic to animal hairs, bird dander, and so on. While cognitively they may define their pets as kin, their bodies more or less emphatically define them as other, and a noxious other to boot. Yet, not all people with animal allergies define the animal as polluting. On a number of occasions I observed pet owners in veterinarians' waiting rooms cheerfully sneezing and crying into their tissues, freely admitting to allergies brought on by interaction with their pets. This uncomfortable condition seemed to them a small price to pay for keeping their pets, and did not deter them from caring for them lovingly.

46 For a species that does not congratulate itself on its sense of smell, it

appears that more of human judgment than we might like to admit may rely on that archaic sense, subliminally registering the 'goodness' or 'badness' of the world. In this as in so many other ways, the universe of human–animal relations reveals vast realms of human experience denied conscious access, and masked by learned ignorance.

47 Douglas 1966: 35.

48 Ibid.: 160: 'In the course of any imposing of order, whether in the mind or in the external world, the attitude to rejected bits and pieces goes through two stages. First they are recognisably out of place, a threat to good order, and so are regarded as objectionable and vigorously brushed away. At this stage they have some identity: they can be seen to be unwanted bits of whatever it was they came from, hair or food or wrappings. This is the stage at which they are dangerous; their half-identity still clings to them ... In the end, all identity is gone. The origin of the various bits and pieces is lost and they have entered into the mass of common rubbish ... So long as identity is absent, rubbish is not dangerous.'

49 Midgley 1978: 194–5.

50 See, e.g., Berger 1980, Berman 1984, and Livingston 1994; for a critique of this position see Williams 1972 and Midgley 1978. Masson (1995: 42) calls this orientation anthropocentric to the core, indulging as it does in an obsession with the repulsive and destructive ways of humans, to which all-virtuous animals are contrasted as the (good) other.

51 See, e.g., Rose, Lewontin, and Kamin 1984, Kitcher 1985, and Midgley 1994.

52 Katcher 1981.

53 In an interesting parallel, Masson reports that male European wildcats and fishing cats, not known to be family-oriented in the wild, have been seen to take on a nurturant and protective role toward their young in zoos. At the Frankfurt Zoo, for instance, '[t]he male not only brought food, but often curled up in the nest box with the rest of the family. He was such a conscientious parent that if he was out of the nest box and the female also came out, he became anxious and went in the nest box with the kittens' (1995: 98). Masson reports that, on observing this repertoire, cat specialist Paul Leyhausen speculated that the artificial condition of captivity may present unaccustomed stimuli that would elicit normally dormant behaviour patterns.

54 Bourdieu 1977: 164.

55 Ortner 1984: 150.

Chapter 4: Manufacturing the Natural Order

1 Kovel 1988: 125.

2 Carson 1972: 13.

3 That is the phrase that stuck in my mind as I watched the spectacle unfolding. In fact, the clerk was a young woman in her late teens or early twenties.
   It is interesting to note that the vast majority of the staff in the chain pet
   stores appeared to be very young. No doubt this sort of job, with its lower
   wages and the opportunity to work with animals, might appeal to younger
   people. However, the marked youthfulness of almost all this staff, compared with the more varied-seeming ages of clerks in smaller, individually
   owned pet shops, seemed to me to be significant. I have wondered whether
   hiring young staff was another marketing tool to complement the neotenous features of the nonhuman living things in the same setting.

4 In this connection Darwin remarked: 'Not one man in a thousand has accu-
   racy of eye and judgement sufficient to become an eminent breeder. If
   gifted with these qualities, and he studies his subject for years, and devotes
   his lifetime to it with indomitable perseverance, he will succeed, and may
   make great improvements; if he wants any of these qualities, he will assur-
   edly fail. Few would readily believe in the natural capacity and years of
   practice requisite to become even a skilful pigeon-fancier' (1968: 91). He
   recounts the claim of a renowned breeder of pigeons, Sir John Sebright, to
   be able to produce any given feather in three years; to obtain a given shape
   of head and beak, however, would take him six years (90).

5 Ralston-Purina # 14, n.d.

6 Tuan 1984: 170.

7 Siegel 1989: 135. Information on the development of the British bulldog
   may be found in Ritvo 1987, and on the Telescope goldfish in Tuan 1984.

8 Kimbrell 1993.

9 Campbell 1996; Kimbrell 1993. See also Haraway 1996 and Rifkin 1991 for
   information on animal patenting in the United States. See as well chapter 5,
   below, for further discussion on this issue.

10 Besso 1990.

11 Midgley 1989: 14–15.

12 Berger 1980: 14, 21. And now, comments Haraway (1989), animals have
    become a spectacle for sale in the world's largest single industry, tourism.
       But we must not take this too sombrely. A study of wild lions revealed
    that the researchers were being observed in turn: 'During the day, ' Masson
    relates, 'the scientists watched the lions sleep. At night, tracks revealed that
    four lions came to the fence and peered at the sleeping scientists. As the
    people examined the scats of the lions, the lions dug up the human latrine
    and inspected its contents, sometimes adding their own' (1995: 225).

13 CBC Radio, 'Patenting Animals,' Quirks and Quarks, 2 May 1987.

14 'How to Understand and Enjoy an Obedience Trial,' Ralston-Purina # 23, n.d.

15 A contrary view is expressed by philosopher and animal trainer Vicki Hearne in her book *Adam's Task: Calling Animals by Name* (1986). She argues that true animal training is based on a relationship of profound interspecies respect and understanding, calling forth capacities and resources from both animal and human beyond their ordinary repertoires: '[D]og trainers and horse trainers insist that training – teaching animals the language games of retrieving, say, or *haute école* in *dressage* – results in ennoblement, in the development of the animal's character and in the development of both the animal's *and the handler's* sense of responsibility and honesty' (1986: 42–3, emphasis in original). In this view, animal training is moral practice. That this is a most unusual view, not held by most laypersons or by all animal trainers, is made clear by the apologetics of the book itself.

It is also a somewhat troubling argument because, while the author recognizes, understands, and honours the individuality and subjectivity of the animal beyond usual folk notions of human–animal relations, even as relations of kin, at the same time she accords human beings indisputable and therefore undisputed dominance in this relation and, by extension, in all human–animal relations. In the end, this treatise is a disquisition on the place of (some) animals in the human moral domain, rather than an inquiry into the moral position of human beings as animals sharing the world with other beings.

16 Noske 1989: 37.

17 It is difficult to avoid comparison of this common human attitude toward animals with the intraspecies anthropological assumption captured by Marshall Sahlins in his famous phrase 'the West and the rest.'

18 Ritvo 1987: 66, 67.

19 Lakoff and Johnson have subsumed metonymy under their examination of metaphor as tropes we 'live by' because, like metaphor, it is a figure of speech that not only enters language but can also change history in the same way. For their purposes, then, this single classification is appropriate. Through the study of different aphasic states, however, linguist and psychologist Roman Jakobson discovered that the association processes of metaphor (similarity) and metonymy (contiguity) are not only different from each other in terms of brain function, but at that level appear to be fundamentally incompatible. He speculated that they might in fact be two very basic processes, expressions of some hardwiring of the brain (Hawkes 1977: 76–7). Nonetheless, as James Fernandez notes, it was Jakobson who pointed out that metonymy has a hint of metaphor and vice versa, that is, they are

not strictly separable in practice. Indeed, Fernandez suggests, in extended discussion their distinctions are difficult to maintain (1986: 48).

20 E.O. Wilson 1984: 115.

21 Writer Edith Cobb, best known for her reflections on the presence of the ecological imagination in childhood, was also a social worker. From this vantage point, she gives us a wonderful sense of the practice of metonymy and its effect on mind in one of the sacred precincts of modern industrial society, the hospital: '[T]he architectural separation of parts of the body and various body functions into distant wings and even buildings made the person-in-the-body and the body in its real world very difficult to conceive. Having an eye in wing A, a limb in R, the heart back in B, and maybe abdominal functioning in X, Y, or Z made the job of the caseworker ... a phenomenal performance' (1977: 21).

22 Winner 1986: 22.

23 Evernden 1985: 67; emphasis in original.

24 Scarry 1985 uses the term 'world alteration,' and Kovel 1988 uses 'transforming nature,' to refer to the effects of the human tendency to make things.

25 Stocking 1987: 3.

26 Foucault 1979; and see Franklin 1992. See Mumford 1963: 4, also Pacey 1983 and Winner 1986 on the role of the machine metaphor in modern technology and industry.

27 Kovel 1988: 151, Tuan 1984: 16, Marcuse 1977: 375.

28 This last point is problematic, because in the West the workforce has in fact responded to extremes of exploitation by forming the union movement, and the union movement has styled itself a strong moral voice in Western culture. Nonetheless, the union movement has never been able to decisively dislodge the compelling central metaphor of the machine from its midst, and indeed, has never seriously or perhaps widely enough confronted the basic issue of this form of labour organization. The fact that work continues to be organized with things in mind – humans or animals as machines or tools, animals as products or factories – seems never to be fundamentally questioned.

29 Mumford 1963: 23; Kovel 1988: 150, also 306, 238, 96.

30 CBC Radio 1998, Franklin 1992. Experimental physicist Ursula Franklin, long a technological critic, notes how important feminist critiques of Western science and technology have been in bringing to consciousness the limits of a machine-conceived ('prescriptive') technology. In seeking alternative technological metaphors to live by, Franklin has suggested as one

possibility the holistic activity of fabric-making, weaving or knitting, for example, where the maker must hold in her or his mind the end as well as the means, the concept and all the associated activities that make up the artifact, and where she or he is responsible for the entire process. Franklin does not, however, appear to be sanguine about any such profound cultural changes in how we organize the making of things in the near future.

31 Evernden 1985: 14; see also Cobb 1977.
32 Thomas 1984: 94.
33 See Noske 1989.
34 Scarry 1985.
35 Ibid.: 49.
36 Evernden 1985.
37 The bibliography that tries to bear witness to human cruelty – that reintroduces the voice, we might say – is long. See especially Terence des Pres, *The Survivor* (1977) and, e.g., Eli Wiesel, *Night* (1969), Joy Kogawa, *Obasan* (1983), and Nien Cheng, *Life and Death in Shanghai* (1986).
38 On 9 May 1998 the *Toronto Star* (see Walkom) reported that American-style hog farming was being adopted increasingly in Canadian pork-raising enterprises. Masson 1995: 57 reports that to date the pain and fear of factory-farmed animals has seldom been the subject of study.
39 Tuan 1984: 107.
40 This is another clear-cut example of embodied metonymy. Dogs are all trained to heel at the human being's left side in order to accommodate the predominance of human right-handedness. This allows a handler to manipulate a leash with the left hand while leaving the dominant hand free to conduct other business. The dog's behaviour, in other words, has been shaped to complement the constitution as well as the desires of the human owner. See 'How to Understand and Enjoy an Obedience Trial,' Ralston-Purina #23, n.d.
41 Hearne 1986, and see note 15 above.
42 Bateson 1972: 369.
43 Scarry 1985: 12.
44 Evernden 1985: 78. See also, e.g., Birke 1994, Langley 1989, Midgley 1989, and Sperling 1988.
45 Fernandez 1986: 12.
46 Marcus and Fischer 1986: 78.
47 Langley 1989: 197.
48 LaFollette and Shanks 1996: 181 and passim.
49 Midgley 1989: 15.
50 Scarry 1985: 57.

51 Haraway 1989: 242. The Harlow quotes are from Harlow et al. 1971 and Harlow and Mears 1979, quoted in Haraway 1989: 238. See also Masson 1995: 102.

52 Scarry 1985: 46.

53 Ritvo 1987: 249. The poaching incident was documented on CBC TV, 'Trophy Hunting,' *The Fifth Estate*, 17 Feb. 1987.

54 Scarry 1985: 20, Ritvo 1987: 265. Compare the fairly recent practices of North American museums. In *Primate Visions* Haraway describes the taking of a bull giraffe for a diorama display at the American Museum of Natural History. She writes: 'When at last the bull was taken as the result of great skill and daring, the minute details of its preservation and recreation were lovingly described' (1989: 40).

55 Scarry 1985: 20.

56 Ibid.: 57.

57 Birke 1994: 54. This anecdote reinforces the observations of Hickrod and Schmitt 1982, cited in the previous chapter, on the psychological aspects involved in the creation of the pet relation. Quite inadvertently in this case, the staff undertook ongoing activities of care simply to permit the creature to eat; the result, as Hickrod and Schmitt might have predicted, was a bonding between members of two species, a relation developed primarily through some durable experience with the other as an individual. Birke relates that the staff were upset when the rat died 'naturally.'

58 Scarry 1985: 44.

59 Ibid.: 310.

60 See Noske 1989.

61 Singer 1975: 27.

Chapter 5: Reordering the Natural World

1 Ingrid Newkirk interviewed by Susan Delacourt: 'Nobody's laughing now,' *Globe and Mail*, 4 May 1987. Historian Gerald Carson agrees that our thinking about animals is oddly compartmentalized. He writes that 'fox hunters are revolted at cruelty to circus animals, bird shooters denounce deer hunters, and loyal members of the RSPCA eat *pâté de fois gras*' (1972: 45).

2 Paul Watson, speaking at the annual general meeting of Action Volunteers for Animals (AVA), Toronto, 16 May 1987.

3 For histories of animal-welfare reforms, see Singer 1975, Turner 1980, Ritvo 1987, and Sperling 1988.

4 Hampson 1989: 220. See also Singer 1985, Midgley 1978, and Langley 1989.

5 Bourdieu 1977: 170; emphases his.
6 For an indispensable outline of the history of the term 'democracy,' see Raymond Williams's generally indispensable *Keywords* (1983).
7 In a recent paper French sociologist Alain Touraine makes a distinction between our contemporary ideological notion of democracy – inherited from the concerns of the nineteenth century to find mechanisms for sharing power – as above all representative, and its practical emphasis in the twentieth century on institutions. Institutional democracy, he suggests, guarantees that no one person will usurp power easily, limiting the threat of totalitarianism, but does not, in and of itself, encourage representativeness or participation. See Touraine 1995.
8 Midgley 1985.
9 Williams 1983: 95.
10 Scarry 1985.
11 Marcus and Fischer 1986: 153; see also Touraine 1977: 141.
12 Touraine 1977.
13 Gerlach and Hine 1970: xvi.
14 Ibid.: 217.
15 See note 7 above. I must at this point underscore the fact that my fieldwork with animal-rights activists was conducted with the grassroots of the movement, made up mostly of people who, passionately committed to the issues, participated on a voluntary basis, and led other lives besides their engagement with this social movement. There is, however, a wide range of animal-rights activist groups throughout Europe and North America, with diverse organizations and levels of public participation. For a critical perspective on animal-rights activism, see, e.g., Jasper and Nelkin 1992.
16 Bourdieu 1977: 170–1, Touraine 1977: 29–31.
17 Lakoff and Johnson 1980: 157, Dahrendorf in Pacey 1983: 33.
18 Touraine 1977: 16.
19 Hollands 1985: 173.
20 In an ironic twist to the present argument, Carson provides us with a grotesque example of the power of metaphor to create persons before the law by describing the prosecution of beasts, a European practice in medieval times. During this era in the development of Western jurisprudence an animal could be arrested, prosecuted, and punished because of some offence it was thought to have perpetrated. Carson tells us, for example, that in the town of Falaise in France in 1386, a sow was dressed up in a suit of men's clothing, mangled about the head and forelegs, and hanged – the penalty for maiming and killing a baby. Animals were even put to the rack to 'extort

confessions.' Although no confession was expected, 'due form' was observed. (See Scarry 1985 for a cogent analysis of the uses of 'confession' under torture.) When a hog was burned because of some felony, it was not then considered 'roast pork': 'To eat an animal caught in blood guilt and elevated by reason of capital punishment to the level of man, would have savored of cannibalism' (Carson 1972: 29–31).

21 Johnson 1987.

22 Interview with Ingrid Newkirk, on 'Animal Rights,' *The Journal*, CBC TV, 28 Jan. 1987.

23 Geertz 1973b.

24 While the figures are disputed, it appears that the worldwide pressure to stop these tests has resulted in a drastic decrease in their use in commercial laboratories. By 1990 many companies in North America, Britain, and Europe had issued statements that they no longer used animals in toxicity testing. Some of my informants suggested, however, that there was evidence these tests continue to be conducted in secret by selected laboratories at the request of a number of companies. It is difficult to corroborate this allegation at present.

25 Scarry 1985: 4–5.

26 People who work in slaughterhouses report that pigs' cries are horrible to hear; they sound very much like human screams (Masson 1995: 229).

27 This is not to deny that the metonymic mode can be used in the service of individual life, as in medical and other emergencies. A veterinary assistant described her emotional state in such emergencies: 'I've dealt with animals that have been in pain in the animal hospitals. There are some things we have to do without an anaesthetic because it is less traumatic in the long run. If they come in and they're in pain and you need to get an X-ray to see what's broken or something ruptured inside and you need to know what to do, you don't give them an anaesthetic. You get them on the X-ray table as fast as you can. Because if you give them an anaesthetic or a tranquilizer, the blood pressure goes down. You can kill them. So you keep them alive, but you know they're in pain. But you're not in pain. You're working as fast as you can. You're aware that you're trying to do things to the animal and you're restraining him. You've got only good intentions for that creature that you're dealing with, that's the only reason you're doing it. I can appreciate that there's something in me that takes over, I have to cut out the emotionalism, get on with the job. You feel for the animals but there is something you can cut out.'

28 Sartre in Bourdieu 1977: 170; my emphasis. A translator's error ('wreck' for 'wreak') has been corrected.

29 David Israelson, in interview with Paul Watson: 'Whaling protester ready to wreck more factories,' *Toronto Star*, 12 Nov. 1986.

30 Watson speaking at annual general meeting of Action Volunteers for Animals (AVA), 16 May 1987.

31 Touraine 1977: 97.

32 Vicki Miller speaking at the AVA annual general meeting, 16 May 1987. Dr Robert Mendelson was interviewed on CBC *Radio Noon*, 9 Apr. 1987.

33 Mike Schwab speaking at AVA annual general meeting, 16 May 1987. See also Noske 1989.

34 The argument based on harm-to-humans is often more compelling to people who are not animal-rights activists than is the ethical argument at the heart of the citizenship metaphor. However, activists recognize that there is a danger in the harm-to-humans argument, for fundamentally it does not challenge the 'animal-as-artifact' model; it merely suggests that some animal-artifacts are potentially toxic to humans and need to be better regulated. Its main value to the animal-rights endeavour is to rattle the unexamined boundaries of doxic thought, to defamiliarize these boundaries by subverting the taken-for-granted nature of animal-artifact 'goods' in Western society, rendering them more accessible to change.

35 Bourdieu 1977: 120.

36 In its choice of symbolic apparel, the Animal Liberation Front is part of a long North American tradition. At some deep level – perhaps the level of practical consciousness, or even deeper, the unconscious level of image schema and dream – activists seem to understand the need in our mythology for some figure such as the black-masked stranger as liberator, symbolizing simultaneously the intrusion of disorder in a closed system and, at a deeper level, the restoration of order. North American iconography recognizes in the black mask, and in the lone masked outsider or pair of outsiders – Zorro, the Lone Ranger and Tonto – the Stranger as Saviour. Currently, there is in North America an enthusiastic camp revival of interest in the horde of masked comic heroes, like Batman, Robin, and Spiderman, who can single-handedly restore order in times of trouble.

37 The title, in English, of Touraine's 1977 book on social movements. See also Regan 1985.

38 As reported on *The Journal*, CBC TV, 28 Jan. 1987.

39 Scarry 1985: 6.

40 Bourdieu 1977: 170.

41 Scarry 1985: 3.

42 Toronto Humane Society board meeting, 12 Nov. 1986.

43 Further, as Masson observes, animals live incident-filled lives every bit as much as we do; they have biographies too (1995: 225).

44 Kovel 1988: 110, Gerlach and Hine 1970: xvi.

45 Bourdieu 1977: 124.

46 Giddens 1984: 53.

47 Scarry 1985: 109.

48 Willis 1974: 28.

49 Bourdieu 1977: 175. Adopting a vegetarian way of life is one way to embody an altered view of human relations to animals. But it can mean something else as well. Some vegetarians 'of conscience' are also aware of practising a thrice-daily rededication to an ethic of *restraint*. In Western culture particularly, with its culinary valorization of meat and critical sectors of its economy devoted to animal husbandry, vegetarianism is perforce a practice of restraint.

   Barbara Noske's 1989 analysis of the animal-industrial complex gives a glimpse of it as an immense, far-flung empire. Bearing this vast multinational 'factory' in mind, vegetarianism could well be considered revolutionary practice: its worldwide implications for drastically altering economics, delicate balances of power, and fundamental cultural models could be quite extraordinary.

50 Kovel 1981: 66.

51 Ortner 1984: 152.

52 Ibid.: 157.

Chapter 6: Missing Metaphors

1 Ferry 1995; see also Ehrenfeld 1978.

2 Aldo Leopold, quoted in Devall and Sessions 1985.

3 See chapter 1, n. 11. In Raymond Williams's many restatements of the idea of the 'long revolution,' we are reminded that all real revolutions, those that achieve new social orders or profound changes in meaning systems, are long ones. The 'long' is the recognition that revolution is not mere 'overthrow,' but a process that takes time, many changes, and much negotiation. A revolution encompasses events preceding and succeeding those specific moments quite often arbitrarily taken as 'deciding events,' in the way the storming of the Bastille is often taken as the pivot of the French Revolution.

   In his elaboration of the 'long revolution' as a contemporary transformative project, Williams goes further, developing this idea to encompass the crucial need for knowledge, participation, and an unending critical consciousness. A long revolution, thus, demands fully conscious, knowledgeable, and engaged participants, people prepared for the long haul. Here he converges with Touraine's view of modern social movements – made up of people who are informed, committed, and willing to stick with the project for the long term – as the primary sources of real cultural change. See Touraine 1977, 1971.

4 Changes in the arena of patenting life forms are moving extremely rapidly, and any assertion today will quickly become obsolete in this fecund age of bioengineering. An article by Charles Hanley, appearing in the Toronto *Globe and Mail* in 1996, entitled, 'Blood lines: Taking a patent on life,' describes the case of the Hagahai people of New Guinea. A Highland people only recently known to the West, the Hagahai appear to have unique blood properties that protect them from a form of adult leukemia. In hopes of helping the Hagahai both medically and economically, Dr Carol Jenkins, an anthropologist working with this community, helped to obtain a United States patent on the blood cells of one member of the group. The patent was issued quietly in 1995, and was revealed to the public only in 1996 through the efforts of a Canadian-based group seeking to protect the rights of developing nations. The issue of patenting human life – indeed, all life – has become a heated topic far from solution. Indeed, Hanley's article makes it disturbingly clear that those involved in deciding the legal aspects of such issues have shied away from addressing the difficult questions. He points out: 'Coming to grips would mean answering some fundamental questions: Should life forms be patentable? Is it ethical to assign commercial rights for human genes, or blood cells, or viruses? Can a foreign government 25,000 kilometres away claim some right over bits of someone's body it finds interesting?' Hanley goes on to observe that United States court decisions have cleared the way for patenting many human genes, DNA sequences, and cell lines to 'protect' them for 'product development' – diagnostic tests, treatments, and so on. See *Globe and Mail*, 11 May 1996, D8; also chapter 4, above.

5 Evernden 1988: 158.

6 Winner 1986: 54. Earlier in his book, Winner says: 'Choosing our terms, we express a vision of the world and name our deepest commitments. The quest for political consensus, however, sometimes leads to atrophy of the imagination. In debates about technology, society, and the environment, an extremely narrow range of concepts typically defines the realm of acceptable discussion. For most purposes, issues of efficiency and risk (or some variant of those) are the only ones to receive a thorough hearing. Any broader, deeper, or more perplexing questions are quickly pushed into the shadows and left to wither. How is it that we have gotten stuck packaging

some of the important issues that face humanity in such conceptually impoverished terms?' (1986: x–xi).

7 Glacken 1967, Thomas 1984, Merchant 1982, Oelschlaeger 1991.

8 Wolf 1982.

9 Thomas 1984: 95 and passim.

10 Ibid.: 96.

11 Ibid.: 126.

12 Ibid.: 128. Darwin seems to have concurred. He wrote in one of his journals: 'It is absurd to talk of one animal being higher than another. *We* consider those, where the cerebral structure, intellectual faculties, most developed, as highest. A bee, doubtless would where the instincts were.' Quoted in Gruber 1981: 21; emphasis Darwin's.

13 Displaying an attitude I imagine to be as old as the association itself, artist Joe Fafard, who grew up on a farm in Saskatchewan in the 1940s and 1950s, describes with some irony the farmers' sense of bondage to the very cattle they are said to own. In Teitelbaum and White's book on Fafard they remark: 'As Fafard has suggested: if this animal provided a means of support through its milk, cheese, butter, meat and hide, it also extracted a high price in the time and effort, little of it pleasant, that went into caring for its considerable needs. "I have spent much of my life working for cows," he has said, not altogether facetiously. "After a while you don't know who is using whom."' Teitelbaum and White 1987: 15–16. Fafard's artistic obsession with cows is famous.

14 Thomas 1984: 98f. One wonders what epithets women used for men. It is a poetry lost to history, alas, twice over: created by people without natural history, and by females, perhaps with a private language of their own. I, for one, remember as a child having overheard women, reared in small European villages, not infrequently refer to men they considered stubborn or stupid as 'horses,' 'oxen,' and 'mules.'

15 Ibid.: 98.

16 Carson 1972.

17 See Kovel 1981: 70, on desire: '[D]esire consists of striving toward an object that cannot yet be named in the languages of history.'

18 Touraine 1977: 55.

19 See, e.g., Devall and Sessions 1985, Evernden 1988, Cayley 1991, Sessions 1995, and Capra 1996 for discussions of the deep ecology position, and Ferry 1995 for a counterpoint.

20 See the United Nations Report of the World Commission on Environment and Development, 1987 (The 'Brundtland Report'). An ambitious, far-sighted, and far-reaching work, this report goes to the edge of exploring

worldwide sustainable development and its limits. Yet it does not step over the edge; it still structures its main arguments around a basically human-centred core. The work does not tackle the heart of the dilemma, the radical questions put forth by the deep ecology movement. The question 'Whose Earth?' is left unasked, and remains unanswered.

21 Evernden 1988: 158, Winner 1986.
22 Cayley 1991: 10.
23 See, e.g., Ferry 1995; also Fox in Sessions 1995.
24 Fox in Sessions 1995, Capra 1996.
25 While the recent image of the earth as 'Gaia,' the Earth Mother, is an intriguing one and might move some of us more definitively toward a holistic vision of the planet, it is still an image that is remote from our everyday lives. Alien to the embodied culture or habitus of our present-day Western society, not least in rendering a powerful, primal, determining source female, it remains a figurative metaphor; it is not – as yet, anyway – one to live by. Paradoxically, too, the image of Gaia renders the complex of concepts embedded in deep ecology, particularly its biocentrism and the non-privileging of the human species – its anti-anthropocentrism – as a human personification, just as Gaia herself was a personification in Greek cosmology.

   For many people the image of earth as Gaia conjures up, not an organic, emergent, self-organizing vision of life more powerful than any of its constituent parts, but (following a basic metaphor we do live by) another kind of *machine*: a perpetual-motion cybernetic bauble in space. Furthermore, it is perceived as a machine that needs to be managed – a machine with a manual, as we might think of Norman Myers's 1984 *Gaia: An Atlas of Planetary Management*, cited by George Sessions (1995: 301). Also, as is everywhere evident, 'Gaia' has already been domesticated as an image for any corporation or entrepreneur with pretensions to global markets. See, e.g., Howard Rheingold's *The Millenium Whole Earth Catalogue*, 1994. Like a Rorschach for a culture, how the image of earth as Gaia has been interpreted and used tells us a lot about the metaphors we still live by as well as those we would like to invent. Where and how far this image will take us, then, has yet to be seen. See Sessions 1995: 300–4.
26 Pacey 1983.
27 LaChapelle in Devall and Sessions 1985: 95.
28 Eliot in Wilson 1984: 79.
29 Masson 1995: 13. *Funkionslust*, he tells us, is an old German term for an animal's pleasure in its capabilities, in what it can do best: run swiftly, fly strongly, burrow deeply.

30 Capra 1996: 9.
31 Ehrenfeld in Cayley 1991: 191–2.
32 Touraine 1971: 20–1.
33 Lovejoy 1964, Williams 1972, Evernden 1985, 1992.
34 Capra 1996: 157. See also Gleick 1987, Waldrop 1992, Casti 1995, and Kellert
    1994.
35 Casti 1995, Kellert 1994, Capra 1996.
36 Capra 1996, Prigogine and Stengers 1984 on thought experiments. See
    Baker 1994 for one of the few attempts to apply dynamical systems theory
    to an ethnographic study, in this case, of Dominica. See also Mitchell Wal-
    drop (1992) on economists and the unpredictable abstractions of the stock
    market studied at the Santa Fe Institute, the current 'temple' of complexity
    theorizing, and N. Katharine Hayles (1991), who has applied complexity
    theory to literary as well as scientific productions.
        For the importance of Bateson to anthropology and to ecological thinking
    in general, see Harries-Jones 1995. Bateson's entire body of work may be
    said to transcend the social or cultural levels of human life, reaching for
    new ways to think about all of the living world. His perspective, still
    largely untapped in anthropology, has much to teach us today. See, e.g.,
    Bateson 1980, 1972.
        I do not want to deny the significance of post-structuralist and post-
    modernist thinking on anthropology and other social-science disciplines.
    Indeed, in its efforts to subvert modernist concerns with hierarchy,
    progress, master narratives, single points of view, history as inevitability,
    and many other aspects of our Enlightenment intellectual inheritance, post-
    modern theorizing displays a great deal of the flavour of complexity theory.
    However, since post-modernist thought concerns itself almost entirely with
    intra-human affairs and has not yet taken up the question that I address
    here – of human relations with the rest of the natural world – in any sys-
    tematic way, this body of work does not figure largely in my analysis.
37 Buber 1970: 58.
38 Because of Geertz's watershed essay, 'Deep Play: Notes on the Balinese
    Cockfight,' no anthropologist can come across the word 'deep' any longer
    without having echoing in her or his brain the notion of deep play that
    Geertz borrowed from Jeremy Bentham: 'play in which the stakes are so
    high that it is, from [the] utilitarian standpoint, irrational for men to engage
    in it at all' (1973a: 432). The idea of 'deep order' suggested here (and
    indeed, 'deep ecology' might fit just as well) demands the adoption of an
    attitude of doubt, bracketing, openness, and unknowingness so profound
    as to threaten the collapse of meaning altogether. In this sense, perhaps the

stakes of living with nature as a more complex system will prove to be too high. On the other hand, deep ecologists might counter that not playing will result in the collapse of nature altogether.

39 Philosopher of science Gaston Bachelard says that we in the West believe in a fundamental order; it is 'a feeling of intellectual repose stemming from the symmetries and certainties inherent in the mathematical analysis' (Bachelard in Kellert 1994: 53).

40 See *Roget's International Thesaurus*, 4th ed., 1977 for animal synonyms for 'obstinacy'; and cf. note 14 above.

41 Williams in Pacey 1983: 169.

42 Wilson 1984: 139–40.

43 Engels in Winner 1986: 31.

44 Evernden 1988: 159–60.

45 See, e.g., Marcus and Fischer 1986 regarding the colonial 'other,' and Rosaldo and Lamphere 1974 for women as 'other.'

46 Lovejoy 1964.

47 Wilson 1984: 7.

48 Rilke 1986 (1904): 78.

Chapter 7: Anthropology as Natural History

1 See chapter 6, n. 38.

2 This is not to suggest that anthropology must inevitably *lead* the long revolution but that it can – and I believe ought to – have a significant role to play, along with other disciplines, that is, other ways of inquiring into the world.

3 Williams 1983: 38, Desmond and Moore 1991. This minimal contestation may have occurred because the deeper, personal implications of Darwinian evolutionary theory for human nature's place in the rest of nature were not then, and have never been since, squarely faced. Indeed, it might fairly be said that the West has never really taken in *Darwin's* Darwinism – with its attention to continuities as well as differences, ecological relationships as well as competition, its multiple, coevolutionary as well as splitting and specializing processes, and, not least, the erasure of judgment – as part of its deepest ethos. It never became part of the West's nature-habitus.

4 Stocking 1992: 350, 22.

5 Kuklick 1991, 1997. Anthropology, she writes, 'is best appreciated as a type of natural history, one species of a class of knowledge – also including geology, botany, zoology, and geography – that could be used to manage the nation's resources of people and land' (1991: 6). The 'nation's resources'

included, of course, all the colonies. She adds elsewhere (1997) that all the natural-history sciences, including anthropology, gained professional status during the latter decades of the nineteenth century largely for this reason, that is, in order to respond to their funders' concern to manage natural resources. See Kuklick 1991, 1997 and Stocking 1992 for the political economy of the development of anthropology as a discipline in Britain and the United States.

6 Freeman 1984, Stocking 1992. See Freeman 1984 for a sociopolitical analysis of the early rift between biological and cultural anthropology.

7 Desmond and Moore 1991, Leaf 1979. Ethnological speculation was useful for the ends of European nationalists who sought to rally individuals to various causes through appeals to putative shared traditions of ancient origin. In North America, cultural evolutionism was used to legitimize the decimation of whole societies of native 'savages' and to take away their land in the name of 'civilization,' that is to say, land-hungry white settlers.

8 A large proportion of philosopher Mary Midgley's corpus of work consists of an extended reflection on this topic. See, e.g., *Beast and Man* (1978) and *The Ethical Primate* (1994). Midgley's reminder that we are not tourists on the planet but native to it bears much repeating, for there is a danger here. When we alienate ourselves from the rest of nature by casting ourselves as more Mephistophelean rather than as more godlike than the others, it is quite as easy to encapsulate our ecological depredations in metaphors of alienation and so, once again, refuse responsibility for them. In this devilish guise we seclude or exclude human practices from human nature by making them sick or criminal: aberrations. Once we 'remove' the problem in this way, however, then we are doomed to project it outward; and once projecting, forget; and once forgetting, repeat.

9 As just a short list of this fascinating area of developing scholarship, see Glacken 1967, Williams 1972, Worster 1977, Merchant 1982, Cronon 1983, 1995, Schama 1995, Crosby 1986, Oelschlaeger 1991, and Evernden 1992.

10 Snyder 1991: 79; my emphasis. See Rodman 1992 for a welcome statement of the need to attend to multilocality as well as multivocality in anthropology; see also Haraway 1991 and in text, below, for situated knowledges.

11 See especially Evelyn Fox Keller's *A Feeling for the Organism* (1983); also Haraway 1989, 1991.

12 For Fabian on classical ethnography, see *Time and the Other* (1983) and *Time and the Work of Anthropology* (1991). For partial and dialogical understanding see the discussion in text, below, and Haraway 1991 on situated knowledges.

13 Bateson 1972: 462.

14 Thoreau 1983.

15 For Latour see especially 1993; for Haraway, 1991 and 1996.

16 As Dassow Walls points out, Thoreau was in the best of company in his inquiries: Alexander von Humboldt, Darwin, and William James were among those scholars who were wrestling then with the same problems we are tackling today.

17 Thoreau in Anderson 1973: 37, 148.

18 Dassow Walls 1995: 232, 245, 238; author's emphasis.

19 Ibid.: 175, 246.

20 Ibid.: 232.

21 Latour 1993: 6 and passim. According to Latour, the West had always viewed pre-modern collectives as making a terrible hash of things and humans, of objects and signs. But the West, while separating these out into neat categories, remixed them below the surface of awareness, permitting them to cause havoc because of our refusal to acknowledge them.

    It is clear that in *We Have Never Been Modern* Latour is presenting a *Savage Mind* for the West, thus completing the circle that started with Lévi-Strauss, showing the 'psychic unity' or the 'intellectual unity' of all humankind. Both have tried to show the capacity of both the West and the Rest to think in savage and civilized terms, while presenting the presumed costs and benefits of inclining toward one style over another.

22 Haraway 1996: 62f., 12. Must it take a poet to find the right metaphors for a self-inventing world to live by? Note the awkwardness of the rather mechanical neologisms of Latour, and the overburdened language of Haraway, compared with the organic, sensuous, more 'real' language of Thoreau. Here, for example, is Haraway: 'Cyborgs are attempts to splice carbon-based life forms to silicon-based computer systems' (1996: 12). The sterility of this kind of machine technology-based language permeates much of the critique of science as well as academia in general. It is as if discourse itself had been turned into technique. Perhaps it does take a poet-naturalist to get closer to properly narrating our structures of feeling. There is no doubt that it is Thoreau's eloquence that comes closest to eliciting not only 'facts' but 'truths' in the subject matter we are dealing with here. He is able to capture the structures of feeling underlying the effort to mend, or rather, collapse, the nature-culture rift in ways seemingly unavailable to Latour and Haraway. To be charitable, some of the difference in style may presumably be left at the door of the latter's disciplinary constraints, whereas Thoreau, as an independent writer, was free of these.

    Yet only in Thoreau do we find playfulness as well, and a true stepping outside of the self toward I–Thou sensibilities. It may take a poet-naturalist to develop the appropriate 'trickster' language we do not have in the West at present, metaphors that can shape-shift with ease, encompassing cyborgs, hybrids, even the stupid genius (or genial stupidity) of species such as our own.

23 Dassow Walls 1995: 249.
24 Ibid.: 227, 143, 226. For extended discussions of nature 'looking back,' see also Dillard 1974, 1982, Berger 1980, Snyder 1991, and Nelson 1993.
25 Dassow Walls 1995: 246, 127.
26 Thoreau in Anderson 1973: 153.
27 Dassow Walls 1995: 168, 39.
28 Haraway 1991, Thoreau in Dassow Walls 1995: 143.
29 Thoreau in Anderson 1973: 34, 114. At these limits of understanding we can sense something of the 'real' beyond human construction. Thoreau and Haraway, at least, evince faith in the real: 'The landscape is indeed something real, and solid, and sincere, and I have not put my foot through it yet,' Thoreau says (in Dassow Walls 1995: 49). There are limits to hybridity, he seems to be saying: nature is real beyond language and beyond human society. Haraway is also clear on this subject: she will not dispense with the reality of nature as something apart from human being. And for Thoreau, as for Haraway and Latour, and for myself, science need not be jettisoned, nor need it objectify nature in order to arrive at truth or useful knowledge.
30 Dassow Walls 1995: 251.
31 Fabian 1991.
32 Haraway 1989: 310, 1996: 8.
33 Bateson has pointed out that the paralinguistics and kinesics of people from strange cultures are at least partly understandable by us even when their verbal utterances remain utterly opaque (1972: 372).
34 The potential of biosemiotics for the enrichment of anthropological theory and practice is evident here. See chapter 2, n. 19.
35 Dassow Walls 1995: 41.
36 Latour 1993: 7.
37 Haraway 1989: 273.
38 See chapter 6, n. 38.
39 Geertz 1983b: 16.

References

Ackerman, Diane. 1990. *A Natural History of the Senses.* New York: Random House.

Anderson, Charles, ed. 1973. *Thoreau's Vision: The Major Essays.* Englewood Cliffs, NJ: Prentice-Hall.

Anderson, Myrdene. 1986a. 'Folk Natural History: Crossroads of Language, Culture, and Environment.' In Peter Bjarkman and Victor Raskin, eds, *The Real-World Linguist: Linguistic Applications in the 1980s,* 185–217. Norwood, NJ: Ablex Publishing.

– 1986b. 'From Predator to Pet: Social Relationships of the Saami Reindeer-Herding Dog.' *Central Issues in Anthropology* 7.

Ardiel, June. 1994. *Sculpture/Toronto.* Toronto: Leidra Books.

Baker, Patrick. 1994. *Centring the Periphery: Chaos, Order, and the Ethnohistory of Dominica.* Montreal: McGill-Queen's University Press.

Bateson, Gregory. 1980 [1979]. *Mind and Nature: A Necessary Unity.* New York: Bantam Books.

– 1972. *Steps to an Ecology of Mind.* New York: Ballantine.

Berger, John. 1980. 'Why Look at Animals?' In *About Looking,* 1–26. New York: Pantheon.

Berlin, Brent. 1992. *Ethnobiological Classification: Principles of Categorization of Plants and Animals in Traditional Societies.* Princeton, NJ: Princeton University Press.

– 1978. 'Ethnobiological Classification.' In Eleanor Rosch and Barbara Lloyd, eds, *Cognition and Categorization,* 9–26. Hillsdale, NJ: Lawrence Erlbaum.

Berman, Morris. 1984 [1981]. *The Reenchantment of the World.* New York: Bantam.

Besso, Verena. 1990. 'Let's curb the obvious abuses.' *Toronto Star,* 4 October.

Birke, Lynda. 1994. *Feminism, Animals and Science: The Naming of the Shrew.* Buckingham, UK: Open University Press.

Blurton-Jones, Nicholas, and Melvin Konner. 1976. '!Kung Knowledge of Animal Behavior.' In Richard B. Lee and Irven DeVore, eds, *Kalahari Hunter-Gatherers*, 325–48. Cambridge: Harvard University Press.

Bohannan, Paul. 1973. 'Rethinking Culture: A Project for Current Anthropologists.' *Current Anthropology* 14:4, 357–72.

Bonner, John Tyler. 1980. *The Evolution of Culture in Animals*. Princeton, NJ: Princeton University Press.

Bourdieu, Pierre. 1977. *Outline of a Theory of Practice*. Cambridge: Cambridge University Press.

Brown, Cecil. 1984. *Language and Living Things: Uniformities in Folk Classification and Naming*. New Brunswick, NJ: Rutgers University Press.

Buber, Martin. 1970. *I and Thou*. Trans. Walter Kaufmann. New York: Charles Scribner's Sons.

Campbell, Jennifer. 1996. 'Can't patent a mouse, Canada says.' *Toronto Star*, 24 February.

Cantor, Paul. 1982. 'Friedrich Nietzsche: The Use and Abuse of Metaphor.' In David Miall, ed., *Metaphor: Problems and Perspectives*, 71–88. Sussex: Harvester Press.

Capra, Fritjof. 1996. *The Web of Life*. New York: Doubleday Anchor.

Carson, Gerald. 1972. *Men, Beasts, and Gods: A History of Cruelty and Kindness to Animals*. New York: Charles Scribner's Sons.

Casti, John. 1995 [1994]. *Complexification: Explaining a Paradoxical World Through the Science of Surprise*. New York: HarperPerennial.

Cayley, David. 1991. *The Age of Ecology*. Toronto: James Lorimer.

CBC Radio. 1998. 'The Progress Myth,' lecture by Heather Menzies. *Ideas*, 21 May.

– 1987a. 'Interview, Dr Robert Mendelson and Dr Jim Kenyon.' *Radio Noon*, 9 April.

– 1987b. 'Patenting Animals.' *Quirks and Quarks*, 2 May.

– 1987c. 'Patenting Animals.' *Sunday Morning*, 10 May.

CBC TV. 1987a. 'Animal Rights.' *The Journal*, 28 January.

– 1987b. 'Trophy Hunting.' *The Fifth Estate*, 17 February.

Cheng, Nien. 1986. *Life and Death in Shanghai*. London: Grafton.

Clutton-Brock, Juliet. 1981. *Domesticated Animals from Early Times*. London: Heinemann.

Cobb, Edith. 1977. *The Ecology of Imagination in Childhood*. London: Routledge and Kegan Paul.

Cronon, William. 1983. *Changes in the Land. Indians, Colonists, and the Ecology of New England*. New York: Hill and Wang.

Cronon, William, ed. 1995. *Uncommon Ground: Toward Reinventing Nature*. New York: W. W. Norton.

Crosby, Alfred. 1986. *Ecological Imperialism: The Biological Expansion of Europe, 900–1900*. New York: Cambridge University Press.

Darwin, Charles. 1968 [1859]. *The Origin of Species*. London: Penguin Books.

Dassow Walls, Laura. 1995. *Seeing New Worlds: Henry David Thoreau and Nineteenth-Century Natural Science*. Madison: University of Wisconsin Press.

Delacourt, Susan. 1987. 'Nobody's laughing now.' *Globe and Mail* (Toronto), 4 May.

Desmond, Adrian, and James Moore. 1991. *Darwin*. New York: W.W. Norton.

des Pres, Terence. 1977 [1976]. *The Survivor*. New York: Pocket Books.

Devall, Bill, and George Sessions. 1985. *Deep Ecology*. Salt Lake City: Peregrine Smith Books.

Diamond, Stanley. 1974. *In Search of the Primitive: A Critique of Civilization*. New Brunswick, NJ: Transaction Books.

Dillard, Annie. 1982. *Teaching a Stone to Talk: Expeditions and Encounters*. New York: HarperPerennial.

– 1974. *Pilgrim at Tinker Creek*. New York: HarperPerennial.

Douglas, Mary. 1975. *Implicit Meanings*. London: Routledge and Kegan Paul.

– 1966. *Purity and Danger*. London: Routledge and Kegan Paul.

Duerr, Hans Peter. 1985. *Dreamtime: Concerning the Boundary between Wilderness and Civilization*. Trans. Felicitas Goodman. Oxford: Basil Blackwell.

Ehrenfeld, David. 1978. *The Arrogance of Humanism*. New York: Oxford University Press.

Evans-Pritchard, Edward. 1981. *A History of Anthropological Thought*. Ed. André Singer. New York: Basic Books.

Evernden, Neil. 1992. *The Social Creation of Nature*. Baltimore: Johns Hopkins University Press.

– 1985. 'Nature in Industrial Society.' In Ian Angus and Sut Jhally, eds, *Cultural Politics in Contemporary America*, 151–64. New York: Routledge.

– 1985. *The Natural Alien*. Toronto: University of Toronto Press.

Fabian, Johannes. 1991. *Time and the Work of Anthropology: Critical Essays 1971–1991*. Chur, Switzerland: Harwood Academic Publishers.

– 1983. *Time and the Other: How Anthropology Makes Its Object*. New York: Columbia University Press.

Fernandez, James. 1986. *Persuasions and Performances: The Play of Tropes in Culture*. Bloomington: Indiana University Press.

Ferry, Luc. 1995. *The New Ecological Order*. Trans. Carol Volk. Chicago: University of Chicago Press.

Fogle, Bruce, ed. 1981. *Interrelations between People and Pets*. Springfield, IL: Charles C. Thomas.

Foucault, Michel. 1979. *Discipline and Punish: The Birth of the Prison*. New York: Vintage Books.

Fox, Warwick. 1995. 'The Deep Ecology – Ecofeminism Debate and Its Parallels.' In G. Sessions, ed., *Deep Ecology for the 21st Century*, 269–89. Boston: Shambhala.

Franklin, Ursula. 1992. *The Real World of Technology*. Toronto: House of Anansi Press.

Freeman, Derek. 1984. *Margaret Mead and Samoa: The Making and Unmaking of an Anthropological Myth*. Harmondsworth: Penguin Books.

Geertz, Clifford. 1983a. 'Common Sense as a Cultural System.' In Geertz, *Local Knowledge*, 73–93 (see below).

– 1983b. *Local Knowledge: Further Essays in Interpretive Anthropology*. New York: Basic Books.

– 1973a. 'Deep Play: Notes on the Balinese Cockfight.' In *The Interpretation of Cultures*, 412–53. New York: Basic Books.

– 1973b. *The Interpretation of Cultures: Essays in Interpretive Anthropology*. New York: Basic Books.

Gerlach, Luther, and Virginia Hine. 1970. *People, Power, Change: Movements of Social Transformation*. Indianapolis: Bobbs-Merrill Co.

Giddens, Anthony. 1984. *The Constitution of Society: Outline of the Theory of Structuration*. Berkeley: University of California Press.

Glacken, Clarence. 1967. *Traces on the Rhodian Shore: Nature and Culture in Western Thought from Ancient Times to the End of the Eighteenth Century*. Berkeley: University of California Press.

Gleick, James. 1987. *Chaos: Making a New Science*. New York: Viking Penguin.

Grady, Wayne. 1995. *Toronto the Wild: Field Notes of an Urban Naturalist*. Toronto: Macfarlane Walter & Ross.

Gruber, Howard E. 1981. *Darwin on Man: A Psychological Study of Scientific Creativity*. 2nd ed. Chicago: University of Chicago Press.

Hallowell, A. Irving. 1975. 'Ojibwa Ontology, Behavior, and World View.' In Dennis Tedlock and Barbara Tedlock, eds, *Teachings from the American Earth: Indian Religion and Philosophy*, 141–78. New York: Liveright.

Hampson, Judith. 1989. 'Legislation and the Changing Consensus.' In Gill Langley, ed., *Animal Experimentation: The Consensus Changes*, 219–51. New York: Chapman and Hall.

Hanley, Charles. 1996. 'Blood lines: Taking a patent on life.' *Globe and Mail* (Toronto), 11 May.

Haraway, Donna. 1996. *Modest_Witness@Second_Millennium. FemaleMan_Meets_OncoMouse: Feminism and Technoscience*. New York: Routledge.

– 1991. 'Situated Knowledges: The Science Question in Feminism and the

Privilege of Partial Perspective.' In *Simians, Cyborgs, and Women: The Re-Invention of Nature*, 183–200. New York: Routledge.

– 1989. *Primate Visions*. New York: Routledge.

Harries-Jones, Peter. 1995. *A Recursive Vision: Ecological Understanding and Gregory Bateson*. Toronto: University of Toronto Press.

Hawkes, Terence. 1977. *Structuralism and Semiotics*. Berkeley: University of California Press.

Hayles, N. Katherine, ed. 1991. *Chaos and Order: Complex Dynamics in Literature and Science*. Chicago: University of Chicago Press.

Hearne, Vicki. 1986. *Adam's Task: Calling Animals by Name*. New York: Knopf.

Herscovici, Alan. 1985. *Second Nature: The Animal-Rights Controversy*. Toronto: CBC Enterprises.

Hickrod, Lucy Jen Huang, and Raymond Schmitt. 1982. 'A Naturalistic Study of Interaction and Frame: The Pet as "Family Member."' *Urban Life*. 11:1 (April), 55–77.

Hoffmeyer, Jesper, and Claus Emmeche. 1991. 'Code-Duality and the Semiotics of Nature.' In Myrdene Anderson and Floyd Merrell, eds, *On Semiotic Modeling*, 117–66. Berlin: Mouton de Gruyter.

Hollands, Clive. 1985. 'Animal Rights in the Political Arena.' In Peter Singer, ed., *In Defense of Animals*, 168–78. New York: Basil Blackwell.

Ingerson, Alice. 1993. 'Tracking and Testing the Nature-Culture Dichotomy.' In Carole Crumley, ed., *Historical Ecology: Cultural Knowledge and Changing Landscapes*, 43–66. Santa Fe, NM: School of American Research Press.

Ingold, Tim, ed. 1988. *What Is an Animal?* London: Unwin Hyman (introduction to paperback ed., 1994).

Israelson, David. 1986. 'Whaling protestor ready to wreck more factories.' *Toronto Star*, 12 November.

Jasper, James M., and Dorothy Nelkin. 1992. *The Animal Rights Crusade: The Growth of a Moral Protest*. New York: Free Press.

Johnson, Mark. 1987. *The Body in the Mind: The Bodily Basis of Meaning, Imagination, and Reason*. Chicago: University of Chicago Press.

Katcher, Aaron. 1981. 'Interactions between People and Their Pets: Form and Function.' In Bruce Fogle, ed., *Interrelations between People and Pets*, 41–67. Springfield, IL: Charles C. Thomas.

Katcher, Aaron, and Alan Beck. 1988. 'Health and Caring for Living Things.' In Andrew Rowan, ed., *Animals and People Sharing the World*, 53–73. Hanover, NH: University Press of New England.

Keller, Evelyn Fox. 1983. *A Feeling for the Organism: The Life and Work of Barbara McClintock*. San Francisco: W.H. Freeman.

Kellert, Stephen H. 1994 [1993]. *In the Wake of Chaos: Unpredictable Order in Dynamical Systems*. Chicago: University of Chicago Press.

Kellert, Stephen R., and Edward O. Wilson, eds. 1993. *The Biophilia Hypothesis*. Washington: Island Press.

Kimbrell, Andrew. 1993. *The Human Body Shop: The Engineering and Marketing of Life*. San Francisco: HarperSanFrancisco.

Kitcher, Philip. 1985. *Vaulting Ambition: Sociobiology and the Quest for Human Nature*. Cambridge, MA: MIT Press.

Knight, David. 1981. *Ordering the World: A History of Classifying Man*. London: Burnett Books.

Kogawa, Joy. 1983 [1981]. *Obasan*. Markham, ON: Penguin Books.

Kovel, Joel. 1988. *The Radical Spirit*. London: Free Association Books.

– 1981. *The Age of Desire*. New York: Pantheon.

Kuklick, Henrika. 1997. 'After Ishmael: The Fieldwork Tradition and Its Future.' In Akhil Gupta and James Ferguson, eds, *Anthropological Locations: Boundaries and Grounds of a Field Science*, 47–65. Berkeley: University of California Press.

– 1991. *The Savage Within: The Social History of British Anthropology, 1885–1945*. Cambridge: Cambridge University Press.

Kuper, Adam. 1983. *Anthropology and Anthropologists: The Modern British School*. Revised ed. London: Routledge and Kegan Paul.

LaFollette, Hugh, and Niall Shanks. 1996. *Brute Science: Dilemmas of Animal Experimentation*. London: Routledge.

Lakoff, George. 1993. 'The Contemporary Theory of Metaphor.' In Andrew Ortony, ed., *Metaphor and Thought*, 202–51. 2nd ed. New York: Cambridge University Press.

Lakoff, George, and Mark Johnson. 1980. *Metaphors We Live By*. Chicago: University of Chicago Press.

Langley, Gill, ed. 1989. *Animal Experimentation: The Consensus Changes*. New York: Chapman and Hall.

Latour, Bruno. 1993. *We Have Never Been Modern*. Trans. Catherine Porter. Cambridge: Harvard University Press.

Lave, Jean. 1988. *Cognition in Practice: Mind, Mathematics and Culture in Everyday Life*. Cambridge: Cambridge University Press.

Lawrence, Elizabeth A. 1984 [1982]. *Rodeo: An Anthropologist Looks at the Wild and the Tame*. Chicago: University of Chicago Press.

Leach, Edmund. 1964. 'Anthropological Aspects of Language: Animal Categories and Verbal Abuse.' In E. Lenneberg, ed., *New Directions in the Study of Language*, 23–64. Cambridge, MA: MIT Press.

Leaf, Murray J. 1979. *Man, Mind, and Science: A History of Anthropology*. New York: Columbia University Press.

Lee, Richard B., and Irven DeVore, eds. 1976. *Kalahari Hunter-Gatherers*. Cambridge: Harvard University Press.

LeGuin, Ursula K. 1988. 'She Unnames Them.' In *Buffalo Gals and Other Animal Presences*, 194–6. New York: New American Library.

Leiss, William. 1974. *The Conquest of Nature*. Boston: Beacon Press.

Levinson, Boris. 1972. *Pets and Human Development*. Springfield, IL: Charles C. Thomas.

Lévi-Strauss, Claude. 1969. *The Elementary Structures of Kinship*. Revised ed. Boston: Beacon Hill Press.

– 1966. *The Savage Mind*. Chicago: University of Chicago Press.

– 1963. *Totemism*. Boston: Beacon Press.

Lewontin, Richard. 1991. *Biology as Ideology: The Doctrine of DNA*. Toronto: House of Anansi Press.

Livingston, John. 1994. *Rogue Primate*. Toronto: Key Porter Books.

Lovejoy, Arthur. 1964. *The Great Chain of Being*. Cambridge: Harvard University Press.

Lovelock, James. 1979. *Gaia: A New Look at Life on Earth*. Oxford: Oxford University Press.

Marcus, George, and Michael Fischer. 1986. *Anthropology as Cultural Critique*. Chicago: University of Chicago Press.

Marcuse, Herbert. 1977. 'Industrialization and Capitalism in the Work of Max Weber.' In Janet Dolgin, David Kemnitzer and David Schneider, eds, *Symbolic Anthropology*, 364–78. New York: Columbia University Press.

Masson, Jeffrey Moussaieff, with Susan McCarthy. 1994. *When Elephants Weep: The Emotional Lives of Animals*. New York: Delacorte Press.

Mays, John Bentley. 1994. *Emerald City: Toronto Visited*. Toronto: Penguin Viking.

Merchant, Carolyn. 1982 [1980]. *The Death of Nature: Women, Ecology, and the Scientific Revolution*. New York: Harper and Row.

Midgley, Mary. 1994. *The Ethical Primate. Humans, Freedom and Morality*. London: Routledge.

– 1989. 'Are You an Animal?' In Gill Langley, ed., *Animal Experimentation: The Consensus Changes*, 1–18. New York: Chapman and Hall.

– 1985. 'Persons and Non- Persons.' In Peter Singer, ed., *In Defense of Animals*, 52–62. New York: Basil Blackwell.

– 1978. *Beast and Man: The Roots of Human Nature*. Ithaca, NY: Cornell University Press.

Mumford, Lewis. 1963 [1934]. *Technics and Civilization*. New York: Harcourt, Brace and World.

Nelson, Richard. 1993. 'Searching for the Lost Arrow: Physical and Spiritual Ecology in the Hunter's World.' In Stephen R. Kellert and Edward O. Wilson, eds. *The Biophilia Hypothesis*, 201–28. Washington: Island Press.

Noske, Barbara. 1989. *Humans and Other Animals: Beyond the Boundaries of Anthropology.* London: Pluto Press.

Oelschlaeger, Max. 1991. *The Idea of Wilderness: From Prehistory to the Age of Ecology.* New Haven, CT: Yale University Press.

Ornstein, Robert, ed. 1973. *The Nature of Human Consciousness.* San Francisco: W.H. Freeman and Co.

Ortner, Sherry. 1984. 'Theory in Anthropology since the Sixties.' *Comparative Studies in Society and History* 26:1, 126–66.

– 1974. 'Is Female to Male as Nature Is to Culture?' In Michelle Zimbalist Rosaldo and Louise Lamphere, eds, *Woman, Culture, and Society,* 67–87. Stanford: Stanford University Press.

Orwen, Patricia. 1987. 'Toronto Humane Society: A century of caring.' *Toronto Star,* 21 February.

Pacey, Arnold. 1983. *The Culture of Technology.* Cambridge, MA: MIT Press.

Perin, Constance. 1981. 'Dogs as Symbols in Human Development.' In Bruce Fogle, ed., *Interrelations between People and Pets,* 68–88. Springfield, IL: Charles C. Thomas.

Poster, Mark. 1980. *Critical Theory of the Family.* New York: Seabury Press.

Prigogine, Ilya, and Isabelle Stengers. 1984. *Order Out of Chaos: Man's New Dialogue with Nature.* New York: Bantam Books.

Ralston-Purina, n.d. *How to Understand and Enjoy a Dog Show.* Form # 14.

– n.d. *How to Understand and Enjoy an Obedience Trial.* Form #23.

Rappaport, Roy. 1968. *Pigs for the Ancestors.* New Haven, CT: Yale University Press.

Regan, Tom. 1985. 'The Case for Animal Rights.' In Peter Singer, ed., *In Defense of Animals,* 13–26. New York: Basil Blackwell.

Rheingold, Howard. 1994. *The Millenium Whole Earth Catalogue.* San Francisco: HarperSanFrancisco.

Rifkin, Jeremy. 1991. *Biosphere Politics.* New York: Crown Publishers.

Rilke, Rainer Maria. 1986 [1904]. *Letters to a Young Poet.* Trans. Stephen Mitchell. New York: Vintage.

Ritvo, Harriet. 1988. 'The Emergence of Modern Pet-Keeping.' In Andrew Rowan, ed., *Animals and People Sharing the World,* 13–31. Hanover, NH: University Press of New England.

– 1987. *The Animal Estate: The English and Other Creatures in the Victorian Age.* Cambridge: Harvard University Press.

Rodman, Margaret C. 1992. 'Empowering Place: Multilocality and Multivocality.' *American Anthropologist* 94(3), 640–56.

Rorty, Richard. 1979. *Philosophy and the Mirror of Nature.* Princeton, NJ: Princeton University Press.

Rosaldo, Michelle Zimbalist, and Louise Lamphere, eds. 1974. *Woman, Culture, and Society.* Stanford: Stanford University Press.

Rose, Steven, Richard Lewontin, and Leon Kamin. 1984. *Not in Our Genes: Biology, Ideology and Human Nature.* London: Penguin.

Roszak, Theodore. 1989. *Where the Wasteland Ends.* Berkeley: Celestial Arts.

Rowan, Andrew. 1988. 'The Power of the Animal Symbol and Its Implications.' In Andrew Rowan, ed., *Animals and People Sharing the World*, 1–12. Hanover, NH: University Press of New England.

Rowan, Andrew, ed. 1988. *Animals and People Sharing the World.* Hanover, NH: University Press of New England.

Rybczynski, Witold. 1996 [1995]. *City Life.* Toronto: HarperPerennial.

Sahlins, Marshall. 1977 [1976]. *The Use and Abuse of Biology: An Anthropological Critique of Sociobiology.* Ann Arbor: University of Michigan Press.

– 1976. *Culture and Practical Reason.* Chicago: University of Chicago Press.

Sarton, May. 1957. *The Fur Person.* New York: Signet.

Scarry, Elaine. 1985. *The Body in Pain: The Making and Unmaking of the World.* New York: Oxford University Press.

Schama, Simon. 1995. *Landscape and Memory.* New York: Knopf.

Schneider, David M. 1980. *American Kinship: A Cultural Account.* 2nd ed. Chicago: University of Chicago Press.

Sebeok, Thomas A. 1972. *Perspectives in Zoosemiotics.* The Hague: Mouton.

Sebeok, Thomas A., ed. 1975. *The Tell-Tale Sign: A Survey of Semiotics.* Lisse, Netherlands: Peter de Ridder Press.

Serpell, James. 1988. 'Pet-Keeping in Non-Western Societies: Some Popular Misconceptions.' In Andrew Rowan, ed., *Animals and People Sharing the World*, 33–52. Hanover, NH: University Press of New England.

– 1986. *In the Company of Animals: A Study of Human-Animal Relationships.* London: Basil Blackwell.

Sessions, George, ed. 1995. *Deep Ecology for the 21st Century.* Boston: Shambhala.

Shepard, Paul. 1978. *Thinking Animals.* New York: Viking Press.

Shepard, Paul, and Daniel McKinley, eds. 1969. *The Subversive Science: Essays toward an Ecology of Man.* Boston: Houghton Mifflin Co.

Siegal, Mordecai, ed. 1989. *The Cornell Book of Cats.* New York: Villard Books.

Singer, Peter. 1975. *Animal Liberation.* New York: Avon.

Singer, Peter, ed. 1985. *In Defense of Animals.* New York: Basil Blackwell.

Snyder, Gary. 1991. *A Place in Space: Ethics, Aesthetics, and Watersheds.* Washington: Counterpoint.

Sperling, Susan. 1988. *Animal Liberators: Research and Morality.* Berkeley: University of California Press.

Stocking, George, Jr. 1992. *The Ethnographer's Magic*. Madison: University of Wisconsin Press.

– 1987. *Victorian Anthropology*. New York: Free Press.

Teitelbaum, Matthew, and Peter White. 1987. *Joe Fafard: Cows and Other Luminaries 1977–1987*. Saskatoon: Mendel Art Gallery and Regina: Dunlop Art Gallery.

Thomas, Keith. 1984 [1983]. *Man and the Natural World: Changing Attitudes in England 1500–1800*. Harmondsworth: Penguin.

Thompson, D'Arcy W. 1961. *On Growth and Form*. Cambridge: Cambridge University Press.

Thoreau, Henry David. 1983 [1854/66]. *Walden and Civil Disobedience*. New York: Viking Penguin.

Touraine, Alain. 1995. 'Beyond Social Movements?' In Stanford M. Lyman, ed., *Social Movements: Critiques, Concepts, Case-Studies*, 371–93. New York: New York University Press.

– 1977. *The Voice and the Eye: An Analysis of Social Movements*. Cambridge: Cambridge University Press.

– 1971. *The Post-Industrial Society*. New York: Random House.

Toynbee, J.M.C. 1971. *Animals in Roman Life and Art*. Ithaca, NY: Cornell University Press.

Tuan, Yi-Fu. 1984. *Dominance and Affection: The Making of Pets*. New Haven, CT: Yale University Press.

Turner, James. 1980. *Reckoning with the Beast: Animals, Pain, and Humanity in the Victorian Mind*. Baltimore: Johns Hopkins University Press.

Waldrop, M. Mitchell. 1992. *Complexity: The Emerging Science at the Edge of Order and Chaos*. New York: Simon and Shuster.

Walkom, Thomas. 1988. 'The whole hog.' *Toronto Star*, 9 May.

White, Lynn, Jr. 1969. 'The Historical Roots of Our Ecological Crisis.' In Paul Shepard and Daniel McKinley, eds, *The Subversive Science*, 341–51. Boston: Houghton Mifflin.

Wiesel, Eli. 1969 [1958]. *Night*. New York: Avon Discus.

Williams, Raymond. 1985. *Towards 2000*. Harmondsworth: Penguin.

– 1983. 'Democracy,' 'Nature,' 'Society.' In *Keywords: A Vocabulary of Culture and Society*. Revised ed. London: Flamingo.

– 1977. *Marxism and Literature*. Oxford: Oxford University Press.

– 1973. *The Country and the City*. London: Chatto and Windus.

– 1972. 'Ideas of Nature.' In Jonathan Benthall, ed., *Ecology: The Shaping Inquiry*, 146–64. London: Longmans.

Willis, Roy. *Man and Beast*. New York: Basic Books.

Wilson, Alexander. 1992. *The Culture of Nature*. Cambridge, MA: Blackwell.

Wilson, Edward O. 1984. *Biophilia*. Cambridge: Harvard University Press.

– 1980 [1975]. *Sociobiology.* Abridged ed. Cambridge, MA: Belknap Press.

Winner, Langdon. 1986. *The Whale and the Reactor.* Chicago: University of Chicago Press.

Wolf, Eric R. 1982. *Europe and the People without History.* Berkeley: University of California Press.

World Commission on Environment and Development. 1987. *Our Common Future: Report of the World Commission on Environment and Development.* Oxford: Oxford University Press.

Worster, Donald. 1977. *Nature's Economy.* New York: Cambridge University Press.

Wrong, Dennis. 1994. *The Problem of Order: What Unites and Divides Society.* New York: Free Press.

Index

Action Volunteers for Animals (AVA) 113, 115, 127. *See also* animal-rights activism, animal-rights movement, social movements

animal communication 41, 203n20; and anthropology 40–1, 184, 203n20; with humans 203n20; among primates 41

Animal Liberation (Singer) 113–14, 131; as manifesto of animal-rights movement 113–14

Animal Liberation Front 127, 217n36

animal research 90–2, 104–9, 123, 126–7; and Amnesty International, torture experiments on pigs 94–5; and animal models, potential harm to humans 126; and debased language 104–6; genetic manipulation in 90–1, 105; (and 'Onco-mouse' 91; and patents 90–1, 140–1; medical research industry and 126; mutilation in 106, 123; pet keeping in, *see* Birke, L.; primate field research as, *see* primatology; and models of human biomedical conditions ('strong models,' transgenic animals as 105; 'weak models,' naturally occurring animals as 105); 'surrogate mother' monkey experiments in 105; toxicity testing and 123, 216n24. *See also* factory domain; Haraway, D.; Harlow, H.; Midgley, M.; pain; primatology; torture

animal-rights activism 112–14, 119, 124–34; and animal slaughter 129; 'direct action' in 125 ('Debbie Campaign' as 129–30); and disorder 124–8; and factory domain 120; habitus and 131. *See also* animal-rights movement; civic domain; social activism; social movements

animal-rights movement 113–15, 130–2, 140; as anti-slavery movement 122; biocentrism and 140; and civic domain 114–18; ethical agenda of 140; history of 113; and media, use of 131–2; as rescue mission 140; scientific legitimacy, desire for 130–1 (and Jane Goodall 131)

animals 53–60, 65–71, 86–96, 101–9;